## WORLDS

. . . a world that turns out to be, quite literally, "heaven"—mixed with just a dash of hell.

. . . a world where a Spitting Contest makes all the difference.

. . . a world where a cubic mile of ice is flown across 700 million miles of uncharted space.

. . . a world where status and success are measured by one's proficiency at swindling.

These, and other worlds—dark yet dazzling, forbidding yet irresistible.

**Also edited by Damon Knight**

Tomorrow X4

**and available in Paperback**

# Worlds to Come

## Nine Science-Fiction Adventures

Edited by

## Damon Knight

CORONET BOOKS
Hodder Fawcett Ltd., London

THIS BOOK CONTAINS
THE COMPLETE TEXT OF THE ORIGINAL
HARDCOVER EDITION


First published in Great Britain by
Victor Gollancz Ltd., London, 1969
Coronet edition 1972

---

*The characters and situations in this book are entirely imaginary and bear no relation to any real person or actual happening*



Printed and bound in Great Britain for
Coronet Books, Hodder Fawcett Ltd,
St. Paul's House, Warwick Lane,
London, E.C.4
By Hunt Barnard Printing Ltd.,
Aylesbury, Bucks.

ISBN 0 340 15849 2

## Contents

## Acknowledgements

*For permission to use the stories in this volume, grateful acknowledgement is made to the following:*

Arthur C. Clarke and Scott Meredith Literary Agency, Inc., for "The Sentinel," copyright 1951 by Avon Periodicals, Inc.; H. B. Fyfe for "Moonwalk," copyright 1952 by Space Publications, Inc.; Ray Bradbury and Harold Matson Co., Inc., for "Mars Is Heaven!" copyright 1948 by Ray Bradbury; Algis Budrys and Russell & Volkening for "The Edge of the Sea," copyright © 1957 by Fantasy House, Inc.; Isaac Asimov for "The Martian Way," copyright 1952 by Galaxy Publishing Corp.; John D. MacDonald and Littauer & Wilkinson for "The Big Contest," copyright 1950 by Hillman Periodicals, Inc.; Robert A. Heinlein and Lurton Blassingame for "Ordeal in Space," copyright 1948 by Hearst Magazines, Inc.; Ballantine Books, Inc., for "That Share of Glory," by C. M. Kornbluth, copyright 1952 by Street & Smith Publications, Inc.; James Blish and Robert P. Mills for "Sunken Universe," copyright 1942 by Fictioneers, Inc.

# INTRODUCTION

Science fiction and prophecy are two different things.

Nobody will pay any attention to this statement. (That's a prediction, but it is fake prophecy, Type A. See the list below.) Newspaper feature writers will go right on asking science-fiction authors what life will be like in the year 2000; and a few good-natured authors will go on telling them that we will have computer libraries, all-purpose disposable garments, wall-to-wall grass in our apartments, and so on, just as if they knew. But they don't.

Let's have some definitions. A *prediction*, let's say, is any statement about the future. A *prophecy* is a prediction that would be astonishing if it came true. If, for example, any fortune-teller or "sensitive" correctly predicted the outcome of all the congressional contests in an election year or the final standings of all the big-league baseball teams, that would be astonishing—and it would be prophecy. (But don't hold your breath.)

Fake prophecy is much more common and breaks down into five types:

A. Predictions of a high order of probability, e.g., "The sun will rise in the east tomorrow." (These are the easiest kind, but there is no money in them.)

B. Scatter-gun predictions. If there are only a certain limited number of possibilities and you predict them all, you can't help winning. (You also can't help losing, but never mind. Keep reminding people about the successes and let them forget the failures.)

C. Vague predictions. (These are the ones the Delphic oracles used.) Make your predictions as vague, general, and ambiguous as possible, and then if anything happens that can be made to fit, you're a prophet.

D. "Predictions" of things that have already happened. (Jules Verne's submarine belongs here.)

E. Predictions that influence the outcome. (Like saying to a nervous golfer, "Watch it, Harry. Your stance is all wrong—you're going to slice.")

Nearly all the predictions in science fiction belong to these five types—in other words, they are fake prophecies.

But what about Cleve Cartmill predicting the atom bomb in such detail that the FBI descended on John W. Campbell, the editor who published his story? What about Jules Verne describing the periscope so accurately that it couldn't be patented later on? Well, both of these stories are myths. Cartmill's story described an atom bomb generally and vaguely. What details it did have were wrong. And as Campbell pointed out to the FBI, science-fiction writers had been using atom bombs in their stories ever since H. G. Wells' *The World Set Free* (1914). As for the periscope, Verne never mentioned it in *20,000 Leagues Under the Sea;* the *Nautilus* didn't have one.

The Cartmill prediction has elements of Types B and D. For the Verne, I guess we'll have to add a Type F: nonexistent predictions.

Now let's go back to Type E, which is the most interesting and least understood. Forty years ago and more, science-fiction writers seemed to be saying "Man will reach the moon," and today this looks like dazzling prophecy. What they really were saying, however, was something slightly different and much more significant: "Man can reach the moon *if he wants to badly enough.*" This is a Type A prediction, the easiest kind. But it is also a Type E prediction—and here, finally, we come to something of which I think science-fiction writers can be justly proud.

What science fiction has been doing for the last forty years is to shake up people's thinking, make them skeptical of dogma, get them used to the idea of change, let them dare to want new things. Nobody will ever know for sure how much effect these stories have had, but it is almost impossible to believe they have had none.

Scientists and engineers today, unlike their counterparts of forty years ago, tend to say "Why not?" instead of "Impossible!" And so we have wingless airplanes, mammals breathing under water, three-color photographs made from two-color negatives, and pictures televised from the moon.

The stories in this anthology, some written as long as twenty-five years ago, may seem startlingly prophetic. But remember that these are Type E predictions, the kind that help bring something about by persuading others to believe in and desire it. Clarke and Fyfe in particular write as if they have been to the moon, but they haven't. No man has. That adventure, like all the others in this book, is still to come.

DAMON KNIGHT

# THE SENTINEL

## by Arthur C. Clarke

*Arthur C. Clarke, a former chairman of the British Interplanetary Society, describes moon exploration in such graphic detail that future generations may have trouble remembering which came first, Clarke or the manned moon landing.*

*This short story was first published in 1951. Fourteen years later, Clarke and a brilliant young motion-picture producer combined their talents to turn it into a movie and a novel—* 2001: A Space Odyssey, *by Arthur C. Clarke and Stanley Kubrick.*

THE next time you see the full moon high in the south, look carefully at its right-hand edge and let your eye travel upward along the curve of the disk. Round about two o'clock you will notice a small, dark oval: anyone with normal eyesight can find it quite easily. It is the great walled plain, one of the finest on the Moon, known as the Mare Crisium—the Sea of Crises. Three hundred miles in diameter, and almost completely surrounded by a ring of magnificent mountains, it had never been explored until we entered it in the late summer of 1996.

Our expedition was a large one. We had two heavy freighters which had flown our supplies and equipment from the main lunar base in the Mare Serenitatis, five hundred miles away. There were also three small rockets which were intended for short-range transport over regions which our surface vehicles couldn't cross. Luckily, most of the Mare Crisium is very flat. There are none of the great crevasses so common and so dangerous elsewhere, and very few craters or mountains of any size. As far as we could tell, our powerful caterpillar tractors would have no difficulty in taking us wherever we wished to go.

I was geologist—or selenologist, if you want to be pedantic—in charge of the group exploring the southern region of the Mare. We had crossed a hundred miles of it in a week, skirting the foothills of the mountains along the shore of what was once the ancient sea, some thousand million years before. When life was beginning on Earth, it was already dying here. The waters were retreating down the flanks of those stupendous cliffs, retreating into the empty heart of the Moon. Over the land which we were crossing, the tideless ocean had once been half a mile deep, and now the only trace of moisture was the hoarfrost one could sometimes find in caves which the searing sunlight never penetrated.

We had begun our journey early in the slow lunar dawn, and still had almost a week of Earth-time before nightfall. Half a dozen times a day we would leave our vehicle and go outside in the space suits to hunt for interesting minerals, or to place markers for the guidance of future travelers. It was an uneventful routine. There is nothing hazardous or even particularly exciting about lunar exploration. We could live comfortably for a month in our pressurized tractors, and if we ran into trouble, we could always radio for help and sit tight until one of the spaceships came to our rescue.

I said just now that there was nothing exciting about

lunar exploration, but of course that isn't true. One could never grow tired of those incredible mountains, so much more rugged than the gentle hills of Earth. We never knew, as we rounded the capes and promontories of that vanished sea, what new splendors would be revealed to us. The whole southern curve of the Mare Crisium is a vast delta where a score of rivers once found their way into the ocean, fed perhaps by the torrential rains that must have lashed the mountains in the brief volcanic age when the Moon was young. Each of these ancient valleys was an invitation, challenging us to climb into the unknown uplands beyond. But we had a hundred miles still to cover, and could only look longingly at the heights which others must scale.

We kept Earth-time aboard the tractor, and precisely at 22:00 hours the final radio message would be sent out to Base and we would close down for the day. Outside, the rocks would still be burning beneath the almost vertical sun, but to us it would be night until we awoke again eight hours later. Then one of us would prepare breakfast, there would be a great buzzing of electric razors, and someone would switch on the shortwave radio from Earth. Indeed, when the smell of frying sausages began to fill the cabin, it was sometimes hard to believe that we were not back on our own world—everything was so normal and homely, apart from the feeling of decreased weight and the unnatural slowness with which objects fell.

It was my turn to prepare breakfast in the corner of the main cabin that served as a galley. I can remember that moment quite vividly after all these years, for the radio had just played one of my favorite melodies, the old Welsh air "David of the White Rock." Our driver was already outside in his space suit, inspecting our caterpillar treads. My assistant, Louis Garnett, was up forward in the control position, making some belated entries in yesterday's log.

As I stood by the frying pan, waiting, like any terrestrial housewife, for the sausages to brown, I let my gaze wander idly over the mountain walls which covered the whole of the southern horizon, marching out of sight to east and west below the curve of the Moon. They seemed only a mile or two from the tractor, but I knew that the nearest was twenty miles away. On the Moon, of course, there is no loss of detail with distance—none of that almost imperceptible haziness which softens and sometimes transfigures all far-off things on Earth.

Those mountains were ten thousand feet high, and they climbed steeply out of the plain as if ages ago some subterranean eruption had smashed them skyward through the molten crust. The base of even the nearest was hidden from sight by the steeply curving surface of the plain, for the Moon is a very little world, and from where I was standing the horizon was only two miles away.

I lifted my eyes toward the peaks which no man had ever climbed, the peaks which, before the coming of terrestrial life, had watched the retreating oceans sink sullenly into their graves, taking with them the hope and the morning promise of a world. The sunlight was beating against those ramparts with a glare that hurt the eyes, yet only a little way above them the stars were shining steadily in a sky blacker than a winter midnight on Earth.

I was turning away when my eye caught a metallic glitter high on the ridge of a great promontory thrusting out into the sea thirty miles to the west. It was a dimensionless point of light, as if a star had been clawed from the sky by one of those cruel peaks, and I imagined that some smooth rock surface was catching the sunlight and heliographing it straight into my eyes. Such things were not uncommon. When the Moon is in her second quarter, observers on Earth can sometimes see the great ranges in the Oceanus Procellarum burning with a blue-white iridescence as the sunlight flashes from their slopes and leaps again from world to world. But I was curious to know what kind of rock could be shining so brightly up there, and I climbed into the observation turret and swung our four-inch telescope round to the west.

I could see just enough to tantalize me. Clear and sharp in the field of vision, the mountain peaks seemed only half a mile away, but whatever was catching the sunlight was still too small to be resolved. Yet it seemed to have an elusive symmetry, and the summit upon which it rested was curiously flat. I stared for a long time at that glittering enigma, straining my eyes into space, until presently a smell of burning from the galley told me that our breakfast sausages had made their quarter-million-mile journey in vain.

All that morning we argued our way across the Mare Crisium while the western mountains reared higher in the sky. Even when we were out prospecting in the space suits, the discussion would continue over the radio. It was absolutely certain, my companions argued, that there had never been any form of intelligent life on the Moon. The only living things that had ever existed there were a few primitive plants and their slightly less degenerate ancestors. I knew that as well as anyone, but there are times when a scientist must not be afraid to make a fool of himself.

"Listen," I said at last, "I'm going up there, if only for my own peace of mind. That mountain's less than twelve thousand feet high—that's only two thousand under Earth gravity—and I can make the trip in twenty hours at the outside. I've always wanted to go up into those hills, anyway, and this gives me an excellent excuse."

"If you don't break your neck," said Garnett, "you'll be the laughingstock of the expedition when we get back to Base. That mountain will probably be called Wilson's Folly from now on."

"I won't break my neck," I said firmly. "Who was the first man to climb Pico and Helicon?"

"But weren't you rather younger in those days?" asked Louis gently.

"That," I said with great dignity, "is as good a reason as any for going."

We went to bed early that night, after driving the tractor to within half a mile of the promontory. Garnett was coming with me in the morning; he was a good climber, and had often been with me on such exploits before. Our driver was only too glad to be left in charge of the machine.

At first sight, those cliffs seemed completely unscalable, but to anyone with a good head for heights, climbing is easy on a world where all weights are only a sixth of their normal value. The real danger in lunar mountaineering lies in overconfidence; a six-hundred-foot drop on the Moon can kill you just as thoroughly as a hundred-foot fall on Earth.

We made our first halt on a wide ledge about four thousand feet above the plain. Climbing had not been very difficult, but my limbs were stiff with the unaccustomed effort, and I was glad of the rest. We could still see the tractor as a tiny metal insect far down at the foot of the cliff, and we reported our progress to the driver before starting on the next ascent.

Inside our suits it was comfortably cool, for the refrigeration units were fighting the fierce sun and carrying away the body heat of our exertions. We seldom spoke to each other, except to pass climbing instructions and to discuss our best plan of ascent. I do not know what Garnett was thinking, probably that this was the craziest goose chase he had ever embarked upon. I more than half agreed with him, but the joy of climbing, the knowledge that no man had ever gone this way before, and the exhilaration of the steadily widening landscape gave me all the reward I needed.

I don't think I was particularly excited when I saw in front of us the wall of rock I had first inspected through the telescope from thirty miles away. It would level off about fifty feet above our heads, and there on the plateau would be the thing that had lured me over these barren wastes. It would be, almost certainly, nothing more than a boulder splintered ages ago by a falling meteor, and with its cleavage planes still fresh and bright in this incorruptible, unchanging silence.

There were no handholds on the rock face, and we had to use a grapnel. My tired arms seemed to gain new strength as I swung the three-pronged metal anchor round my head and sent it sailing up toward the stars. The first time it broke loose and came falling slowly back when we pulled the rope. On the third attempt, the prongs gripped firmly and our combined weights could not shift it.

Garnett looked at me anxiously. I could tell that he wanted to go first, but I smiled back at him through the glass of my helmet and shook my head. Slowly, taking my time, I began the final ascent.

Even with my space suit, I weighed only forty pounds here, so I pulled myself up hand over hand without bothering to use my feet. At the rim I paused and waved to my companion, then I scrambled over the edge and stood upright, staring ahead of me.

You must understand that until this very moment I had been almost completely convinced that there could be nothing strange or unusual for me to find here. Almost, but not quite; it was that haunting doubt that had driven me forward. Well, it was a doubt no longer, but the haunting had scarcely begun.

I was standing on a plateau perhaps a hundred feet across. It had once been smooth—too smooth to be natural—but falling meteors had pitted and scored its surface through immeasurable eons. It had been leveled to support a glittering, roughly pyramidal structure, twice as high as a man, that was set in the rock like a gigantic, many faceted jewel.

Probably no emotion at all filled my mind in those first few seconds. Then I felt a great lifting of my heart, and a strange, inexpressible joy. For I loved the Moon, and now I knew that the creeping moss of Aristarchus and Eratosthenes was not the only life she had brought forth in her youth. The old, discredited dream of the first explorers was true. There had, after all, been a lunar civilization—and I was the first to find it. That I had come perhaps a hundred million years too late did not distress me; it was enough to have come at all.

My mind was beginning to function normally, to analyze and to ask questions. Was this a building, a shrine—or something for which my language had no name? If a building, then why was it erected in so uniquely inaccessible a spot? I wondered if it might be a temple, and I could picture the adepts of some strange priesthood calling on their gods to preserve them as the life of the Moon ebbed with the dying oceans, and calling on their gods in vain.

I took a dozen steps forward to examine the thing more closely, but some sense of caution kept me from going too near. I knew a little of archaeology, and tried to guess the cultural level of the civilization that must have smoothed this mountain and raised the glittering mirror surfaces that still dazzled my eyes.

The Egyptians could have done it, I thought, if their workmen had possessed whatever strange materials these far more ancient architects had used. Because of the thing's smallness, it did not occur to me that I might be looking at the handiwork of a race more advanced than my own. The idea that the Moon had possessed intelligence at all was still almost too tremendous to grasp, and my pride would not let me take the final, humiliating plunge.

And then I noticed something that set the scalp crawling at the back of my neck—something so trivial and so innocent that many would never have noticed it at all. I have said that the plateau was scarred by meteors; it was also coated inches deep with the cosmic dust that is always filtering down upon the surface of any world where there are no winds to disturb it. Yet the dust and the meteor scratches ended quite abruptly in a wide circle enclosing the little pyramid, as though an invisible wall was protecting it from the ravages of time and the slow but ceaseless bombardment from space.

There was someone shouting in my earphones, and I realized that Garnett had been calling me for some time. I walked unsteadily to the edge of the cliff and signaled him to join me, not trusting myself to speak. Then I went back toward that circle in the dust. I picked up a fragment of splintered rock and tossed it gently toward the shining enigma. If the pebble had vanished at that invisible barrier, I should not have been surprised, but it seemed to hit a smooth, hemispheric surface and slide gently to the ground.

I knew then that I was looking at nothing that could be matched in the antiquity of my own race. This was not a building, but a machine, protecting itself with forces that had challenged Eternity. Those forces, whatever they might be, were still operating, and perhaps I had already come too close. I thought of all the radiations man had trapped and tamed in the past century. For all I knew, I might be as irrevocably doomed as if I had stepped into the deadly, silent aura of an unshielded atomic pile.

I remember turning then toward Garnett, who had joined me and was now standing motionless at my side. He seemed quite oblivious to me, so I did not disturb him but walked to the edge of the cliff in an effort to marshal my thoughts. There below me lay the Mare Crisium—Sea of Crises, indeed—strange and weird to most men, but reassuringly familiar to me. I lifted my eyes toward the crescent Earth, lying in her cradle of stars, and I wondered what her clouds had covered when these unknown builders had finished their work. Was it the steaming jungle of the Carboniferous, the bleak shoreline over which the first amphibians must crawl to conquer the land—or, earlier still, the long loneliness before the coming of life?

Do not ask me why I did not guess the truth sooner—the truth that seems so obvious now. In the first excitement of my discovery, I had assumed without question that this crystalline apparition had been built by some race belonging to the Moon's remote past, but suddenly, and with overwhelming force, the belief came to me that it was as alien to the Moon as I myself.

In twenty years we had found no trace of life but a few degenerate plants. No lunar civilization, whatever its doom, could have left but a single token of its existence.

I looked at the shining pyramid again, and the more I looked, the more remote it seemed from anything that had to do with the Moon. And suddenly I felt myself shaking with a foolish, hysterical laughter, brought on by excitement and overexertion: For I had imagined that the little pyramid was speaking to me and was saying, "Sorry, I'm a stranger here myself."

It has taken us twenty years to crack that invisible shield and to reach the machine inside those crystal walls. What we could not understand, we broke at last with the savage might of atomic power and now I have seen the fragments of the lovely, glittering thing I found up there on the mountain.

They are meaningless. The mechanisms—if indeed they are mechanisms—of the pyramid belong to a technology that lies far beyond our horizon, perhaps to the technology of paraphysical forces.

The mystery haunts us all the more now that the other planets have been reached and we know that only Earth has ever been the home of intelligent life in our Universe. Nor could any lost civilization of our own world have built that machine, for the thickness of the meteoric dust on the plateau has enabled us to measure its age. It was set there upon its mountain before life had emerged from the seas of Earth.

When our world was half its present age, *something* from the stars swept through the Solar System, left this token of its passage, and went again upon its way. Until we destroyed it, that machine was still fulfilling the purpose of its builders; and as to that purpose, here is my guess.

Nearly a hundred thousand million stars are turning in the circle of the Milky Way, and long ago other races on the worlds of other suns must have scaled and passed the heights that we have reached. Think of such civilizations, far back in time against the fading afterglow of Creation, masters of a universe so young that life as yet had come only to a handful of worlds. Theirs would have been a loneliness we cannot imagine, the loneliness of gods looking out across infinity and finding none to share their thoughts.

They must have searched the star clusters as we have searched the planets. Everywhere there would be worlds, but they would be empty or peopled with crawling, mindless things. Such was our own Earth, the smoke of the great volcanoes still staining the skies, when that first ship of the peoples of the dawn came sliding in from the abyss beyond Pluto. It passed the frozen outer worlds, knowing that life could play no part in their destinies. It came to rest among the inner planets, warming themselves around the fire of the Sun and waiting for their stories to begin.

Those wanderers must have looked on Earth, circling safely in the narrow zone between fire and ice, and must have guessed that it was the favorite of the Sun's children. Here, in the distant future, would be intelligence; but there were countless stars before them still, and they might never come this way again.

So they left a sentinel, one of millions they scattered throughout the Universe, watching over all worlds with the promise of life. It was a beacon that down the ages patiently signaled the fact that no one had discovered it.

Perhaps you understand now why that crystal pyramid was set upon the Moon instead of on the Earth. Its builders were not concerned with races still struggling up from savagery. They would be interested in our civilization only if we proved our fitness to survive —by crossing space and so escaping from the Earth, our cradle. That is the challenge that all intelligent races must meet, sooner or later. It is a double challenge, for it depends in turn upon the conquest of atomic energy and the last choice between life and death.

Once we had passed that crisis, it was only a matter of time before we found the pyramid and forced it open. Now its signals have ceased, and those whose duty it is will be turning their minds upon Earth. Perhaps they wish to help our infant civilization. But they must be very, very old, and the old are often insanely jealous of the young.

I can never look now at the Milky Way without wondering from which of those banked clouds of stars the emissaries are coming. If you will pardon so commonplace a simile, we have set off the fire alarm and have nothing to do but to wait.

I do not think we will have to wait for long.

# MOONWALK

## by H. B. Fyfe

*Here is another story about the moon, written with the same sort of convincing realism as Clarke's* The Sentinel.

*The explorer Roy Chapman Andrews used to say that he did not have adventures, because an adventure is something that goes wrong. Sometimes, even in the best-planned expeditions, something does go wrong. Then the time for planning and preparation is over; the time has come for heroism.*

THE radio operator stopped sending out his call and slumped back in the folding chair of canvas and aluminum. Concern showed through the impassivity of his broad, Mexican features.

The footsteps in the corridor outside the radio room pattered lightly because of the Lunar gravity, but with a haste that suggested urgency. Two men entered. Like the operator, they wore dungarees and heavy sweaters, but the gray-haired man had an air of authority.

"Dr. Burney wanted to check with you himself, Mike," said the youth with him.

The operator shrugged.

"Tractor One is okay, Doctor," he reported, "but as Joey must have told you, we've lost Two."

"When was the last time they called in?" asked Burney.

Mike gestured at the map on the side wall, and the elder man stepped over to study it. The area shown was that surrounding the fifty-mile-wide crater of Archimedes.

"The blue line is One and the red is Two," said Mike. "I guess you know the planned routes. Well, the little *x*'s show the positions reported and the times."

Burney glanced briefly at the blue line. From the black square near the northern side of the crater that represented the first major base on Luna, it climbed slantingly over the ringwall. After zigzagging down the broken outer slope and skirting a ridge of vein mountains, the line swept in a wide curve north of Aristillus and Autolycus, the next largest craters of the region, and moved into that subregion of the Mare Imbrium, whimsically christened "Misty Swamp." Thereafter, the blue trail led toward possible passes through the Lunar Apennines to the Mare Serenitatis.

"I could expect to lose One," muttered the operator, "in spite of our tower here. But Two shouldn't be blocked by anything yet."

The red line was more direct. Parting from the blue north of the ringwall of Archimedes, it pushed out across the level plain, avoiding isolated mountain ridges and the seven-mile craters of Kirch and Piazza Smyth. After something like three hundred miles, it passed the towering lonely Mt. Pico and probed a dotted delta of possible routes up the ringwall of Plato. This route was *x*'ed almost to Pico.

"They were supposed to report before attempting the descent," mused Burney. "Maybe the depression of the Mare Imbrium isn't quite what we estimated. The normal curvature would put a lot of rock between us, in that case. An awful lot of rock."

"Maybe they went over the ringwall in a hurry," suggested Joey.

Burney considered that in a short silence. He ran a hand absently over his balding temple. His lean face became a mask of lines as he puckered up his eyes in thought.

"Number Two has Hansen driving, hasn't it? And Groswald, the mechanic . . . Van Ness, the astronomer . . . and who else?"

"Fernandez from Geology," said Joey.

The entire personnel of the base numbered scarcely fifty. They were just beginning their surface exploration projects after completing the low domes of their buildings. With such scanty resources, Burney was naturally worried about four men and one of the precious tractors.

"They were with us an hour ago," said Mike, fingering his microphone. "Their set must have gone sour."

When no one replied, he hitched around to face his own controls.

"Or else, they're in trouble—"

On the ledge atop the ringwall of Plato, Hansen teetered and tried to maintain his balance by pressing a gauntleted hand against an outcropping of gray Lunar rock. The thermal-eroded surface crumbled slightly beneath the metal-tipped mitten.

In his bulky space suit, he found it difficult to lean very far forward, but he could not bear not seeing. The landslip tumbled down the inner slope of the ringwall with horrible deliberation.

"I told them 'Don't move her till I find a way down!' " Hansen muttered. "I told them, I *told* them!"

He was hardly conscious of speaking aloud. Somewhere in the churning mass was the vacuum tractor in which he had driven from Archimedes. Inside, unless it had already been split open, were Van Ness, Groswald, and Fernandez.

The collection of loose rock and dust passed out of sight for a moment over the edge of a terrace. It reappeared farther down. Once, Hansen thought he saw a glint of bright metal, but the slide almost immediately plunged down another sheer drop.

The phase of Luna being closer to "new" than to "first quarter," the sun was far too low on the horizon to light the floor of the crater, or even the three mountain peaks on the ringwall to Hansen's right front. The light from the gibbous Earth, however, was bright enough for him to see quite clearly the surface around him.

The slide finally reached the bottom, at this point nearly three thousand feet below the man's precarious position. He breathed deeply and tried to straighten the ache from his shoulders.

"Must have taken five minutes," he murmured, realizing that he had frozen in a cramped position as he stared.

It had seemed more like an hour. In the dim shadows of the crater floor, the dust settled rapidly because of the lack of air, but the debris remained heaped at an angle much steeper than would have been possible on Earth. Even the slight vibration Hansen had felt through his boots ceased.

He was alone in the dead silence of a world for eons dead.

He stood there, a spot of color in the chrome yellow of the protective chafing suit. The transparent faceplate of his unpainted helmet revealed a blond young man, perhaps twenty-six, with a lean, square-jawed face. Against the tanned skin, his eyebrows were ludicrously light, but the gray eyes under them were wide with horror.

He was of medium height, but the bulkiness of the suit hid his welterweight trimness; and the pack of oxygen tank and batteries for powering radio, heat pads, and air circulator increased the appearance of stubbiness.

The quiet hiss of the air being circulated through his suit finally aroused him. With painstaking care, he climbed from the ledge to the level terrace on which the tractor was to have remained while he scouted the route down. A hundred yards away, a great bite seemed to have been snapped out of the ridge.

"All the way from Archimedes, and we didn't even get a look at the floor," he whispered.

For a moment, following the raw scar of the slide with his eye, he considered climbing all the way down and venturing out onto the crater floor to examine the ground. For centuries, the floor of Plato had been reported by Earth observers to darken with the rising sun until at noon it was nearly black. Occasionally, there were stories of misty clouds obscuring the surface, and of shifts in the pattern of light streaks and spots.

One of the expedition's first assignments, therefore, had been the investigation of Plato, to check the unlikely possibility that there might be some primitive, airless form of life present. But the present sortie was clearly ended.

"Not one damn chance," Hansen told himself as he squinted downward. "None of them had a suit on when I got out."

On a terrace about a third of the way down lay an object with an oddly regular shape. It gleamed in the blue-green earthlight, and Hansen peered more intently. It looked like one of the spare oxygen cylinders that had been carried on top of the tractor.

Hansen abruptly became sensitive about the supply of his suit tank. Before he did anything, even sitting down to think the situation over, he wanted to get down there and find out if the cylinder was full.

Despite his eagerness, he held back until he thought he had spied a reasonable path. It involved going two or three hundred feet out of his way, but Hansen managed to work his way down to the lower level without serious difficulty. Once or twice, he slithered a few feet when loose rock shaled off under his grip, but even with his suit and equipment, he weighed little over forty pounds. As long as he did not drop very far, he could always stop himself one-handed.

He walked back along the level strip which was about fifty yards wide at this point, until he approached the path of the landslip. Near it, apparently having been scraped off as the tractor rolled, lay the cylinder.

He checked it hurriedly.

"Whew! Well, that's some help, anyway," he told himself, discovering that the tank had not been tapped.

He left the cylinder and walked over to the inner limit of the level band. Scanning the steep slope and the debris of the slide, he thought he could pick out two or three scraps of twisted metal. There was nothing to be done.

"I'd better get back up and think this out," he decided.

He took the broken chain that had held the tank to the tractor and hooked a broken link through it to make a sling. For the time being, he contented himself with using it as a handle to drag the lucky supply of oxygen after him.

After regaining his original position, the going was easier to the top of the ringwall. They had come over one of the several passes crossing the southern part of the cliffs, and Hansen walked through in a few minutes. The thickness of the ringwall here was only a mile or so, although at the base it probably approached ten miles.

He came out onto a little plateau, and the dim plain of the Mare Imbrium spread out before him. Hansen suddenly felt tiny, lost, and insignificant.

"What am I gonna do?" he asked himself.

For the first time, he had admitted his predicament to himself. His gauntlet crept up to his chest where the switch of his radio protruded through the chafing suit.

"Hello Base! Tractor Two to Base! Tractor Two to Base. Over."

He waited several minutes, and repeated the call five or six times. He screwed his eyes shut to throw every ounce of concentration into listening.

No human voice broke into the quiet hissing of the earphones. Hansen sighed.

"Never reach them, of course!" he grumbled. "This set is made to reach about your arm's length."

He remembered that Van Ness had complained about the reception the last time they had called in, and asked Hansen to maneuver to the top of a ridge of vein mountains near the hulking silhouette of Pico. Hansen was higher now, but also much farther from home.

"Mike Ramirez and Joey Friedman aren't the kind to miss a call," he muttered. "It seems to me, Paul E. Hansen, my boy . . . that you are . . . on your own!"

The radio had been but a faint hope, inspired by his height and tales of freak reception. He was not too disappointed. Looking down the rough outer slope of the ringwall, he saw that it was not by any means as steep as the inner, and that fact settled it.

"Guess I'd better see how far I can get," Hansen decided. "When they don't get the regular report over the tractor radio, they'll probably send out another crew to follow the trail. If I can meet them out a way, maybe even as far as Pico, it'll save that much time."

After considerable fumbling, he balanced the large cylinder on his back atop the other equipment with the chain sling across his chest. He started along the series of gentle slopes the tractor had climbed earlier. Deliberately, he pushed to the back of his mind the possibility he would have to face sometime: Base might decide the crew had been too eager to negotiate the ringwall to call back before being blanked out by the mass of rock.

He had to restrain a temptation to rush headlong down to the plain across miles of rough grades. Even with his tremendous load of equipment, he might still travel in twenty-foot bounds in Lunar gravity; but he had no desire to plunge all the way to the bottom with one misstep.

"It'll be easy enough going down," he murmured. "And after that, I can judge the direction well enough from Earth."

He looked up at the brightness of the planet. Earth

was rather high in the Lunar sky, although not overhead because of his position far north. It would indicate roughly his southerly course toward Archimedes. As he looked, he noticed that much of the eastern coast of North America, which to his view was almost centered on the hemisphere, was blanketed in clouds.

"Wish I was there right now," he sighed. "Rain and all!"

He wondered about the next step as he worked his way around ridges radiating from the sizable minor craterlet in Plato's ringwall. He still had a good view of the gray plain at the foot of the heights. Although reasonably flat—probably leveled by the colossal flow of lava that had formed the Mare Imbrium, filling older craters and melting down or inundating existing mountains until merely their crests showed—it contained many hills and irregularities that would be even more apparent to a man on foot than from the tractor.

He worked past the craterlet, leaving it to his right. Whenever he struck a reasonably level stretch, he moved at a bounding trot. The first time he tried this, he tumbled head over heels and gave himself a fright lest he rupture the space suit on a projecting rock. Thereafter, he was more careful until he got used to being so top-heavy because of the huge oxygen tank.

Finally, scrambling down the last ridges of old debris, he found himself on the level floor of the Sea of Showers, in the region between Plato and the jutting, lonely Mt. Pico. Off to his right, an extension of the ringwall behind him thrust out to point at the group of other peaks known as the Teneriffe Mountains, which were somewhat like a flock of lesser Picos. The ground on which he stood had perhaps once been part of another crater, twin in size to Plato, but now only detectable by faint outlines and vein mountains. In the past, some astronomers had called it Newton, before deciding upon a more worthy landmark for Sir Isaac.

It had taken Hansen nearly half an hour, and he paused now to catch his breath.

"I feel pretty good," he exclaimed with relief. "I'm carrying quite a lot to go at that speed, but I don't seem to get tired." He thought a moment, and warned himself, "You'd better not, either!"

He turned partly to look at the ringwall towering behind him. It loomed grimly, scored with deep shadows of cracks into which the rays of Earth, seventy times brighter than moonlight it received from Luna, could not penetrate.

Hansen turned away hastily. The mountainous mass made him uneasy; he remembered how easily a landslip had started on the inner slope.

"I'd better get moving!"

He struck out at a brisk, bounding pace, a trot on Luna without the effort of a normal trot. The ground was fairly level, and he congratulated himself upon making good time. Once or twice, he staggered a little, having overbalanced; but he soon got into the rhythm of the pace and the load on his back ceased to bother him. He bore slightly to the right, toward the jutting point of the ringwall.

The footing was like powdery gray sand. Alternating extremes of temperature during the two-week Lunar day or night had cracked the rock surface until successive expansions and contractions had affected the crystalline structure of the top layers. When these had flaked off, the powder had formed an insulating layer, but the result as far as Hansen was concerned was that he trotted on a sandy footing. When he looked back, he could see the particles kicked up by his last few steps still above the surface. They fell rather neatly, there being no air to whirl them about.

Gradually, he realized that the unobtrusive noises of his space suit had risen a notch in tone. The clever little machines were laboring to dispel the effects of his faster breathing. He dropped down to an easy walk, which was still a goodly pace in the light gravity.

"Guess I'm sweating more, too," he told himself. "Now that I think of it, my mouth's a little dry."

He twisted his neck until he could get his lips on the thin rubber hose sticking up to the left of his chin. He closed his teeth on the clamp, and sucked up a few swallows of water from his tank. It was not particularly tasty, but at least it was cool. It would have been a lot colder if carried uninsulated, he reflected. The night temperature of Luna was something like minus one-fifty Centigrade, and it dropped like a shot as soon as the surface was shaded from the sun.

Refreshed, he started out again at a bounding run, rejoicing in his strength. He felt as if he were just jogging along, but the ground rolled back under his feet swiftly. Had he been on such a bleak desert on Earth, he knew he would be slogging ankle-deep in sand—if he could move at all. His own weight was between a hundred and fifty and a hundred and sixty pounds. With what he was wearing and carrying, he was probably close to three hundred. It did not bother him here.

"It isn't bad at all," he thought with satisfaction. "Feels like jogging around the track in school, warming up for a race. One . . . two . . . three . . . four —still got pretty good form! Not even breathing hard!"

It occurred to him that it resembled a footrace in one other particular. He was deliberately putting off consideration of the finish while he still felt good.

"Oh, I'll meet them somewhere along the way," he said aloud, despite a momentary doubt that he was talking too much to himself. "Pretty soon, I'll cross the tractor trail. I'll follow it out maybe as far as Pico and wait for them to pick me up. The relief crew can't miss a landmark like that. It's damn near nine thousand feet high, straight up out of the flat plain."

He slowed down somewhat to scrutinize a ridge ahead. It turned out to be an easy grade and he skimmed over it easily. Otherwise, however, he was beginning to lose his recent feeling of satisfaction. Now that he moved out into the flat, empty plain, the essential grimness of Lunar landscape was more apparent than when disguised by the majesty of the view from atop the ringwall. It was a study in gray and black, the powdery sand and the deep shadows groping toward him as he trotted into the earthshine. Above was the deep black of an airless sky, lit by the bright Earth and chilly stars.

Gray, black, green, white—and all of it cold and inhospitable.

"I feel like I'm not wanted here," Hansen thought. "Well, that makes it mutual, I guess!"

He looked back, and was amazed at the distance he had covered. Already, Plato looked more like a range of towering mountains than it did like a barrier of cliffs.

"This won't take so long," he reassured himself. "I must have covered five miles running like this. Maybe almost ten."

He circled a tiny craterlet, or "bead," a few hundred yards across. In the precise center, it had a tiny peak, corresponding to the central mountain masses found in nearly half the craters of Luna. For the first time, Hansen regretted the camera that had gone down with the tractor.

"Too busy driving to take any pix on the way," he growled, "and now that I come across a perfect miniature, I have no camera. A fine spare photographer for an expedition this size!"

He diverted himself for a few minutes by considering what a fool he was to come to Luna in the first place. He had not really wanted to, and he was sure there were plenty of others who would have been better qualified and better pleased at the opportunity. Still, it was strange sometimes how a man would do things he did not want to because someone else was doing them.

He glanced up at Earth, and kept moving southward with the shining globe on his left front.

Mike and Joey sat before their radio, on a folding chair and empty crate respectively, maintaining whenever not directly addressed an almost sullen silence. Their tiny cubicle was becoming entirely too crowded to suit them.

Dr. Burney paced up and down before the wall map of the Mare Imbrium. Opposite him, the lower section of the radiomen's double bunk—canvas and aluminum like their single chair—had collected an overload of three. Dr. Sherman, the chief astronomer, sat between Bucky O'Neil and Emil Wohl. Besides heading the geologists, Wohl was Burney's second in command; and O'Neil was present in case it was decided to send out a rocket to photograph the Plato region.

"Ya'd think they could use their own rooms," Joey whispered into Mike's ear. "All but Bucky got singles. How we gonna catch an incoming call with all this racket?"

The "racket" at the moment consisted mostly of sighs, finger drumming, and a tortured semiwhistle from where Sherman sat staring at the map with his chin cupped in one hand.

"There's little doubt of the general location," repeated Burney, once more reaching a familiar impasse. "But I hate to hold up the other work to send out a crew when we cannot with any certainty agree that something has gone wrong."

"Let's see," said Wohl. "There was some difficulty, was there not, the last time they communicated?"

When no one answered, Mike finally repeated his previous testimony.

"Van Ness said they drove up a sort of mountain to get us. Complained a little about reception. He might've been getting to the limit."

"Then," said Wohl, "there is really no reason for alarm, is there? They could just as well have decided that continuing the mission was more important than running around looking for a good radio position, couldn't they?"

Mike considered that glumly.

"It's funny they didn't back up far enough to make *one* call to let me know they were going out of reach," he grumbled. "The speed they make in that rig, it wouldn'ta taken them long."

"That would have been the proper action," admitted Burney, "but we must not demand perfect adherence to the rules when a group is in the field and may have perfectly good reasons for disregarding them. No, I think we had best—Who's that coming?"

Bucky O'Neil bounded up from the end of the bunk

and stuck his head out the door. When he looked around, his freckled face was unhappy.

"Johnny Pierce from the map section," he announced. "He's got Louise with him. I guess you don't need me any more."

He edged out the door as two others of the base staff came in. The one who acted as if he had business there was a lean, bespectacled man who managed to achieve a vaguely scholarly air despite rough clothing.

Trailing him was a girl who looked as if the heating economy that necessitated the standard costume of the base also had the effect of cheating the male personnel of a brightening influence. The shapeless clothing, however, did not lessen the attractiveness of her lightly tanned features or lively black eyes. She wore her dark hair tucked into a knit cap that on Earth probably would have been donned only as a joke.

"We've looked at the photo maps," Pierce reported in a dry, husky voice. "They might very well be out of range. Lots of curvature in that distance, even with the depression caused by a mass of lava like that Mare Imbrium."

Burney accepted this with an expression of relief.

"I heard them talking about the Plato crew," the girl put in. "What's going on?"

Her voice was warm and, like a singer's, stronger than her petite outline would have suggested.

"Oh . . . just checking the radio reception," said Burney. "You can get the details from Mike, I suppose, if you have time off from the observatory. The rest of us are through here."

Mike scowled, and the girl looked puzzled; but Burney, Wohl, and Sherman crowded through the door as if intent upon some new project. Sherman muttered something about the problem of erecting a transparent dome for direct observations, and the voices receded down the corridor. Pierce slipped out after them.

"Did I say something?" inquired Louise. "I only thought there might be news."

"I guess they're just busy, Louise," Mike said. He turned to the radio, unplugged the speaker, and donned a set of earphones. "You know how it is. Why don't you catch Bucky? *He's* got nothing to do for a while."

Louise had started to show her even white teeth in a smile which now faded. Joey picked up his empty crate and busily moved it around to the other side of the radio setup.

"Sorry," said the girl, her dark eyes beginning to smolder. "I'll ask somebody else."

They listened to her footsteps as they faded away in the corridor. Mike looked at Joey and shrugged.

"What was I gonna tell her?" he asked. "That her husband either forgot to call in—or got himself quick-frozen when something in his tractor popped?"

Joey shook his head sympathetically. "Tough on her."

"Dunno why she had to come to Luna in the first place," Mike complained. "I can see a nurse like Jean doin' it, and a typewriter pusher like old Edna oughta be classed expendable. But a babe like Louise!"

"It's her science," said Joey. "She wants to see the stars better."

"We got enough astronomers now. She's a smart girl, all right—can't take that away from her. But if she was *my* woman, she wouldn'ta come up here!"

"If she was mine," countered Joey, "I wouldn'ta taken a second-rate job just to follow her up here either! But you're dreaming about the past, Boss."

"*Uh*-unh," grunted Mike, plugging in the speaker again. "I just believe in equal rights for men. How'd you like to be married to a dame like that and have to trail her to a place where there's three women to forty-eight men?"

"Ask me how I'd like to be married to a dame like that, period!" Joey invited him.

Mike adjusted the shade on the light so as to shadow half the room. He straightened the blanket where the three visitors had sat, appropriated the one from the upper bunk to cover himself, and lay down.

"Your watch," he announced coldly. "Wake me up if anything comes in!"

The rope lacing of the canvas creaked as he settled himself; then Joey was left with only the quiet hiss of the radio. He leaned back in the folding chair and relaxed.

Hansen paused and turned to survey the ground he had covered in the past half hour. The hiss of his air circulator and the whine of the tiny motors within his suit were a comfort in the face of his bleak surroundings.

He had found himself trotting along at such an easy pace that he had kept going past Mt. Pico. Now he wondered if he ought to stop.

"Might as well go on," he muttered. "Now that I've picked up the tractor trail from Archimedes, I can hardly be missed by the relief crew."

He eyed the twin tracks in the gray sand. Flanked by his own wide-spaced footprints, they stretched away into the dim distance. As a sign that man had passed, they did little but accentuate the coldness of the scene.

"Maybe I'll stop at the big triple peak," Hansen planned. "That's about thirty-five or forty miles . . . they ought to be along by then if they started right away."

Careful not to admit to himself that relief might be slow in starting from Archimedes, he took a last look at Pico. Rearing starkly upward, it projected a lonely, menacing grandeur, like a lurking iceberg or an ancient monument half buried in the creeping sands of a desert. In the light of the nearly full Earth, it was a pattern of gray angles and inky black patches—not a hospitable sight.

"Come on, come on!" Hansen reproved himself. "Let's get moving. You want to turn into a monument too?"

He had stopped just before reaching Pico to replenish his suit tank from the big cylinder, and still felt good at having managed the valves without the mishap he had feared. He did not feel like a man who had traveled seventy miles.

"Why, on Earth," he thought, "that would be a

good three-day march! I feel it a little, but not to the point of being tired."

He looked up at Earth as he started out again. The cloudy eastern coast of North America had moved around out of sight in the narrow dark portion. Hansen guessed that he had been on the move for at least four or five hours.

"I'd like to see their faces when they meet me way out here," he chuckled.

It occurred to him that he might be more tired than he thought, and as he went on he tried to save himself by holding his pace to a brisk walk. He found that if he got up on his toes a bit, he could still bound along that way.

The gray sand flowed under his feet, relieved occasionally by a stretch of yellowish ground. Hansen kept his eyes on his path and avoided the empty waste. When he did glance into the distance, he felt a twinge of loneliness. It was like the wide plainsland of the western United States, but grimly bare of anything so living as a wheat field.

He tried to remember as he moved along where it was that they had driven the tractor up a mountain ridge. He decided that he would rather avoid the climb, and kept an eye open for the chain of vein mountain beyond Pico.

"It ought to be faster to go around the end of them," he thought. "I can always pick up the tracks again."

When he finally sighted the rise ahead, he bore to his right. He remembered from the maps he had studied that the mountains curved somewhat toward another isolated peak, and he watched for that. As far as he knew, it had no name, but although only half the height of Pico, it was an unmistakable landmark.

The mountains on his left gradually dwindled into ragged hills and sank beneath the layer of lava. Hansen turned toward the last outcroppings as the triple mountain he sought came into sight. He climbed onto a broad rock and started to sit down.

The end of the big cylinder slung across his back

clanged on the back of his helmet. Hansen lost his balance and tumbled over the side of the rock. Under his groping hands, the heat-tortured surface of it flaked away, and he bounced once on the ground before sprawling full length.

"Damn!" he grunted. "When'll I learn to watch my balance with this load?"

He picked himself up and unslung the tank. Then, allowing for the normal bulk of his backpack of tank and batteries, he backed against the outcropping until he was resting at a comfortable angle.

"Maybe I ought to relax a few minutes," he told himself. "Give the air circulator time to filter out some of the sweat. Then, too, I don't want to get tired and miss them when they come along."

He idly scanned the arc between the peak toward which he was heading and Mt. Pico, still easily visible off tó his right. The northern part of the Mare Imbrium drew his gaze coaxingly into the distance until he felt an insane desire to thrust his head forward. It almost seemed that if he could get beyond the double glass of his insulated faceplate, if he could escape from the restraint of his helmet, he might perceive his bleak surroundings with a better, more real sense of proportion.

There was nothing out there, of course, he forced himself to realize. Except for shadows of craterlets that looked like low mountains, there was nothing to see for fifty miles, and nothing even then more noteworthy than a couple of minor craters.

"Then what are you looking for?" Hansen snapped. "You want it to get on your nerves? And quit talking to yourself!"

He suppressed, however, the sudden urge to spring up and break into a run. Instead, he hitched around to stare along the ridge at whose end he sat.

He was far enough south to be able to see the side lit by earthlight. The ridge climbed higher the farther it went, like the back of some sea monster rising from placid waters. Several miles away, a spur seemed to project out to the south; and Hansen thought he could remember a mile-wide crater on the maps.

He was a bit more comfortable inside his suit by now. He shifted his position to expedite the drying of the coveralls he wore under the space suit. Then he raised his arms and tried to clasp his hands behind his neck, but found that his garb was not that flexible.

"Shouldn't kick, I guess," he thought. "Without plenty of springs in the joints, I wouldn't be able to bend anything, considering the pressure difference."

He spent a minute admiring the construction of the suit that alone stood between him and instant extinction. That led him to think of the marvelous mechanism of the vacuum tractor that had carried him so comfortably—though he had not appreciated it at the time—across the Lunar plain. That, logically, recalled the men who had come with him and now were buried beneath one of Plato's many landslips.

"Talk about borrowed time!" he thought. "I wonder how long I'll stay lucky? Any little thing might do it—"

He had already taken three or four tumbles, or was it more? On any one of them, had he rolled the wrong way perhaps, he might have cracked that faceplate on a projecting rock. It was made as tough as possible, true, but if he ever cracked the outer pane, the insulating sheet of air would spurt out to leave him with a slow leak. The inner plate would lose heat and cloud up from his breath, so that he would end up without even knowing where he was dying.

Or if he had slid over a surface jagged enough to tear through his yellow chafing suit, and then to rip the tough material of the inner suit—

A puncture here would be a real blowout!

He reminded himself to be careful about stepping into shadows, especially if they were more or less straight-edged. He did not remember encountering on the way out any of the canyonlike rills that ran like long cracks straight through all other surface features of Luna—except occasional small craters slammed into the rock after the rill had been formed—but there was always the chance that he might step into some other kind of a hole.

Fortunately, the earthlight shone into his face, so that he should be able to tell a shadow resulting from some elevation ahead of him.

"I'm getting the jitters squatting here," Hansen thought. "It won't do any harm to move on a little way. At least out past that mountain, where I'll have a good view toward Archimedes."

He arose and slung the big cylinder over his back again, jiggling on the toes of his boots to jockey it into place. With one last look over his shoulder at the trail of his footprints splotched in the ashy sand, he started off.

He was surprised to discover that the rest had stiffened him slightly, but that soon worked out. As soon as he was warmed up, he moved out in a brisk walk which on Luna sent him bounding along with fifteen-foot strides. Swinging his arms to keep his balance, he concentrated upon the footing ahead of him. Once more he was alone with the hissing and humming of his suit and the sound of his own breathing, undisturbed by either memory or anticipation.

Mike Ramirez stirred on his bunk with the change of the quiet hissing of the radio. Something more than the occasional crackle or creak of Joey's chair or footfall in the corridor brought him up with eyes still half closed. To his sleep-drugged mind, it seemed that nothing had existed until a second ago, when a faint, dreamlike voice had started to speak.

He started to push back his blanket—Joey's blanket—and said, "Joey! You got a call!"

". . . to Archimedes Base. Hello Base! Over."

"I hear him!" snarled Joey. "Go back to sleep!"

He pushed his switch and the rushing noise that had partly muffled the weak voice gave way before the surge of his own transmitter.

"Archimedes Base to Tractor One!" Joey answered, and Mike leaned back on one elbow and sighed.

He did not listen while Joey took the message, but swung his feet to the floor and sat up. Wiggling his toes uncomfortably, he wished he had taken off his shoes; but he had expected to lie down only half an hour or so. Until the call came in, he had been sound asleep.

Joey acknowledged the message and turned to Mike after dropping his pencil.

"The Serenitatis bunch," he said. "They left two of them at Linné to take photos and poke around while the other pair brought the tractor back through between the Apennines and Caucasus to call in."

"Everything okay?"

"Yeah, they're on the way back already, but they say Linné didn't look as if it was ever a volcano after all."

"Very true if interesting," said Mike. "Okay, take it to Burney. I'll bend an ear a while."

He tossed the blanket back onto the upper bunk and walked over to the chair. He stretched, and sat down as Joey's footsteps departed down the corridor.

He sat there, staring moodily at the softly lighted dials of the radio, wishing he had a cigarette. That was one habit he had had to cut off short when joining the expedition.

"I think I'm getting over it some," he congratulated himself. He looked up at the sound in the corridor, thinking that Joey had made good time to Burney's compartment and back. He raised an eyebrow as Louise entered.

"I just saw Joey go by," she announced hastily. "Did some news come in?"

"Tractor One reported—just routine. What are you doing, picketing this dive?"

"I—I just happened to be passing the Junction, and I saw the paper in Joey's hand."

"Uh-huh," grunted Mike.

What the members of the expedition had come to call the Junction was an intermediate dome equipped with the main airlock. The other buildings connected with it through safety doors so as to localize any danger of air loss in the event of a rupture in one of the domes. It was, in effect, the front hall of the whole base.

*And if you stand there long enough,* thought Mike, *everyone you know on Luna will pass by, and you'll find out everything that's going on.*

"Where is number Two now?" demanded Louise quietly.

*Scared,* thought Mike, noting the overcontrolled tenseness of her voice.

"I don't know for sure," he answered, not looking at her. "It's time they were inside Plato, and we can't expect to hear them from in there."

Louise walked jerkily to the bunk and sat on the foot of the lower section. She crossed her legs. Seeing the nervous manner in which she twitched her foot, Mike turned to his radio.

After a moment, she spoke again, and his shoulders quivered at the agonized harshness of her tone.

"Don't string me along, Mike! I want to know! You were worried about them hours ago, weren't you?"

Mike licked his lips.

"That don't mean anything," he muttered.

"The others backtracked to report, didn't they? To call in, I mean. Something happened to number Two, didn't it?"

"Now, take it easy, Louise!" Mike squirmed in his chair, then forced himself to sit still. It was not the sort of furniture that would stand much squirming. "Burney kinda considered that as a possibility, but in the end they decided things were probably okay."

"Then why did they have Bucky in here?" she demanded.

"Just in case they thought it worth the trouble of scouting the Plato region. Nothing special."

Louise bounced up from the bunk. She stood beside it, stiff, with her little fists clenched tightly at her sides.

"They wouldn't let this long a time go by without calling in and you know it!" she declared. "Even if they did, there ought to be a tractor on the way to check."

"You might have a point there," admitted Mike.

"It could always be called back."

"It's probably been thought of," said Mike. "Look, Louise, why don't you calm down and let the worryin' get done by the people supposed to do it?"

She did not look at him. The darkness of her eyes surprised him, and he realized how she had paled beneath her tan.

"I can't help it," she said. "It's my fault, in a way. He only came along because I got so excited about the expedition I couldn't stay down on Earth. He didn't want to come, and now he's out there—"

Mike rose and shoved his chair aside with his foot. He thought the girl was going to faint. Watching her narrowly, he reached out to put his hand on her arm.

He sighed with relief as he heard Joey whistling outside. Louise straightened and moved away from his hand as the younger operator entered.

"Why don't you go see Burney?" suggested Mike. "He'll explain how he figures the odds; or if you want to argue, it's more sense to do it with him than me. I got nothing to do with it."

The girl pulled herself together with a visible effort.

"I know, Mike. Thanks for listening, anyway."

"Joey, go along with her to Burney's quarters!"

"That's all right," said Louise. "I can find my way farther than that."

They watched her leave.

Once more, Joey took the chair before the set and the pair of them sat in glum silence. The ventilation system came to life in one of its efforts to homogenize the base atmosphere, and its sigh partly drowned out the hiss of the radio.

"You know something, Joey?" grunted Mike.

"What?"

"I got a feelin' we're not gonna see those guys again."

"Hope you're wrong," said Joey. "It's awful tough digging around here, after the first few inches."

Hansen trotted along steadily with the four-thousand-foot mountain rising in a sheer sweep out of the lava "sea" over to his right. There were three distinct peaks, he knew, but they ran in a line away from him so that the whole thing appeared one towering mass to him. Most of it, from his position, was black with the deepness of Lunar shadows, although he was gradually reaching a location where he could see the splashes of earthlight on the tortured rocks.

"Pretty soon I'll be out in the real flat, with nothing but a scattering of little craters to steer by," he reflected. "If I don't want to stop, how had I better head?"

Just in case the problem should arise, he began to estimate the direction he should take and the sort of ground he would find.

The first thing would be to bear slightly left until he picked up the trail of the tractor once more. Then he could expect a region of fairly frequent craterlets, leading up to Kirch, a modest but respectable seven miles in diameter. If he passed to the right of Kirch, he would be kept from wandering aimlessly out into the Mare Imbrium by a range of vein mountains. He might go farther astray by passing Kirch to the left, but there the going would probably be easier.

"Then what?" he murmured, trying to recall the map and the journey in the tractor.

There was another open area, he seemed to remember, and then the forty-mile string of peaks called the Kirch Mountains, bordered on the right by an even longer ridge of vein mountains which might once have been part of the range.

And then, another thirty miles or so would bring him to the ringwall of Archimedes!

Hansen shook his head.

"That would be going a little too far," he muttered.

His voice sounded husky to his own ears, and he paused to suck up a few swallows of water through the hose. He must have been half hypnotized by the steady streaming of the gray surface under his feet, for he suddenly realized that he had gone considerably beyond the triple peak.

Without his steady forward speed, he found it difficult for a moment to stand erect. He braced against the movement of the big tank on his back, and turned around to look back.

He stared at the dark, earthlit ground over which he had been trotting. With the looming mountain in the foreground, and the upthrust ringwalls of smaller craterlets here and there above the level, aseptic frigidity of the plain, it was a scene of complete desolation. It was more naked of life or any kind of softness than any desert on Earth; yet to Hansen, it did not really seem like a desert. There was some further overtone plucking at the fringe of his consciousness.

Then it came to him.

"It's like an *ocean!*" he exclaimed. "There's something about it that's like . . . like a cold, gray, winter sea smashing in on a rocky coast!"

There was the same monstrous, chilling power, the same effect upon the beholder that here was a massive, half-sentient entity against whose callous strength and cruelty nothing human could stand. It was a *thing* to observe from a safe distance, to cower from lest it somehow become aware of the puny structure of bone, blood, and flesh spying upon it. Then there would be no escape, no withstanding the crushing force of its malice. But he was on no safe cliff. He was down *in* the sea.

He looked around. Gray everywhere, mottled with inky shadows. Gray ash underfoot, gray-and-black lumps thrusting up from the surface like colossal vertebrae, gray distance in all directions.

"Been going for hours," he thought, "and there's no sign, really, that I'll ever get anywhere! I might as well be in the middle of the far side of Pluto!"

The huge mountain towered behind him, like a hulking beast from some alien world stalking the only object in all its frozen world that dared to move. Hansen suddenly could not bear to have his back turned to it. He faced it and edged clumsily away. The helmet that reduced his field of vision was his prison. If that black-shadowed mass of rock chose to topple over, it would easily reach him, and more. He would be ground under countless tons of weight, mangled and frozen in one instant—

Hansen whirled about and bolted.

On his first stride, he caught the toe of his right foot in the sand and sprawled forward with flailing arms. He plowed into the ground, throwing up spurts of sand like a speedboat tossing spray.

Somehow, he was up immediately, running in long, wobbling, forty-foot bounds. His eyes bulged and the breath rasped between his lips as he strove desperately to keep his balance.

It was like running in a dream, the nightmare come true. More than once, until he adapted to the pace, he found himself churning two or three steps at the zenith of his trajectory, too impatient to wait for the touch of boot on sand. There was sudden, dynamic power in his tiring muscles. All his joints felt loose.

His chest began to labor and he stumbled slightly. With a quick spasm, he blew his lungs and sucked in a deeper breath. After a few repetitions, he felt a trifle easier. In a minute he began to get his second wind. All this came like a half-perceived process of instinct, while he concentrated narrowly upon speeding ahead.

He flew up a slight grade and took off in a soaring leap to the next crest of an undulating stretch of pale yellow ash. The next thing he knew, he was rushing upon a long shadow that barred his path.

A hasty glance each way warned him there was no use trying to skirt it, for the shadow or hole or whatever it was ran for hundreds of yards right and left. Hansen stamped hard at the near edge and kicked off for at least sixty feet. Something seemed to snap in his right knee, but he came down all right and kept running, well clear of the shadow.

How long he ran, dodging this way and that to avoid hills and shadows obstructing his path, he did not know. In the end, the tiny motors of his suit fell behind the rate at which he consumed oxygen and gave off carbon dioxide and copious moisture.

When he began to feel like an underwater swimmer reaching his limit with writhing chest, Hansen gave up. He stopped.

That felt worse. He moved on at a gentle walk, accomplishing it mostly by motion from the ankles down. Amid the stifling warmth and stickiness inside his space suit, it was borne in upon him how badly he had lost his head.

He looked back, panting. Where was the mountain? Then, following the trail of isolated scars on the surface beyond where they faded into the gray distance, he saw a small knob of gray against the star-dotted black of the horizon.

"I guess . . . I've . . . really been traveling!" he panted. "Twenty minutes or half an hour—wonder how fast I went to put a mountain out of sight? Of course . . . I was well past when I started."

That reminded him of his bolt, and he closed his eyes in a paroxysm of shame.

The sweat beading his forehead began to trickle down his cheekbones or nose. Now and then, a drop rolled into his eyes, despite efforts to shake his head inside the confines of the helmet. It stung, but he was too blown to get excited over that.

"Why did I have to go and do that?" he groaned inwardly.

He remembered how levelheaded he had been in the first minutes of the catastrophe. Calmly, he had judged the odds of there being any survivors; calmly, he had climbed down for the prime requisite, the tank of oxygen; calmly, he had started off by a well-chosen route that led him accurately to landmarks so plain that they could be spotted from Earth with a good pair of field glasses.

He had intended to go only as far as Pico, or perhaps the triple peak. Or had he?

Somewhere back there, he remembered, he had

begun planning a further march. There could be no reason for that except—

Except that he was secretly aware that he could count upon no help to reach him in time!

"Why should they send anybody out yet?" he asked himself. "For all they know, we're still inside Plato, camping on the nice level lava floor. I *must* have been thinking that, underneath, when I was figuring which side to pass Kirch."

He had been skating on thin ice and should have expected a crack-up. For a moment, he considered the possibility that it would have been better had he broken down on the spot. But then he might have quit while still on the ringwall of the great crater.

"As it is," he said aloud, "I'll at least get the most possible mileage out of this suit. If I live long enough, I might even walk in on them at base, for a surprise."

He grinned a bit as he considered that pleasant fantasy:

*"Hi, Paul; where you been?"*

*"Oh, just out for a little walk on the moon."*

*"And where did you go on your little moon walk?"*

*"Took a turn around Plato. Pretty boring but 'toujours gai, whatthehell whatthehell!' "*

He managed a deeper breath as his equipment caught up somewhat to his physical needs. The half grin on his lean features faded, and he stepped up his plodding pace.

"Why kid myself?" he snorted. "I'm just about scared senseless! And I've got a right to be!"

Bucky O'Neil, as the pilot who was to take the scouting rocket, occupied the only extra chair in Dr. Burney's headquarters room. Burney sat across from him at the folding table and circled the proposed search area continuously with the butt of his pencil. Both men eyed the map reflectively. Burney looked as if he were trying to guess the precise location of his tractor crew. O'Neil, tracing his route with a blunt forefinger, was obviously attempting to estimate where he would have to punch his flare release in order to have his camera working by the time he whipped across Plato.

"Just to save us the wait," said Burney, leaning back in the silent, crowded room, "report by radio as soon as you loop back. Have you checked your set with Mike?"

The radio operator, standing to the rear of the little group, spoke up, "Joey's checking with the field now."

"Good!" approved Burney. "Does anyone have anything to add?"

He looked about. Sherman whistled quietly and tonelessly. Wohl shook his head. Johnny Pierce hovered, waiting to get his hands on his photomap again. Louise leaned against one wall near the door, worrying a pencil end between her white teeth.

"All right, then," said Burney, "you can get into your suit, Bucky. Good luck!"

The gathering broke up. Burney signaled for Wohl and Dr. Sherman to stay behind, and forestalled Johnny's move to reappropriate the map.

"We may want to consider further," he offered as an excuse, and Pierce left with Mike.

Outside, they watched Louise follow Bucky in the opposite direction.

"Wonder how it feels to have her man out there and maybe not coming back?" murmured Johnny.

His long face looked sad.

"What do you think their chances are?" he persisted after a brief pause as they turned a corner in the corridor.

Mike shrugged.

"Tractor One is starting back already," he said simply.

Hurrying along the other end of the corridor, Bucky was unable to shake off the following footsteps without putting on an obvious burst of speed. It sounded like Louise, and he wanted to think about his flight plan.

Finally, as he passed through the safety door—a double mounting that could be used in an emergency as an airlock—he had to pause long enough to acknowledge her presence.

"Do you mind if I ask you something, Bucky?" Louise inquired.

"Of course not, but I have to—"

"I know; I won't take more than a minute. The thing I don't like is that they just want you to photograph Plato."

Bucky released the door which swung shut automatically. He looked puzzled.

"Don't you think it's worth doing?" he asked.

"Oh, yes! Yes, I do. But how about all the other places?"

The pilot fidgeted.

"I can't take shots of the whole Mare Imbrium, Louise."

"You might take a few of the section this side of Plato, though. How do we know they ever reached the crater? If tracks show up on your pictures, we'll know how far they got."

"That's a good point," admitted Bucky, scratching his head. "But why didn't you bring it up in the meeting?"

Louise looked away. She shrugged slightly.

"Well, maybe Burney would have talked you out of it," Bucky conceded. "We all know you're worried."

"I know what everybody thinks," Louise replied. "I'm getting excited because one of the four happens to be my husband. I'm not thinking calmly about what's best for the base as a whole, whether it's worth taking people off other jobs to play hide-and-seek out on the surface. I probably shouldn't have come to Luna in the first place."

Bucky looked around, but there was no one passing through the Junction. Louise stepped closer and put a trembling hand on his arm.

"All right, Bucky, it's true enough. I'm frightened. I wish I'd never thought of coming here and making Paul feel he had to trail along! Are you married, Bucky, or engaged?"

"Well, there's a little blonde waiting down there for me—I hope. She'd better wait."

"How would you like it if *she* were out there?"

"Ummm," murmured the pilot. "I see what you mean."

He saw more than that. He saw how close she was to losing her grip, how she was keeping back the tears with an effort, trying to use every ounce of self-discipline so as to keep from being ignored as hysterical. Getting a few little things done, like influencing him to take extra photos, was all she could do at the moment to look out for her man. He remembered hearing from Pierce that Burney had refused her offer to take out a tractor herself.

"Well . . ." he yielded, "I'll see if I have a chance. I figure to cover the approaches to the ringwall anyway; maybe I can get a shot out around Pico, or thereabouts."

She did not thank him, but hid her face against his shoulder for a second. Bucky looked around again, touched her lightly on the head with one big, freckled hand, and disengaged himself gently.

When he glanced back over his shoulder, Louise was opening the safety door to go back.

"Heading for Mike and the radio, I bet," he thought. "Wonder when she slept last?"

He reminded himself that he had a job to do which involved delicate judgments at high speed, and he had no business going into it with hindering worries on his mind. If that girl did not watch herself, she would wind up under the care of Jean and "M.D." McLeod.

"I'm liable to, myself," he muttered, "if I don't snap out of it now! I wonder who'll pick me up if I zig out there when I ought to zag?"

He stopped at a phone connection and called the field control dome to learn if they were ready for him.

Dazzling glints of light flashed here and there from that part of the Pacific Ocean still in bright sunlight as Hansen came in sight of Kirch. The coast of California had faded into the darkness and Asia was partly in view. He estimated that he had been moving for nearly eight hours.

His pace was still a rhythmic lope, but the feeling of

having vigorous reserves of strength had worn off. Hansen knew that he must rest soon. In traversing the flat, crater-speckled plain since his panic, he had paused only once when he took a few minutes to recharge the oxygen tank of his suit.

"But I'm due for a good half hour off my feet," he decided.

His legs, he noticed, had lost some of their snap, so that his bounding trot was less exuberant. On the other hand, this resulted in his getting slightly better control of his stride; he no longer broke his rhythm by bouncing too high. The thing that bothered him most was the growing ache across the small of his back.

He skirted the ringwall of the last of a series of small craters and saw the shadowed side of the seven-mile wall. He was approaching the left curve of it, for he had hours ago decided to abandon the tractor tracks when he had crossed them again.

"No use running up the right and getting into the Kirch Mountains," he had muttered. "I'd have to zigzag through them and I doubt I'll feel like making any extra distance by then."

His guess now, from the angle of Earth in the starry sky, was that he was heading a shade left of his generally southerly route. He reminded himself that he must change after rounding Kirch.

"I'll keep going till I'm past," he promised himself. "Then I'll sit down and relax a while."

He could not see much point in making another few miles out into the empty wasteland beyond Kirch. The crater was a natural goal to mark a section of his journey. About halfway between Plato and Archimedes, it was farther than he had dreamed of going. Even now, after he had seen how fast he could travel in the light gravity, it struck him as almost unbelievable that he could have covered such a distance. It was nearly a hundred and fifty miles.

Yet here he was, not in bad shape at all. He glanced at the outer slope of the ringwall on his right, and mentally cataloged his various irritations. There was, of course, the general clamminess that resulted from spending hours in a space suit, plus the fact that his bladder was beginning to bother him and there was nothing he could do about it. The overheating due to his exertions had been partially adjusted when he had discovered during his last halt that he could regulate the heating unit by a small dial in his battery pack, which discovery left him slightly aggrieved at not having had the finer points of the care and handling of space suits more exhaustively explained to him.

"But then," he reflected, "I was probably expected to spend a lot of time in the darkroom as a spare photographer."

He could not say he was hungry, although he supposed that sooner or later he would discover feelings of weakness. His suit seemed to be functioning as well as could be expected, except for something that had given way in the right knee on that one leap. He wondered if a spring was working loose.

"That could end up giving me a beautiful limp," he thought. "With fourteen pounds inside, and no air at all outside, it'd be tough to bend a joint without some mechanical help."

By now he could see light-streaks along the ring-wall, and knew that he was rounding it. The lighting gradually increased as he continued, until when he began to move out into the open plain some time later, the walls were mostly gray with earthlight. Kirch had a "new" appearance, as craters went. Its floor was not lava-filled, nor its ringwall seemingly as long exposed to thermal erosion, so that the probability was that it had been formed after the "sea" around it.

Hansen began to keep an eye out for a suitable place to sit down. Presently, he located a rock the size of an auto.

"Time for a drink, and then I'll pick out a good spot," he sighed.

The second he stopped to grope with his lips for the little hose, he knew he was really tired.

The water, cool from being only partly surrounded by heating coils to protect it from the exterior cold, refreshed him but slightly. The running had left a thick taste in his mouth.

Hansen unslung the big cylinder he had carried on his back and set it down beside a comfortable indentation in the rock. He then unfastened his backpack of tank and batteries. The metal-covered connection protecting the hose and wires was long enough to permit the pack to be set at his side.

He lowered himself to the fine sand and leaned his back against the rock with a sigh of relief. He squirmed into a more comfortable position.

"Wish I hadn't drunk all that water," he growled.

He leaned the back of his neck against the neckpiece of his suit. It was not uncomfortable except that he found himself staring directly into the light of Earth.

"I'm getting used to it all right, if I think that's too bright," he thought. "Bet my pupils are big as a cat's now."

Ironically, his feet had not started to hurt until his weight was off them. It felt as if he were developing blisters. The coveralls he wore under the space suit, moreover, had begun to chafe in a few places—around the armpits as he swung his arms, behind his right knee, on the inside of his thighs.

He also was reminded of the sweat that had trickled around or into his eyes, for the lids felt sore.

"I want a different view," he grunted, picking himself up. "Facing the other way, maybe I can rest my eyes."

Carrying his backpack, he started around the rock, then prudently went back for his big oxygen cylinder. He could think of no good reason for dragging this with him, but he somehow felt more comfortable with it beside him.

The other face of the rock was blackly shadowed, and he was forced to find a convenient spot by groping about. With a sigh, he settled down, squirmed again into an easy position, and found himself contemplating the ringwall of Kirch a few miles away. The regular sough of air through his suit and the quiet hum of the mechanisms that were keeping him alive were so familiar by now that he hardly noticed them. It was the cessation of movement, not any diminishment of the normal sounds, that lent an impression of quiet to the scene.

He looked at the ringwall, squinting against the sting in his eyes that caused them to water occasionally. The left extremity was dim in the distance, but to the right, he could clearly see the slope of the wall as it curved to meet the plain. There was no feeling of a towering, insecurely balanced mass like that of the mountain.

"Although a crater at a distance does look like a mountain range," he thought. "Not so close as this; it goes up too steeply."

In a way, it was almost like looking at the skyscrapers of a big city, like looking at Manhattan from across the Hudson River. Except that there were no lights.

He closed his eyes for a moment and tried to visualize the sharp peak a little to his left atop the wall as it might look with a thousand lighted windows gleaming white and yellow.

It was hard to do. The stark fact was that there was only Lunar dimness, relieved by earthlight but tending to be uniform in intensity without the rays of the sun. If the silhouette of Kirch was like that of a city, the metropolis it resembled was a dead one.

A dead city in the midst of a cold, frozen sea of lava. A ghost city that had never lived, yet rose up from the gray sea over which no ship had sailed and whispered and whined ghostly warnings. "Stay with me, Man! I am dry and lonely. There are no people to warm me with light and sound. . . . There is none to see my massive strength and, by seeing, make it into reality. . . . Stay where you are, Man!"

"But it's dead," thought Hansen. "More than dead—sterile!"

"But you, Man, you too are dead. You are already turning cold. You will slowly congeal . . . become solid . . . a monument . . . a symbol of the tribute brought by folly and life to the sea of coldness and gray death—No, do not shake your head. . . . It is too late. . . . My shadows are about you. . . . You have no light. . . . All your prayers and wishes will not turn on a single light. The shadows reach you . . . touch you. . . . The pain in your leg is the cold of space. . . . You will sit there forever . . . drowned in the gray sea of frozen lava . . . imagining lights for me in the blackness . . . imagining life in me in the noon glare. . . . But now there is no light unless you have the force to see it . . . but you are cold . . . cold . . . cold . . . cold. . . ."

The sky flared with flickering light. It turned black while the image of light still remained in Hansen's eyes. Then a new light, tinier and higher streaked overhead. Hansen awoke with the hairs tingling on his neck and leaped to his feet with a hoarse shout.

*"A rocket!"*

In the stillness of the radio room, the incoming call from Bucky's rocket made Mike jump in his chair before the set. Hastily, he turned down the volume he had kept up in hope of picking up faint calls from Plato.

When he had answered and relayed the message by phone to the landing area, he turned to the others in the room.

Joey had been sleeping in the upper bunk. Louise had asked to stay and Mike had offered his bunk for her to sit on. She had not slept, as far as he knew; but he had turned to the radio and maintained a lengthy silence.

"Maybe I ought to talk to her," he thought, "but what is there to say? Four good guys; but they're awful late checking in."

But when he looked around, they were both watching him; and he had to tell them.

"Bucky's coming in," he said.

"Did he find anything?" demanded Louise.

"Don't know yet," Mike told her. "He said he took

a snap of Plato coming and going and three more on the way back."

Louise moved toward the door.

"Thanks a lot, Mike," she said.

Joey slipped down from the bunk as she disappeared into the corridor.

"Never mind," advised Mike. "With Louise and Bucky in that hole they call a darkroom, dodging the photographer's elbow every time he breathes in, they won't have any place for you but up on a shelf."

"I just thought I'd—"

"We'll get told. Now, stay with me, kid, an' make sure *I* don't go wanderin' off to have a look too!"

Hansen stood stiffly by the rock and painfully tried his neck muscles. He searched the sky, but nothing moved among the stars.

"Now, *did* I see something?" he asked himself slowly. "Or was I still dreaming?"

He grimaced, and raised a hand to the back of his head before he remembered that he was still in his space suit. His neck was stiff and sore from lying across the rigid neckpiece of his suit, and he was chilled to the bone.

"Must have been asleep quite a while," he thought. "Maybe I ought to turn up the heating again—or should I just warm up as I walk?"

He paused a moment to stare in open-mouthed amazement at the ringwall of Kirch, rearing up three thousand feet toward the stars.

"When am I going to do something right?" he asked. "Why couldn't I stay where I was, facing Earth, and go to sleep dreaming I was home?"

He went on to wish that he had not gone to sleep at all. The aches that were irritations when he was warm from walking were now centers of agony.

He was sure he had blisters, and the chafed places under the suit jabbed little warnings of tenderness as he tried to move. Reaching for his battery pack, he nearly toppled over because his right leg was asleep.

Even after he recovered and took a few steps to restore the circulation, the knee did not feel right.

"I wonder if I pulled a muscle?" he mused. "Or is it in the suit?"

He looked up at Earth. India was moving into the arc of shadow, but he could see Africa, the Mediterranean, and Europe.

When he realized he must have been out for three or perhaps four hours, he immediately checked his oxygen. It was none too soon. He refilled his suit tank and examined the pressure of the big cylinder. He guessed that he could do the trick once more.

"I wonder how long a man can live in a space suit?" he muttered. "Hansen, why aren't you dead?"

Groaning with stiffness, he adjusted his battery pack and tank and slung the cylinder atop the load. Although he seemed as wet as ever, he sucked up a drink of water while he listened to the hiss of his air circulator.

"Wish I wasn't so thirsty," he said. "I'll have to watch it. Beginning to feel lack of food, too."

He started off, moving mincingly to favor his sore muscles, and immediately felt the weakness brought on by hunger. It was hard to believe that a nightmare could last so long, but he remembered that it was almost a full day since he had eaten a sandwich in the tractor.

Gradually, as he moved along, marching away from Kirch into the open wasteland, he began to warm up. The stiffness left his muscles, although the chafing remained annoying. His feet felt sticky in the thick socks, suggesting that he would have trouble. He thought they might be bleeding.

What the hell was the matter with that knee? he wondered.

He thought of stopping to examine it, but the likelihood of his falling over on his face if he bent to feel the joint deterred him. He kept on. In half an hour, it became clear that a spring had snapped.

Not only was the knee harder to bend than it should

have been, but something began to dig through his coveralls behind the knee.

"That's not so good," he told himself, but there was nothing he could think of to do.

He finally mustered the ambition to get up on his toes and bound along at a fairly brisk pace. The miles again floated under his feet, but he found that he could not maintain the trot the way he had earlier. Then, he had congratulated himself on his freshness, but he had come a long way since those few hours of immunity to fatigue.

The end of an hour found him moving at a moderate walk. One more, and he stopped noticing the pace particularly. There were few landmarks about him. He did not even strain ahead to catch a glimpse of the Kirch Mountains.

Finally, the nagging pain behind his knee became bad enough to make him stop.

"This is damn silly!" he growled. "I can't go along until that point of metal saws through a vein or something! Must be something I can do about it."

He thought it over, but it seemed that there simply was nothing he *could* do. The broken bit of metal was beyond his reach; he could not even feel it through the thickness of the space suit and the protective yellow chafing suit. Even if he should remove the latter by some weird contortion, the knee joint, as an obvious trouble spot, was reinforced by a bulge of metal. He would not be able to pinch or prod through that.

"Of course," he muttered, "I might take it off entirely. That would make things easy right away. A lot easier than just sitting down to wait for my air to run out."

He shook that out of mind with a jerk of his head, and struck out across the plain once more.

He had come to a stretch of gently rolling rises, and he tried to get most of his upward push from his left leg. Coming down the slopes, he hopped stiff-legged on his right. It was not too long before this became more tiring than it was worth.

"To hell with it!" he growled, and grimly drove onward with a more normal gait despite the sharp dig . . . dig . . . dig into his flesh at every stride.

Burney and Bucky again sat across the table in the former's room. Instead of the map they had consulted earlier, they gazed down at the new photographs. The room, as before, was crowded with others who had edged in to watch silently. Even "M.D." McLeod, so nicknamed to distinguish him from all the doctors of philosophy and doctors of science among the expedition, lingered with his stethoscope dangling after giving Bucky a routine, postflight check.

Johnny Pierce stood lankily behind Burney's shoulder, holding a spare magnifying glass and squinting down at the photos. Sherman, Wohl, and Joey stood around the table with the photographers who had developed and enlarged the pictures. Louise watched from behind Bucky, resting her hands on his shoulders.

Burney nodded slowly, examining the picture of the interior of Plato through his lens.

"I very much fear," he said, tapping a forefinger on the half-lit heap of material at the foot on the ringwall, "that there is only one conclusion. That is a new slide, is it not?"

"It is," said Dr. Sherman, gesturing slightly with an older photograph of the region.

"And it is quite clear that they reached the crater," Burney continued. "These are excellent pictures, and the trail of the tractor treads shows very definitely."

"How about this one, Dr. Burney?" asked Bucky, pushing across another photo.

It showed the region around Mt. Pico, and had been enlarged until tracks of the tractor could be clearly seen. Burney frowned when he looked at it.

"To be perfectly frank," he murmured, "I do not know what to make of it. Those marks accompanying the trail *could* be footprints, I suppose, as has been suggested. But why . . . or how?"

"A man running could make marks that far apart in this gravity," said Bucky. "I know Johnny estimates those little dots are twenty and thirty feet apart, but it's possible."

"It is also possible that they are nothing of the sort. You notice that they leave the trail after a time."

Louise spoke up.

"That at least rules out one interpretation," she said. "They certainly aren't footprints made by someone on the surface on the way *to* Plato. Anybody walking beside the tractor would have left a trail starting and ending at the tread tracks."

There was silence. Some of the men looked at her with pity, others stared very hard at the photographs on the table.

Burney prodded another picture with his finger.

"Bucky took this where the tracks passed Kirch," he reminded them. "There are none of these so-called footprints there. I regret to point out the obvious conclusion—"

"But can't you do something to make sure?" Louise burst out. "You aren't just going to leave them out there. You couldn't!"

"Of course not," said Burney, biting his lip uncomfortably. "As soon as the Serenitatis crew get a few hours' rest, I shall send them out to recover . . . ah . . . to check. But the time element has already become such that—Well, my dear, there is simply no use in rushing things. Either there is no need, or it is already too late."

There was not much doubt as to which possibility seemed the more likely. The meeting began to break up in unhappy silence.

Hansen trudged along with his chin on the neckpiece of the suit. Every so often, when he lurched in the shifting sand, his forehead bumped against the faceplate of his helmet.

"And that's not so easy to do," he thought foolishly. "Takes a supple neck to accomplish it."

He concentrated for perhaps a hundred paces, and slowly arrived at the corollary.

"Takes a pretty soft and supple head to get out here

in the first place. Shoulda stood at home in bed. Should've stayed on Plato and tried to build some kind of a marker. Base'll send out somebody . . . wonder if that was a rocket I saw? Maybe I'd be dead . . . but I'm gonna be dead anyway. Why don't I just sit down and wait? At least, it won't hurt anymore. And, I'll be easy."

No arguments to the contrary occurred to him, but some deep impulse refused to let him quit.

He had to pause again; his stops for rest were becoming frequent. He did not sit down.

Never get up again, he realized.

He planted his feet wide apart and stood there, panting and letting his hands hang limply at his sides. His face felt stiff as he bared his teeth against the throb of the cut behind his knee. By now, he was so used to the wetness of the leg that he could not be sure the blood trickled down any faster.

He saw that he was standing on ground lighter than usual, and tinted pale yellow. Remembering passing several such areas, he slowly realized that they must be rays from Aristillus, traces of vaporized minerals blown out across the surrounding territory when the crater had been formed. It meant, for what it might be worth, that he was getting near Archimedes. Some of the rays of Aristillus reached the larger crater.

He gritted his teeth and took the first step forward. A glance to his right assured him that the jagged peaks of the Kirch Mountains were where they should be. Once, as he walked along half awake, he had discovered himself turning away on a course that would have sent him circling back into the Mare Imbrium.

"Sea of Showers," he thought. "I wish there were some. I wish I even had a glass of water to pour over my head. Just a glass of water to rinse out these eyes. I wouldn't even care about a shave."

He began to notice his footsteps, besides the hiss of the air circulator and the laboring of the suit's motors. Through his boots, they had a distant, swishing sound that insidiously lowered his puffed eyelids little by little. His head bumped against the faceplate again.

Hansen jerked upright with a start. Clumsily, he turned to look back. His tracks were long, dragging gashes in the sandy surface.

"Hell! Going to sleep again," he croaked.

With the effort of speaking aloud—it was getting difficult to think clearly otherwise—the corner of his lower lip cracked. He opened his dry mouth, making a face at the morning-after taste, and gently touched the tip of his tongue to the spot. It stung.

No harm in taking a little water, he decided, though he knew it would offer only a fleeting relief. But he needed that.

He turned his head to the left and got the thin rubber tube between his teeth. The cracked lip stung as he sucked on the tube.

The water was cool. His tired eyes closed with the sheer pleasure of the sensation.

On the third swallow, it stopped flowing.

"Oh, *no!*" Hansen groaned.

He drew harder on the hose and eked out another mouthful. That was all. The tank was empty. It was supposed to be partly replenished by moisture removed from the air in the suit, but he had apparently reached the limit. The suit was not designed to be worn for twenty hours. It was a wonder that nothing had yet broken down.

He held the last mouthful without swallowing, letting it roll slowly about his mouth.

"Come on!" he thought. "That's all there is. What are you waiting for?"

He knew it was silly to feel angry at this latest pinprick. His growing rage was a sign of exhaustion, and some part of his mind recognized that fact; but he deliberately let his temper go . . . and drew extra strength from it.

The swallow of water gradually slipped down as he surged forward. With the stiff right knee, he staggered once and came so near falling flat that he skidded on all fours under him again.

"Dammit!" he raged. "What are they doing at base?

Waiting for a weather report? Anybody with an ounce of brain would know by now things went sour!"

He lurched down a gentle slope and charged the next rise.

"I'll show them!" he grunted. "I don't need them, if they're too chicken to come out for me. I'll get there. . . . I don't know how I'll get up the goddamned wall . . . but I'll get *to* it! I'll get there!"

Mike sat before his radio and looked at the other three in the room.

Pierce looked thoughtful, Joey was frankly excited, and Louise Hansen paced nervously back and forth.

"The crew from Tractor One say they saw no tracks of any kind," he said, "but that doesn't prove a thing. They came nowheres near the line between Plato and Archimedes."

"Then you think we're justified in not waiting for the same crew?" asked Louise.

"Sure," said Mike. "I don't like to sound like I'm egging you on to something I wouldn't do myself, but—"

"Of course, Mike, of course," interrupted Johnny. "One of you has to stay on the radio, or we couldn't call back. We could get Bucky to take Joey's place, I guess, but why wake him up?"

"He did his share," Joey put in quickly.

Mike looked from face to face.

"Well, Joey can say I gave him permission," he said. "I don't know what you will say, but it'd be better if you got going and figured that out on the way back."

The shadowed ringwall loomed up before the yellow speck on the plain. Just enough earthlight reached this face to show where the seven-mile-wide outer slope was terraced by gentle inclines. Several of these led upward toward the pass used by the scouting expedition. Against the black sky, Hansen could not see the radio tower that had been erected, but he was no longer interested in that. He had jettisoned his radio batteries back on the plain to be rid of their weight as he tackled the long slope leading to Archimedes.

"There you are . . . there you are!" he mumbled. "Eureka, eureka! Damn near three hundred miles . . . maybe more the way I came. That's navigating, ain't it?"

The ringwall stood passively before him.

"Well, ain't it?" snarled Hansen thickly. "All right, here we go!"

He lurched forward. Despite having abandoned every bit of excess gear—the empty oxygen cylinder lay back beside the last craterlet he had passed—he could walk no faster than if he had been on Earth. It probably meant that on Earth he would have long since collapsed, but he was beyond thinking of that.

He found he could not climb the first seven-foot ledge he came to, and had to walk along it to a lower spot.

"No time, no time," he muttered against the delay. "You're on your last tankful now . . . in fact, well into it. You get up there . . . now . . . . or not ever."

He found a long lateral slope and followed it up several hundred yards. He was cold and sluggish, and it seemed that his heating batteries were close to exhausted.

The ache across his back seemed normal. Even the dull misery of his legs, chafed, cut, rubbed raw, and the sogginess of his bleeding feet had come to be merely part of his general limpness.

He found himself finishing the last few yards of the slope on hands and knees.

"Funny," he croaked. "Don't remember fallin'."

He reached out for an outcropping of rock to pull himself up. The broken spring twisted in the mangled spot on the back of his thigh as he tried to rise. Getting both hands on the rock, he inched upward little by little.

It took him all of five minutes before he was on his feet again. At first, he thought he was dreaming again. The rock seemed to move under him.

Then he saw, peering blearily upward, that it was part of an old landslide. One slip on his part now might set it off again, and send him crashing down to the bottom of the ringwall again. Hansen groaned and stepped away as carefully as he could.

He was faced by a forty-five degree slope. If he could negotiate it for about thirty feet, he would reach another ramp. He looked down, and wondered if it would be easier to slide down to a lower terrace which would eventually lead higher than his present position.

"No time," he said dazedly.

He began to scrabble his way up the incline, not one too difficult to climb on Luna. The sun-powdered rock flaked off beneath his hands, elbows, knees, and feet. He slid back about as fast as he climbed.

With a sob, he lunged for a projection the size of a man's head and got one mitten on it. The rock cracked off and he slid to the foot of the incline.

*"Oh, God! It's too much!"*

His face twisted up and he expected to feel tears running down his face. Apparently, however, he was too dried out for that.

He sat there dully, staring at the lower ramp and trying to tell himself he could always try that.

He knew better.

"This is the end of the line," he told himself. "Last stop. . . . You're done."

Even his conscience did not twitch at his surrender. He only wished he could see Earth and look at North America again where it was centered on the globe once more.

It was too much effort to turn around.

"Wonder if they'll find me," he mumbled. "Dunno if I want to get buried or not. . . ."

Something moved to his left. A light.

"I'm seeing things," he muttered. "Not long now."

But the light swung up and down, it lit the slope below him, and it kept moving.

Nothing looked like that but a tractor.

But it would pass a hundred yards below him. The driver would have his eyes glued to the ground ahead, watching for holes or cracks.

Hansen started to laugh and managed to catch himself.

"The chance after the last chance!" he thought he said aloud, although his lips barely moved.

The effort of pulling himself to his knees brought out sweat he did not know he had left.

He waited for the tractor to reach a point below him. Waited . . . lifting the head-sized rock in both hands.

The tiny weight tired him, and he lowered the stone to his knees. The tractor lumbered along, heading down the slope into the plain.

Hansen swayed where he knelt, but concentrated everything upon estimating the distance.

With a grunt, he raised the rock and thrust it away from his chest, outward over the slope on which he sprawled with the motion.

He raised himself on his elbows and looked to see what happened. The tractor had slid to an abrupt halt.

Dimly, he could see the shattered pieces of his missile bouncing in and out of patches of earthlight below the vehicle. The driver could not have missed it crossing his path.

"Gotta get up . . . up!" Hansen thought desperately.

He did not realize that his air was turning foul, but the simple feat of getting his feet under him left his heart pounding wildly.

He planted his feet somehow until the light swept up the slope as those in the tractor searched for a possible slide.

Brightness filled his helmet. He was dazzled, and felt himself falling.

"Paul, try to help!"

"Paul, can't you get some grip when I shove you in? I can't keep you from sliding out the airlock. Paul!"

The voice was young and desperate.

When the other man backed away, parting the contact of their helmets, Hansen saw the features of Joey, the radio operator, through the other faceplate.

He stirred feebly.

"That's it, Paul," said the faraway voice as Joey bent to lift him again. "Just a little bit of help till I get you inside the airlock."

Something clanged, leaving him in blackness.

The next thing he knew, he was gulping in sobbing breaths of fresh, oxygen-rich air. His head ached, but he felt better.

Someone was mopping his sweaty face with a wet handkerchief. The handkerchief dripped, and the drops were salty.

He could not see Louise, because she held his head cradled against her breast, but Joey was looking at him wide-eyed over the back of another seat.

"How long ago did you start?" asked someone else, and Hansen saw that Johnny Pierce was driving.

"Right after we got to Plato," said Hansen. "Everything but me and a tank of oxygen went down in a slide."

"Musta been nearly twenty-four hours ago!" exclaimed Joey.

"Gol-darn!" said Pierce primly. "Three hundred miles, give or take a few!"

"You ain't human, Paul!" said Joey.

"Do you want your suit off now?" asked Louise. "We could only get your helmet loose in this space."

Without seeing her face, he could tell that she had been crying.

"Just leave it on," said Hansen. "Wait till we're in, and I can go right from the suit to a bath."

"We're coming over the crest," announced Johnny. "Louise, you better hold him in case I hit a few bumps."

Hansen relaxed with a sigh as he felt her hands tighten against him.

"Hold tight, honey!" he whispered as he closed his eyes against the lights in the tractor. "I . . . I'm a little tired."

# MARS IS HEAVEN!

## by Ray Bradbury

*The first two steps in Man's conquest of space have been mapped out for over a generation—first the moon, then Mars.*

*This story, unlike the two that precede it, is anything but sober or realistic—it is a vivid nightmare. Surely, when we get to Mars, we will not find anything like this. Yet can we really be that sure?*

THE ship came down from space. It came from the stars and the black velocities, and the shining movements, and the silent gulfs of space. It was a new ship; it had fire in its body and men in its metal cells, and it moved with a clean silence, fiery and warm. In it were seventeen men, including a captain. The crowd at the Ohio field had shouted and waved their hands up into the sunlight, and the rocket had bloomed out great flowers of heat and color and run away into space on the *third* voyage to Mars!

Now it was decelerating with metal efficiency in the upper Martian atmospheres. It was still a thing of beauty and strength. It had moved in the midnight waters of space like a pale sea leviathan; it had passed the ancient moon and thrown itself onward into one nothingness following another. The men within it had been battered, thrown about, sickened, made well again, each in his turn. One man had died, but now the remaining sixteen, with their eyes clear in their heads and their faces pressed to the thick glass ports, watched Mars swing up under them.

"Mars!" cried Navigator Lustig.

"Good old Mars!" said Samuel Hinkston, archaeologist.

"Well," said Captain John Black.

The rocket landed on a lawn of green grass. Outside, upon this lawn, stood an iron deer. Farther up on the green stood a tall brown Victorian house, quiet in the sunlight, all covered with scrolls and rococo, its windows made of blue and pink and yellow and green colored glass. Upon the porch were hairy geraniums and an old swing which was hooked into the porch ceiling and which now swung back and forth, back and forth, in a little breeze. At the summit of the house was a cupola with diamond leaded-glass windows and a dunce-cap roof! Through the front window you could see a piece of music titled "Beautiful Ohio" sitting on the music rest.

Around the rocket in four directions spread the little town, green and motionless in the Martian spring. There were white houses and red brick ones, and tall elm trees blowing in the wind, and tall maples and horse chestnuts. And church steeples with golden bells silent in them.

The rocket men looked out and saw this. Then they looked at one another and then they looked out again. They held to each other's elbows, suddenly unable to breathe, it seemed. Their faces grew pale.

"I'll be damned," whispered Lustig, rubbing his face with his numb fingers. "I'll be damned."

"It just can't be," said Samuel Hinkston.

"Lord," said Captain John Black.

There was a call from the chemist. "Sir, the atmosphere is thin for breathing, but there's enough oxygen. It's safe."

"Then we'll go out," said Lustig.

"Hold on," said Captain John Black. "How do we know what this is?"

"It's a small town with thin but breathable air in it, sir."

"And it's a small town the like of Earth towns," said Hinkston, the archaeologist. "Incredible. It can't be, but it *is.*"

Captain John Black looked at him idly. "Do you think that the civilizations of two planets can progress at the same rate and evolve in the same way, Hinkston?"

"I wouldn't have thought so, sir."

Captain Black stood by the port. "Look out there. The geraniums. A specialized plant. That specific variety has only been known on Earth for fifty years. Think of the thousands of years it takes to evolve plants. Then tell me if it is logical that the Martians should have: one, leaded-glass windows; two, cupolas; three, porch swings; four, an instrument that looks like a piano and probably *is* a piano; and five, if you look closely through this telescopic lens here, is it logical that a Martian composer would have published a piece of music titled, strangely enough, 'Beautiful Ohio'? All of which means that we have an Ohio River on Mars!"

"Captain Williams, of course!" cried Hinkston.

"What?"

"Captain Williams and his crew of three men! Or Nathaniel York and his partner. That would explain it!"

"That would explain absolutely nothing. As far as we've been able to figure, the York expedition exploded the day it reached Mars, killing York and his partner. As for Williams and his three men, their ship exploded the second day after their arrival. At least the pulsations from their radios ceased at that time, so we figure that if the men were alive after that they'd have contacted us. And anyway, the York expedition was only a year ago, while Captain Williams and his men landed here some time during last August. Theorizing that they are still alive, could they, even with the help of a brilliant Martian race, have built such a town as this and *aged* it in so short a time? Look at that town out there; why, it's been standing here for the last seventy years. Look at the wood on the porch newel; look at the trees, a century old, all of them! No, this isn't York's work or Williams'. It's something else. I don't like it. And I'm not leaving the ship until I know what it is."

"For that matter," said Lustig, nodding, "Williams and his men, as well as York, landed on the *opposite* side of Mars. We were very careful to land on *this* side."

"An excellent point. Just in case a hostile local tribe of Martians killed off York and Williams, we have instructions to land in a further region, to forestall a recurrence of such a disaster. So here we are, as far as we know, in a land that Williams and York never saw."

"Damn it," said Hinkston, "I want to get out into this town, sir, with your permission. It may be there *are* similar thought patterns, civilization graphs on every planet in our sun system. We may be on the threshold of the greatest psychological and metaphysical discovery of our age!"

"I'm willing to wait a moment," said Captain John Black.

"It may be, sir, that we're looking upon a phenomenon that, for the first time, would absolutely prove the existence of God, sir."

"There are many people who are of good faith without such proof, Mr. Hinkston."

"I'm one myself, sir. But certainly a town like this could not occur without divine intervention. The *detail*. It fills me with such feelings that I don't know whether to laugh or cry."

"Do neither, then, until we know what we're up against."

"Up against?" Lustig broke in. "Against nothing, Captain. It's a good, quiet green town, a lot like the old-fashioned one I was born in. I like the looks of it."

"When were you born, Lustig?"

"Nineteen-fifty, sir."

"And you, Hinkston?"

"Nineteen fifty-five, sir. Grinnell, Iowa. And this looks like home to me."

"Hinkston, Lustig, I could be either of your fathers. I'm just eighty years old. Born in nineteen-twenty in Illinois, and through the grace of God and a science that, in the last fifty years, knows how to make *some* old men young again, here I am on Mars, not any more tired than the rest of you, but infinitely more suspicious. This town out here looks very peaceful and cool, and so much like Green Bluff, Illinois, that it frightens me. It's too *much* like Green Bluff." He turned to the radioman. "Radio Earth. Tell them we've landed. That's all. Tell them we'll radio a full report tomorrow."

"Yes, sir."

Captain Black looked out the rocket port with his face that should have been the face of a man eighty but seemed like the face of a man in his fortieth year. "Tell you what we'll do, Lustig; you and I and Hinkston'll look the town over. The other men'll stay aboard. If anything happens they can get the hell out. A loss of three men's better than a whole ship. If something bad happens, our crew can warn the next rocket. That's Captain Wilder's rocket, I think, due to be ready to take off next Christmas. If there's something hostile about Mars we certainly want the next rocket to be well armed."

"So are we. We've got a regular arsenal with us."

"Tell the men to stand by the guns then. Come on, Lustig, Hinkston."

The three men walked together down through the levels of the ship.

It was a beautiful spring day. A robin sat on a blossoming apple tree and sang continuously. Showers of petal snow sifted down when the wind touched the green branches, and the blossom scent drifted upon the air. Somewhere in the town someone was playing the piano and the music came and went, came and went, softly, drowsily. The song was "Beautiful Dreamer." Somewhere else a phonograph, scratchy and faded, was hissing out a record of "Roamin' in the Gloamin'," sung by Harry Lauder.

The three men stood outside the ship. They sucked and gasped at the thin, thin air and moved slowly so as not to tire themselves.

Now the phonograph record being played was: *"Oh, give me a June night, The moonlight and you. . . ."*

Lustig began to tremble. Samuel Hinkston did likewise.

The sky was serene and quiet, and somewhere a stream of water ran through the cool caverns and tree shadings of a ravine. Somewhere a horse and wagon trotted and rolled by, bumping.

"Sir," said Samuel Hinkston, "it must be, it *has* to be, that rocket travel to Mars began in the years before the First World War!"

"No."

"How else can you explain these houses, the iron deer, the pianos, the music?" Hinkston took the captain's elbow persuasively and looked into the captain's face. "Say that there were people in the year nineteen-five who hated war and got together with some scientists in secret and built a rocket and came out here to Mars—"

"No, no, Hinkston."

"Why not? The world was a different world in nineteen-five; they could have kept it a secret much more easily."

"But a complex thing like a rocket, no, you couldn't keep it secret."

"And they came up here to live, and naturally the houses they built were similar to Earth houses because they brought the culture with them."

"And they've lived here all these years?" said the captain.

"In peace and quiet, yes. Maybe they made a few trips, enough to bring enough people here for one small town, and then stopped for fear of being discovered. That's why this town seems so old-fashioned. I don't see a thing, myself, older than the year nineteen twenty-seven, do you? Or maybe, sir, rocket travel is older than we think. Perhaps it started in some part of the world centuries ago and was kept secret by the small number of men who came to Mars with only occasional visits to Earth over the centuries."

"You make it sound almost reasonable."

"It has to be. We've the proof here before us; all we have to do is find some people and verify it."

Their boots were deadened of all sound in the thick green grass. It smelled from a fresh mowing. In spite of himself, Captain John Black felt a great peace come over him. It had been thirty years since he had been in a small town, and the buzzing of spring bees on the air lulled and quieted him, and the fresh look of things was a balm to the soul.

They set foot upon the porch. Hollow echoes sounded from under the boards as they walked to the screen door. Inside they could see a bead curtain hung across the hall entry, and a crystal chandelier and a Maxfield Parrish painting framed on one wall over a comfortable Morris chair. The house smelled old, and of the attic, and infinitely comfortable. You could hear the tinkle of ice in a lemonade pitcher. In a distant kitchen, because of the heat of the day, someone was preparing a cold lunch. Someone was humming under her breath, high and sweet.

Captain John Black rang the bell.

Footsteps, dainty and thin, came along the hall, and a kind-faced lady of some forty years, dressed in the sort of dress you might expect in the year 1909, peered out at them.

"Can I help you?" she asked.

"Beg your pardon," said Captain Black uncertainly. "But we're looking for—that is, could you help us—" He stopped. She looked out at him with dark, wondering eyes.

"If you're selling something—" she began.

"No, wait!" he cried. "What town is this?"

She looked him up and down. "What do you mean, what town is it? How could you be in a town and not know the name?"

The captain looked as if he wanted to go sit under a shady apple tree. "We're strangers here. We want to know how this town got here and how you got here."

"Are you census takers?"

"No."

"Everyone knows," she said, "this town was built in eighteen sixty-eight. Is this a game?"

"No, not a game!" cried the captain. "We're from Earth."

"Out of the *ground,* do you mean?" she wondered.

"No, we came from the third planet, Earth, in a ship. And we've landed here on the fourth planet, Mars—"

"This," explained the woman, as if she were addressing a child, "is Green Bluff, Illinois, on the continent of America, surrounded by the Atlantic and Pacific oceans, on a place called the world, or, sometimes, the Earth. Go away now. Good-bye."

She trotted down the hall, running her fingers through the beaded curtains.

The three men looked at one another.

"Let's knock the screen door in," said Lustig.

"We can't do that. This is private property. Good God!"

They went to sit down on the porch step.

"Did it ever strike you, Hinkston, that perhaps we got ourselves somehow, in some way, off track, and by accident came back and landed on Earth?"

"How could we have done that?"

"I don't know, I don't know. Oh, God, let me think."

Hinkston said, "But we checked every mile of the way. Our chronometers said so many miles. We went past the Moon and out into space, and here we are. I'm positive we're on Mars."

Lustig said, "But suppose, by accident, in space, in

time, we got lost in the dimensions and landed on an Earth that is thirty or forty years ago."

"Oh, go away, Lustig!"

Lustig went to the door, rang the bell, and called into the cool, dim rooms; "What year is this?"

"Nineteen twenty-six, of course," said the lady, sitting in a rocking chair, taking a sip of her lemonade.

"Did you hear that?" Lustig turned wildly to the others. "Nineteen twenty-six! We *have* gone back in time! This *is* Earth!"

Lustig sat down, and the three men let the wonder and the terror of the thought afflict them. Their hands stirred fitfully on their knees. The captain said, "I didn't ask for a thing like this. It scares the hell out of me. How can a thing like this happen? I wish we'd brought Einstein with us."

"Will anyone in this town believe us?" said Hinkston. "Are we playing with something dangerous? Time, I mean. Shouldn't we just take off and go home?"

"No. Not until we try another house."

They walked three houses down to a little white cottage under an oak tree. "I like to be as logical as I can be," said the captain. "And I don't believe we've put our finger on it yet. Suppose, Hinkston, as you originally suggested, that rocket travel occurred years ago? And when the Earth people lived here a number of years they began to get homesick for Earth. First a mild neurosis about it, then a full-fledged psychosis. Then threatened insanity. What would you do as a psychiatrist if faced with such a problem?"

Hinkston thought. "Well, I think I'd rearrange the civilization on Mars so it resembled Earth more and more each day. If there was any way of reproducing every plant, every road, and every lake, and even an ocean, I'd do so. Then by some vast crowd hypnosis I'd convince everyone in a town this size that this really *was* Earth, not Mars at all."

"Good enough, Hinkston. I think we're on the right track now. That woman in that house back there just *thinks* she's living on Earth. It protects her sanity. She and all the others in this town are the patients of the greatest experiment in migration and hypnosis you will ever lay eyes on in your life."

"That's *it,* sir!" cried Lustig.

"Right!" said Hinkston.

"Well." The captain sighed. "Now we've got somewhere. I feel better. It's all a bit more logical. That talk about time and going back and forth and traveling through time turns my stomach upside down. But *this* way—" The captain smiled. "Well, well, it looks as if we'll be fairly popular here."

"Or will we?" said Lustig. "After all, like the Pilgrims, these people came here to escape Earth. Maybe they won't be too happy to see us. Maybe they'll try to drive us out or kill us."

"We have superior weapons. This next house now. Up we go."

But they had hardly crossed the lawn when Lustig stopped and looked off across the town, down the quiet, dreaming afternoon street. "Sir," he said.

"What is it, Lustig?"

"Oh, sir, *sir,* what I see—" said Lustig, and he began to cry. His fingers came up, twisting and shaking, and his face was all wonder and joy and incredulity. He sounded as if at any moment he might go quite insane with happiness. He looked down the street and began to run, stumbling awkwardly, falling, picking himself up, and running on. "Look, look!"

"Don't let him get away!" the captain broke into a run.

Now Lustig was running swiftly, shouting. He turned into a yard halfway down the shady street and leaped up onto the porch of a large green house with an iron rooster on the roof.

He was beating at the door, hollering and crying, when Hinkston and the captain ran up behind him. They were all gasping and wheezing, exhausted from their run in the thin air. "Grandma! Grandpa!" cried Lustig.

Two old people stood in the doorway.

"David!" their voices piped, and they rushed out to embrace and pat him on the back and move around him. "David, oh, David, it's been so many years! How you've grown, boy; how big you are, boy. Oh, David boy, how are you?"

"Grandma, Grandpa!" sobbed David Lustig. "You look fine, fine!" He held them, turned them, kissed them, hugged them, cried on them, held them out again, blinking at the little old people. The sun was in the sky, the wind blew, the grass was green, the screen door stood wide.

"Come in, boy, come in. There's iced tea for you, fresh, lots of it!"

"I've got friends here." Lustig turned and waved at the captain and Hinkston frantically, laughing. "Captain, come on up."

"Howdy," said the old people. "Come in. Any friends of David's are our friends too. Don't stand there!"

In the living room of the old house it was cool, and a grandfather clock ticked, high and long and bronzed in one corner. There were soft pillows on large couches and walls filled with books and a rug cut in a thick rose pattern, and iced tea in the hand, sweating, and cool on the thirsty tongue.

"Here's to our health." Grandma tipped her glass to her porcelain teeth.

"How long you been here, Grandma?" said Lustig.

"Ever since we died," she said tartly.

"Ever since you what?" Captain John Black set down his glass.

"Oh, yes." Lustig nodded. "They've been dead thirty years."

"And you sit there calmly!" shouted the captain.

"Tush." The old woman winked glitteringly. "Who are you to question what happens? Here we are. What's life, anyway? Who does what for why and where? All we know is here we are, alive again, and no questions asked. A second chance." She toddled over and held out her thin wrist. "Feel." The captain felt. "Solid, ain't it?" she asked. He nodded. "Well, then," she said triumphantly, "why go around questioning?"

"Well," said the captain, "it's simply that we never thought we'd find a thing like this on Mars."

"And now you've found it. I dare say there's lots on every planet that'll show you God's infinite ways."

"Is this Heaven?" asked Hinkston.

"Nonsense, no. It's a world and we get a second chance. Nobody told us why. But then nobody told us why we were on Earth, either. That other Earth, I mean. The one you came from. How do we know there wasn't *another* before *that* one?"

"A good question," said the captain.

Lustig kept smiling at his grandparents. "Gosh, it's good to see you. Gosh, it's good."

The captain stood up and slapped his hand on his leg in a casual fashion. "We've got to be going. Thank you for the drinks."

"You'll be back, of course," said the old people. "For supper tonight?"

"We'll try to make it, thanks. There's so much to be done. My men are waiting for me back at the rocket and—"

He stopped. He looked toward the door, startled.

Far away in the sunlight there was a sound of voices, a shouting and a great hello.

"What's that?" asked Hinkston.

"We'll soon find out." And Captain John Black was out the front door abruptly, running across the green lawn into the street of the Martian town.

He stood looking at the rocket. The ports were open and the crew was streaming out, waving their hands. A crowd of people had gathered, and in and through and among these people the members of the crew were hurrying, talking, laughing, shaking hands. People did little dances. People swarmed. The rocket lay empty and abandoned.

A brass band exploded in the sunlight, flinging off a gay tune from upraised tubas and trumpets. There was a bang of drums and a shrill of fifes. Little girls with golden hair jumped up and down. Little boys shouted, "Hooray!" Fat men passed around ten-cent cigars. The town mayor made a speech. Then each member of the crew, with a mother on one arm, a father or sister on the other, was spirited off down the street into little cottages or big mansions.

"Stop!" cried Captain Black.

The doors slammed shut.

The heat rose in the clear spring sky, and all was silent. The brass band banged off around a corner, leaving the rocket to shine and dazzle alone in the sunlight.

"Abandoned!" said the captain. "They abandoned the ship, they did! I'll have their skins, by God! They had orders!"

"Sir," said Lustig, "don't be too hard on them. Those were all old relatives and friends."

"That's no excuse!"

"Think how they felt, Captain, seeing familiar faces outside the ship!"

"They had their orders, damn it!"

"But how would you have felt, Captain?"

"I would have obeyed orders—" The captain's mouth remained open.

Striding along the sidewalk under the Martian sun —tall, smiling, his eyes amazingly clear and blue— came a young man of some twenty-six years. "John!" the man called out, and broke into a trot.

"What?" Captain John Black swayed.

"John, you old son of a bitch!"

The man ran up and gripped his hand and slapped him on the back.

"It's you," said Captain Black.

"Of course, who'd you *think* it was?"

"Edward!" The captain appealed now to Lustig and Hinkston, holding the stranger's hand. "This is my brother Edward. Ed, meet my men, Lustig, Hinkston! My brother!"

They tugged at each other's hands and arms and then finally embraced. "Ed!" "John, you bum, you!" "You're looking fine, Ed, but Ed, what *is* this? You haven't changed over the years. You died, I remember, when you were twenty-six and I was nineteen. Good

God, so many years ago, and here you are and, Lord, what goes on?"

"Mom's waiting," said Edward Black, grinning.

"Mom?"

"And Dad too."

"Dad?" The captain almost fell as if he had been hit by a mighty weapon. He walked stiffly and without coordination. "Mom and Dad alive? Where?"

"At the old house on Oak Knoll Avenue."

"The old house." The captain stared in delighted amaze. "Did you hear that, Lustig, Hinkston?"

Hinkston was gone. He had seen his own house down the street and was running for it. Lustig was laughing. "You see, Captain, what happened to everyone on the rocket? They couldn't help themselves."

"Yes. Yes." The captain shut his eyes. "When I open my eyes, you'll be gone." He blinked. "You're still there. God, Ed, but you look *fine!*"

"Come on, lunch's waiting. I told Mom."

Lustig said, "Sir, I'll be with my grandfolks if you need me."

"What? Oh, fine, Lustig. Later, then."

Edward seized his arm and marched him. "There's the house. Remember it?"

"Hell! Bet I can beat you to the front porch!"

They ran. The trees roared over Captain Black's head; the earth roared under his feet. He saw the golden figure of Edward Black pull ahead of him in the amazing dream of reality. He saw the house rush forward, the screen door swing wide. "Beat you!" cried Edward. "I'm an old man," panted the captain, "and you're still young. But then, you *always* beat me, I remember!"

In the doorway, Mom, pink, plump, and bright. Behind her, pepper-gray, Dad, his pipe in his hand.

"Mom, Dad!"

He ran up the steps like a child to meet them.

It was a fine, long afternoon. They finished a late lunch and they sat in the parlor and he told them all about his rocket and they nodded and smiled upon him and Mother was just the same and Dad bit the end off a cigar and lighted it thoughtfully in his old fashion. There was a big turkey dinner at night and time flowing on. When the drumsticks were sucked clean and lay brittle upon the plates, the captain leaned back and exhaled his deep satisfaction. Night was in all the trees and coloring the sky, and the lamps were halos of pink light in the gentle house. From all the other houses down the street came sounds of music, pianos playing, doors slamming.

Mom put a record on the victrola, and she and Captain John Black had a dance. She was wearing the same perfume he remembered from the summer when she and Dad had been killed in the train accident. She was very real in his arms as they danced lightly to the music. "It's not every day," she said, "you get a second chance to live."

"I'll wake in the morning," said the captain. "And I'll be in my rocket, in space, and all this will be gone."

"No, don't think that," she cried softly. "Don't question. God's good to us. Let's be happy."

"Sorry, Mom."

The record ended in a circular hissing.

"You're tired, Son." Dad pointed with his pipe. "Your old bedroom's waiting for you, brass bed and all."

"But I should report my men in."

"Why?"

"Why? Well, I don't know. No reason, I guess. No, none at all. They're all eating or in bed. A good night's sleep won't hurt them."

"Good-night, Son." Mom kissed his cheek. "It's good to have you home."

"It's good to *be* home."

He left the land of cigar smoke and perfume and books and gentle light and ascended the stairs, talking, talking with Edward. Edward pushed a door open, and there was the yellow brass bed and the old semaphore banners from college and a very musty raccoon coat which he stroked with muted affection. "It's too much," said the captain. "I'm numb and I'm tired. Too much has happened today. I feel as if I'd been out in a pounding rain for forty-eight hours without an umbrella or a coat. I'm soaked to the skin with emotion."

Edward slapped wide the snowy linens and flounced the pillows. He slid the window up and let the night-blooming jasmine float in. There was moonlight and the sound of distant dancing and whispering.

"So this is Mars," said the captain, undressing.

"This is it." Edward undressed in idle, leisurely moves, drawing his shirt off over his head, revealing golden shoulders and the good muscular neck.

The lights were out; they were in bed, side by side, as in the days how many decades ago? The captain lolled and was nourished by the scent of jasmine pushing the lace curtains out upon the dark air of the room. Among the trees, upon a lawn, someone had cranked up a portable phonograph and now it was playing softly, "Always."

The thought of Marilyn came to his mind.

"Is Marilyn here?"

His brother, lying straight out in the moonlight from the window, waited and then said, "Yes. She's out of town. But she'll be here in the morning."

The captain shut his eyes. "I want to see Marilyn very much."

The room was square and quiet except for their breathing.

"Good-night, Ed."

A pause. "Good-night, John."

He lay peacefully, letting his thoughts float. For the first time the stress of the day was moved aside; he could think logically now. It had all been emotion. The bands playing, the familiar faces. But now . . .

How? He wondered. How was all this made? And why? For what purpose? Out of the goodness of some divine intervention? Was God, then, really that thoughtful of his children? How and why and what for?

He considered the various theories advanced in the first heat of the afternoon by Hinkston and Lustig. He let all kinds of new theories drop in lazy pebbles down through his mind, turning, throwing out dull flashes of light. Mom. Dad. Edward. Mars. Earth. Mars. Martians.

Who had lived here a thousand years ago on Mars? Martians? Or had this always been the way it was today?

Martians. He repeated the word idly, inwardly.

He laughed out loud almost. He had the most ridiculous theory quite suddenly. It gave him a kind of chill. It was really nothing to consider, of course. Highly improbable. Silly. Forget it. Ridiculous.

But, he thought, just *suppose* . . . just suppose, now, that there were Martians living on Mars and they saw our ship coming and saw us inside our ship and hated us. Suppose, now just for the hell of it, that they wanted to destroy us, as invaders, as unwanted ones, and they wanted to do it in a very clever way, so that we would be taken off guard. Well, what would the best weapon be that a Martian could use against Earth Men with atomic weapons?

The answer was interesting. Telepathy, hypnosis, memory, and imagination.

Suppose all of these houses aren't real at all, this bed not real, but only figments of my own imagination, given substance by telepathy and hypnosis through the Martians, thought Captain John Black. Suppose these houses are really some other shape, a Martian shape, but, by playing on my desires and wants, these Martians have made this seem like my old home town, my old house, to lull me out of my suspicions. What better way to fool a man, using his own mother and father as bait?

And this town, so old, from the year nineteen twenty-six, long before *any* of my men were born. From a year when I was six years old and there *were* records of Harry Lauder, and Maxfield Parrish paintings *still* hanging, and bead curtains, and "Beautiful Ohio," and turn-of-the-century architecture. What if the Martians took the memories of a town *exclusively* from *my* mind? They say childhood memories are the clearest. And after they built the town from my mind, they populated it with the most-loved people from all the minds of the people on the rocket!

And suppose those two people in the next room, asleep, are not my mother and father at all. But two Martians, incredibly brilliant, with the ability to keep me under this dreaming hypnosis all of the time.

And that brass band today? What a startlingly wonderful plan it would be. First, fool Lustig, then Hinkston, then gather a crowd; and all the men in the rocket, seeing mothers, aunts, uncles, sweethearts, dead ten, twenty years ago, naturally, disregarding orders, rush out and abandon ship. What more natural? What more unsuspecting? What more simple? A man doesn't ask too many questions when his mother is suddenly brought back to life; he's much too happy. And here we all are tonight, in various houses, in various beds, with no weapons to protect us, and the rocket lies in the moonlight, empty. And wouldn't it be horrible and terrifying to discover that all of this was part of some great clever plan by the Martians to divide and conquer us, and kill us? Sometime during the night, perhaps, my brother here on this bed will change form, melt, shift, and become another thing, a terrible thing, a Martian. It would be very simple for him just to turn over in bed and put a knife into my heart. And in all those other houses down the street, a dozen other brothers or fathers suddenly melting away and taking knives and doing things to the unsuspecting, sleeping men of Earth. . . .

His hands were shaking under the covers. His body was cold. Suddenly it was not a theory. Suddenly he was very afraid.

He lifted himself in bed and listened. The night was very quiet. The music had stopped. The wind had died. His brother lay sleeping beside him.

Carefully he lifted the covers, rolled them back. He slipped from the bed and was walking softly across the room when his brother's voice said, "Where are you going?"

"What?"

His brother's voice was quite cold. "I said, where do you think you're going?"

"For a drink of water."

"But you're not thirsty."

"Yes, yes, I am."

"No, you're not."

Captain John Black broke and ran across the room. He screamed. He screamed twice.

He never reached the door.

In the morning the brass band played a mournful dirge. From every house in the street came little solemn processions bearing long boxes, and along the sun-filled street, weeping, came the grandmas and mothers and sisters and brothers and uncles and fathers, walking to the churchyard, where there were new holes freshly dug and the new tombstones.

The mayor made a little sad speech, his face sometimes looking like the mayor, sometimes looking like something else.

Mother and Father Black were there, with Brother Edward, and they cried, their faces melting now from familiar faces into something else.

Grandpa and Grandma Lustig were there, weeping, their faces shifting like wax, shimmering as all things shimmer on a hot day.

The coffins were lowered. Someone murmured about "the unexpected and sudden deaths of sixteen fine men during the night—"

Earth pounded down on the coffin lids.

The brass band, playing "Columbia, the Gem of the Ocean," marched and slammed back into town, and everyone took the day off.

# THE EDGE OF THE SEA

## by Algis Budrys

*The stories in this book so far have been about visits by Man to other planets. The one that follows tells about an event at least as interesting and perhaps only slightly less probable—a visit to our planet by a thing from Elsewhere—and about a man's lonely fight to keep it for himself.*

THE Overseas Highway, two narrow white lanes on yellowed old concrete piers, lay close to the shallow water, passed over the little key, and went on.

All afternoon the sea had been rising. Long, greasy faced, green swells came in from the Atlantic Ocean and broke on the sharp rocks with a sudden upsurge of surf. At midday the water had been far down among the coral heads. But now it was in the tumbled limestone blocks and concrete prisms that had been dumped there to build up the key. In a little while it would be washing its spume over the highway itself, and it might well go farther, with the increasing wind.

It was dark with twilight, and darker with clouds thick as oil smoke covering the sun over the Gulf of Mexico. The gulf was stirring too, and bayous were flooding in Louisiana. But it was over the Atlantic that the hurricane was spinning. It was the broad, deep, deadly ocean that the tide and wind were pushing down through the gloom onto the side of the key where Dan Henry was struggling grimly, his massive back and shoulders naked and running with spray.

His pale eyes were red-rimmed with salt and his hide slashed shallowly in a dozen places where he had lost his balance on the tumbled stones and fallen. He had been lurching through the surf all afternoon, working frantically to save what he had seen, leaden and encrusted, rolling ponderously at the edge of the water. His shirt, the seat covers from his car—the fan belt too—and what few scraps of rope and wire had been in the trunk, all had gone for him to twist into an incredible rag of a hawser.

The men who built the Overseas Highway on the old railroad right-of-way had built up the little key, but it was still no more than a hundred feet in diameter. If the thing trapped on the rocks had chosen any other islet to wash against, there would have been a reasonable chance of saving it. But there was no one living here, and nothing to use for tools or anchors. The thing was rolling and grinding against the rocks, too heavy to float but too bulky to resist the push of storm-driven water. There were bright silver gouges on its thick metal flanks, and in a little while it would break up or break free, and be lost either way. The rope—the stubborn, futile rope passed around the two stubby struts at its nose and wrapped around the great concrete block it was now butting at with brute persistence—was as much use as though Dan Henry had been a spider and tried to hold this thing in a hurriedly created web. But he had had to try, and he was trying now in another way. He jammed the soles of his feet against one concrete block and pushed his bare shoulders against another. With his belly ridged and his thighs bulging, his face contorted and his hands clenched, he was trying to push another massive piece of stone into place behind the plunging metal thing, though his blood might erupt from his veins and the muscles tear open his flesh.

The thing was as thick through as a hogshead, and as long as two men. There was a thick-lipped, scarred opening a foot across at one end, where the body rounded sharply in a hemispheric compound curve. There were the three stumpy fins rooted in the curve, their tips not extending beyond the bulge of the body, and two struts at the blunt nose like horns on a snail but bent forward so that the entire thing might have been fired out of a monstrous cannon or launched from the tubes of some unimaginable submarine. There were no visible openings, no boltheads, no seams. The entire thing might have been cast of a piece—might have been solid, except for the tube in the stern—and though barnacles clung to it and moss stained it, though the rocks gouged it and other blows had left their older scars on its pitted surface, still the thing was not visibly damaged.

Dan Henry strained at the rock, and sand grated minutely at its base. But the world turned red behind his eyes, and his muscles writhed into venomous knots, and his breath burned his chest with the fury of fire. The sea broke against him and ran into his nose and mouth. The wind moaned, and the water hissed through the rocks, crashing as it came and gurgling as it drew back. The thing groaned and grated with each sluggish move. The day grew steadily darker.

Dan Henry had stopped his car on the key at noon, pulling off the highway onto the one narrow space of shoulder. He had opened the glove compartment and taken out the waxed container of milk and the now stale sandwich he had bought in Hallandale, above Miami, at ten that morning. He lit a cigarette and unwrapped the sandwich, and began to eat. The milk had turned warm in the glove compartment and acquired an unpleasant taste, but Dan Henry had never cared how his food tasted. He paid no attention to it as he chewed the sandwich and drank the milk between drags on the cigarette. He had bought the food when he stopped for gas, and when he finished it he planned to go on immediately, driving until he reached Key West.

There was nothing specific waiting for him there. Nothing in his life had ever been waiting for him anywhere. But everywhere he went, he went as directly and as efficiently as possible because that was his nature. He was a physically powerful, reasonably intelligent, ugly man who drew his strength from a knowledge that nothing could quite overcome him. He asked no more of the world. He was thirty years old, and had been a construction foreman, a police officer, an MP sergeant in Germany, and a long-haul trailer-truck driver. In addition to these things he had been born into a derrick rigger's family in Oklahoma and raised in his father's nomadic, self-sufficient tradition.

When he first saw the dull color of metal down among the rocks, he got out of the car to see what it was. He was already thinking in terms of its possible usefulness when he reached the thing. Once near it, the idea of salvage rights came naturally.

Looking at it, he felt immediately that it had to be a military instrument of some kind. The Navy, he knew, was constantly firing rockets from Cape Kennedy, up in central Florida. But the longer he looked at the thing, the longer he doubted that possibility. The thing was too massive, too obviously built to take the kind of vicious punishment it was receiving at the hands of the sea, to be the light, expendable shell that was a missile prototype or a high-altitude test rocket. There were tons of metal in it, and the barnacles were thick on it. He wondered how long it had been surging along the bottom, urged and tumbled by the great hidden forces of the ocean, drifting this way and that until finally this morning the first high tide had heaved it up here to lie caught and scraping on the rocks, steaming as it dried under the early sun.

He did not know what it was, he decided finally. Rocket, torpedo, shell, bomb, or something else, whatever it was, it was valuable and important. The Navy or the Army or Air Force would need it or want it for something.

There was nothing on it to mark it as anyone's property. If anything had ever been written or engraved on that hull, it was gone now. He began to think of how he might establish his rights until he could reach a Navy installation of some kind. The only reason he had for going to Key West was that he had a friend in the sponge-diving business down there. The friend did not know he was coming, so there was no reason not to delay for as long as this business might take him.

He had begun with nothing more than that to urge him on, but as the afternoon grew, the sea and the thing between them had trapped him.

The thing lay awash with half its length over the usual high watermark, and even when he found it, at low tide, the water curled among the rocks above it. He had thought about that too, but he had not thought that a hurricane might have taken an unexpected turn during the night, while he drove his old car without a radio to tell him so. Only when the clouds turned gray and the water swirled around his knees like a pack of hounds grown hungry did he stop for a moment and look out to sea.

He had been clearing the smaller rocks away from around the thing and piling them in an open-ended square enclosing its forward sections, and had been scraping a clean patch in the barnacles with a tire iron. It had been his intention to make it obvious someone was working on the thing, so he could then leave it and report it with a clear claim. The few cars going by on the highway had not stopped or slowed down—there was no place to stop, with his car on the bit of shoulder, and no real reason to slow down—and after a while the cars had stopped coming entirely.

It was that, telling him the storm had probably caused the highway to be blocked off at either end, together with the look of the sea, that made him go up to the car and try to make a hawser. And by then he could not have left the thing. It was too obvious that a man had begun a job of work here. If he left it now, it would be too plain that someone had let himself be backed down.

If he had gotten in his car and driven away, he would not have been Dan Henry.

The water was almost completely over the thing now. He himself was working with the waves breaking over his head, trying to dislodge him. More important, the thing was rocking and slipping out of its trap.

The next nearest key was a third of a mile away, bigger than this one, but still uninhabited. The nearest inhabited place was Greyhound Key, where the rest stop was for the buses, and that was out of sight. It would be battened down, and probably evacuated. Dan Henry was all alone, with the highway empty above him and the sea upon him.

He set his back once more, and pushed against the concrete block again. If he could wedge the thing, even a storm tide might not be able to take it away from him. He could untangle his homemade rope and put the fan belt back on his car. Then he could drive away to some place until the storm died down.

The blood roared in Dan Henry's ears, and the encrusted concrete block opened the hide over his shoulders. A coughing grunt burst out of his mouth. The block teetered—not much, but it gave a little way. Dan Henry locked his knees and braced his back with his palms, pushing his elbows against the block, and when the next wave threw its pressure into the balance, he pushed once more. The block slipped suddenly away from him, and he was thrown aside by the wave, flung into the wet rocks above. But the thing was wedged. It could roll and rear as much as it wanted to, but it could not flounder back into the sea. Dan Henry lay over a rock, and wiped the back of his hand across his bloody mouth in satisfaction.

It was over. He could get out of here now, and hole up somewhere. After the storm, he would come back and make sure it was still here. Then he would make his claim, either at one of the little Navy stations along the chain of keys, or at the big base at Boca Chica.

And that would be that, except for the check in the mail. The bruises and breaks in his skin would heal over, and become nothing more than scars.

He took his rope off the thing and took it apart far enough to pick out the fan belt. He let the rest of it wash away, shredded. As he got out of the surging water at last, he scowled slightly because he wondered if the car's spark plugs weren't wet.

It was dark now. Not quite pitch-black, for the hurricane sky to the west was banded by a last strip of sulfur-colored light at the horizon, but dark enough so that his car was only a looming shape as he climbed up to it. Then, suddenly, the wet finish and the rusty chrome of the front bumper were sparkling with the first pinpoint reflections of faraway lamps. He turned to look southward down the highway, and saw a car coming. As it came nearer, its headlights let him see the clouds of spray that billowed across the glistening road, and the leaping white heads of breakers piling up on the piers and rebounding vertically to the level of the highway. The storm was building up even more quickly than he'd thought. He wondered what kind of damned fool was crazy enough to drive the stretches where the highway crossed open water between keys, and had his answer when a spotlight abruptly reached out and fingered him and his car. Either the state or the county police were out looking to make sure no one was trapped away from shelter.

The police car pulled up, wet and hissing, half blocking the highway, and the driver immediately switched on his red roof-beacon, either through force of habit or force of training, even though there was no oncoming traffic to warn. The four rotating arms of red light tracked monotonously over the road, the key, and the water. By their light, Dan Henry realized for the first time that it was raining furiously. The spotlight was switched off, and the headlights pointed away, up the highway. It was the red beacon that lit the scene and isolated the two men inside its color.

The officer did not get out of the car. He waited for

Dan Henry to come around to his side, and only then cranked his window down halfway.

"Trouble with the car?" he asked, hidden behind the reflection on the glass. Then he must have thought better of it, seeing Dan Henry's broken skin. He threw the door open quickly, and slid out with his hand on the bone-gripped butt of his plated revolver. He was thick-bodied, with a burly man's voice and brusqueness, and he kept his eyes narrowed. "What's the story here, Mac?"

Dan Henry shook his head. "No trouble. I was down on the rocks. Waves threw me around some."

The officer's uniform pants and leather jacket were already sodden. Water ran down his face, and he wiped it annoyedly out of his eyes. "What were you doin' down there? No brains?" He watched carefully, his hand firm on his gun.

Dan Henry had been a policeman himself. He was not surprised at the officer's attitude. A policeman was paid to be irritated by anything that didn't have a simple answer.

"I've got something down there I was salvaging," he said reasonably. "Storm caught me at it and knocked me around some before I got finished." Telling about it made him realize he was tired out. He hoped this business with the policeman would be over in a hurry, so that he could fix his car and get into its shelter. The wind was chilly, and the constant impact of driven water on his skin was beginning to make him numb.

The officer risked a quick glance down at the thrashing surf before he brought his hard eyes back to Dan Henry. "I don't see nothin'. What kind of a thing was it? What're you carryin' that belt around for?"

"It's metal," Dan Henry said. "Big. Never seen anything just like it before. I was using the belt to hold it."

The officer scowled. "What's holdin' it now? What d'you mean, big? How big? And how come I can't see it?"

"I pushed a rock behind it," Dan Henry said patiently. "It's damn near as big as a car. And it's under water, now."

"Buddy, that don't begin to sound like a likely story." The policeman pulled his gun out of the holster and held it down alongside his thigh. "What kind of a lookin' thing is it?"

"Kind of like a rocket, I guess."

"Now, why the hell didn't you say so!" the policeman growled, relaxing just a little bit. "That makes sense. It'll be one of those Navy jobs. They've got 'em droppin' in the ocean like flies. But you ain't goin' to get anything out of it, Buddy. That's government property. You're supposed to turn it in. It's your duty."

"I don't think so."

"What d'you mean, you don't think so?" The policeman's gun arm was tense again.

"It doesn't look like a Navy rocket. Doesn't look like anybody's rocket, that I know of. I said it was *kind* of like a rocket. Don't know what it is, for sure." Now Dan Henry was growing angry himself. He didn't like the way things were going. He kept his attention carefully on the gun.

"Know all about rockets, do you?"

"I read the papers. This thing isn't just a piece. It isn't the bottom stage or the top stage. It's one thing, and it never was part of anything bigger. And it's been in the water maybe a couple of years without getting broken up. You show me the Navy rocket that's like that."

The policeman looked at him. "Maybe you're right," he said slowly. "Tell you what—suppose you just step over here and put my spotlight on it. Reach through the window." He stepped back casually.

Dan Henry reached around and switched the spot on. He swept it down across the water, a little startled to see how far up the breakers had come. Under the light, the water was a venomous green, full of foam, rain-splotched and furiously alive. A gust of wind rocked the car sharply, and the light with it. The pale beam shot over the sea before it fell back, reaching beyond the swinging cross of red from the roof beacon, and out there the lashing waves disappeared in a mist of rain.

He found the thing, finally, after having to hunt for it. For an instant he thought it had been swept away after all, and felt a stab of sharp anger. But it was still there, heaving insensately under the waves, with only the dim, broad mottling of its back near enough to the surface to be seen at all, that and a constant stirring in the water, roiling it like an animal. "There it is." He was surprised how relieved he felt. "See it?"

"Yeah. Yeah, I seen enough of it," the officer said. "You got somethin' down there, all right." There was a sudden hardness in his voice that had been waiting all along for him to make the decision that would bring it completely out. "I got my gun on you, buddy. Just step back from the car easy. Anybody foolin' around out here in a hurricane must want somethin' awful bad. If that somethin's a Navy rocket, I guess I know what kind of a son of a bitch that would be."

"Jesus Christ," Dan Henry whispered to himself. He was angry with the fine-drawn kind of rage that is almost a pleasure. And not because the cop thought he was a Commie, either, Dan Henry suddenly realized, but because he persisted in not understanding about the rocket. Or whatever it was.

He turned around with a jump. The fan belt in his hand whipped out with all the strength in his arm and all the snap in his wrist, and snatched the cop's gun out of his hand. It skittered across the wet concrete of the highway, and Dan Henry pounced after it. He scooped it up with a scrape of his fingertips, and crouched with the muzzle pointed dead at the cop's belly.

"Back off," he said. "Back off. You're not takin' that thing away from me. I sweated blood to hang on to it, and you're not goin' to come along and throw me in jail to get it away."

The cop retreated watchfully, his hands up without his being told, and waited for his chance. Dan Henry backed him up the highway until the cop was past the cars, and opened the door of his own car. He threw the gun inside, together with the belt. He slammed the door and said, "You can get that back later. Or you can try and take it away from me now, barehanded." He was shaking with the tension in his bunched shoulders, and his arms were open wide. He was crouched, his broad chest deep as his lungs hunted for more and more oxygen to wash the rush of blood his heart was driving through his veins. The red flood of revolving beacon on the police car swept over him in regular flashes.

"I'll wait," the cop said.

"Now," Dan Henry said, "I want to use your radio. I want you to call in and report this. Only I want you to report it to the Navy before you call your headquarters."

The cop looked at him with a puzzled scowl. "You on the level?" he asked, and Dan Henry could see him wondering if he hadn't made a mistake, somewhere, in his thinking about what was going on here. But Dan Henry had no more time for him. The wind was a steady, strong pressure that made him brace his left leg hard against it. The water flying across the highway was coming in solid chunks, instead of spray, and the two cars were rocking badly on their springs. The rain was streaming over them, leaving the officer's jacket a baggy, clinging mess and pounding on the top of Dan Henry's head. The sea was smashing violently into the highway piers, thundering to the wind's howl, and even here on solid ground the shock of the impacts was coming clearly up through Dan Henry's bones.

His throat was raw. Bit by bit, he and the officer had had to raise their voices until they had been shouting at each other without realizing it. "Get in the car and do it!" he yelled, and the officer came forward as he backed away to give him room.

The policeman got into his car, with Dan Henry standing watchfully a little behind the open door frame, and switched on his radio. "Tell them where we are," Dan Henry said. "Tell them my name—Daniel Morris Henry—tell them what I said about its not being one of their rockets—and tell them I'm claiming salvage rights. Then you tell them the rest any way you see it."

The officer grudgingly turned the dials away from their usual settings. After a minute, he picked his microphone out of the dashboard hanger and began calling Boca Chica in a stubborn voice. At intervals, he said, "Over," and threw the Receive switch. They heard the peculiar, grating crackle of radiotelephone static, trapped in the small speaker. And only that.

"Look, buddy," the policeman said at last, "we're not goin' to get any answer. Not if we ain't got one by now. Boca Chica radio may be knocked out. Or maybe my transmitter's shorted, with all this wet. Could be anything." He jerked his head toward the water. "How much longer you want us to stay out here?" Probably because he had seen so many hurricanes, he was beginning to grow nervous.

"Try it again," Dan Henry said. He watched the officer closely, and couldn't see him doing anything wrong. Dan Henry didn't know the Boca Chica frequency; that was where the trouble might be. But he'd used a police radio often enough so that any other trick wouldn't have gotten by him.

The officer called Boca Chica for another five minutes. Then he stopped again. "No dice. Look, buddy, you've had it. Maybe you're just a guy looking for some salvage money, like you say you are. Maybe not. But there's goin' to be waves coming across this road in a little while. Why don't we get out of here and straighten things out when this blows over?"

Dan Henry set his jaw. "Get the vibrator out of that radio. Do it." Now he had no choice. If he went with the cop, that was that. They'd throw him in some jail for resisting arrest and assaulting an officer, and keep him there until they were good and ready to let him out. By then, whatever happened to the thing down here, somebody would have figured out some way to get that Navy check instead of him. The only thing to do was to cripple the cop's radio and send him down the highway until he reached a phone. There was no guarantee that radio wouldn't work on the police frequency.

Maybe the cop would call the Navy right after he

called his headquarters. Or maybe, even if he didn't, some higher brass at the headquarters would report to the Navy. Either way—if you believed it was a Navy rocket or if you didn't—it was government business. Then, maybe, the Navy would get here before the cops did. Or soon enough afterward so he'd still be here to talk to them. Once he got taken away from here, that chance was gone.

On that decision, he was ready to cling to a hundred-foot key in the middle of an Atlantic hurricane. "Let's have that vibrator. Right now."

The officer looked at him, and reached slowly under the dash. He fumbled in the narrow space where the radio hung, and pulled the sealed aluminum cylinder out of its socket. But he was getting ready to grab for Dan Henry if he could reach him quickly enough.

"Okay," Dan Henry said, "drop it on the road and get out of here. You can get it back along with your gun. And just in case you get some brains in your head, when you get to a phone, call the Na—"

The policeman had dropped the vibrator, and the wind had rolled it under Dan Henry's Chevrolet. Dan Henry had been in the act of letting the open police car door close, when a sharp thread of brilliant violet fire punched up from down in the green water, through the red light, up through the rain, up through the black clouds, and out to the stars beyond.

"There's something *in* that thing!" the officer blurted.

Dan Henry threw the door shut. "Get out of here, man!"

Down in the drowned rocks, an arc hissed between the two struts in the thing's nose. The water leaped and bubbled around it, but for all the breakers could do, the blaze of light still illuminated the thing and the rocks it ground against, turning the sea transparent; and from the crown of the arc the thin violet column pointed without wavering, without dispersing, straight as a line drawn from hell to heaven.

The police car's tires smoked and spun on the pavement. "I'll get help," the officer shouted dimly over the squeal and the roar of his engine. Then he had traction and the car shot away, headlights slashing, glimmering in the rain and the spray, lurching from side to side under the wind's hammer, roof beacon turning at its unvarying pace, the siren's howl lost quickly in the boom of the water. And Dan Henry was left in the violet-lanced darkness.

Without the windbreak of the police car in front of him, he was pushed violently backward until his own car's fender stopped him. Water struck his eyes, and the night blurred. He bent forward and rubbed his face until the raw ache of the salt was dulled to a steady throbbing, and then he staggered across the highway to the guardrail on the Atlantic side. The tops of the incoming waves washed over his shoes, just as the surf at noon had lapped at him, twelve feet below.

The rain and the spray steamed over him. He cupped one hand over his nose, to breathe, and hung on the rail.

There was nothing more to see. The pillar of light still shot up from the arc, and the bulk of the thing loomed, gross and black, down there in the water. It was feet below the surface now, cushioned from the first smash of the waves, and it stirred with a smooth, regular motion like a whale shark in a tank.

The radio, he thought. It had felt the radio in the police car. Nothing else had happened to bring it to life at that particular moment. It had waited a little—perhaps analyzing what it had encountered, perhaps then noticing the regular flash of the car's roof beacon for the first time. And for the first time since the day, years ago, when it entered the sea, it had found a reason for sending out a signal.

To where? Not to him or the policeman. The light was not pointed toward the highway. It went up, straight up, going out of sight through the clouds as his eyes tried to follow it before the lash of water forced his head down again.

There was no one inside the thing, Dan Henry thought. There couldn't be. He had scraped on the side with regular, purposeful strokes, clearing an exactly square patch, and gotten no response. And the thing had lain in the ocean a long time, sealed up, dragging its armored hide over the bottom as the currents pushed and pulled it, rolling, twisting, seamless, with only those two horns with which to feel the world about it.

He could be wrong, of course. Something could be alive in there, still breathing in some fantastic way from a self-contained air supply, eating tiny amounts of stored food, getting rid of its wastes somehow. But he didn't see how. It didn't seem logical that anything would trap itself like that, not knowing if it was ever going to escape.

He could be wrong about it all. It might not have been reacting to anything that happened on the highway. It might be ignoring everything outside itself, and following some purpose that had nothing to do with this world or its people. But whether it was that, or whether he was at least partly right, Dan Henry wondered what was sending things to drop down on the Earth and make signals to the stars.

The water came higher. It came up the key too quickly to split and go around it, and spilled over the highway to plunge into the rocks on the gulf side. It broke halfway up the side of his car. He remembered the policeman's vibrator. That would be far to the west of him by now, skipping at a thrown stone's velocity over waves whose tops were being cut off by the wind. Dan Henry's mouth twisted in a numb grimace. Now he'd have to buy one. They probably wouldn't let him get away that cheaply. They could make that stick for a robbery charge. And destroying public property. While on the other hand, if he was swept off this key they wouldn't even have to pay for his burial. He laughed drunkenly.

A wave broke over him. He had made a sling for himself by knotting the legs of his dungarees around one of the guardrail uprights, and when the wave was past, he lolled naked with the bunched tops of the dungarees cutting into his chest, under his arms. The wind worked at him now, with a kind of fury he had never felt by simply putting his head out through the window of a speeding car, and then the next wave came. It was warm, but the wind evaporating it as soon as he was exposed again made his skin crawl and his teeth chatter. He reached behind him with a wooden arm and felt the knot in the dungaree legs to make sure it was holding. The pressure had tightened it into a small hard lump.

That was good, at any rate. That and the blessed practicality of the engineers who built the highway. When they laid the roadway where the hurricane-smashed railroad had been, they had cut the rusted rails up with torches, set the stumps deep in the concrete, and welded the guardrails together out of T-shaped steel designed to hold a locomotive's weight.

Dan Henry grinned to himself. The rail would hold. The dungarees would hold, or the trademark was a liar. Only about Dan Henry was there any doubt. Dan Henry—hard, sure Dan Henry, with his chest being cut in half, with his torn skin being born again as the waves beat him against the highway, with his head going silly because he was being pounded into raw meat.

Dear God, he thought, am I doing this for *money?* No, he thought as a wave filled his nostrils, no, not any more. When that thing turned its light on and I didn't jump in the car with that cop, that's when we found out I wasn't doing it for the money. For what? God knows.

He floundered half over on his side, arched his neck, and looked at the violet arrow through the clouds. Signal, you bastard! Go ahead and signal! Do anything. As long as I know you're still there. If you can stay put, so can I.

Well, what *was* he doing this for? Dan Henry fought with the sling that held him, trying to take some of the pressure off his chest. God knew, but it was up to Dan Henry to find out for himself.

It wasn't money. All right—that was decided. What was left—vanity? Big Dan Henry—big, strong, Dan

Henry—take more than a hurricane to stop big, strong, wonderful Dan Henry . . . was that the way his thoughts were running?

He croaked a laugh. Big, strong Dan Henry was lying here limp as a calico doll, naked as a baby, praying his pants wouldn't rip. The storm had washed the pride out of him as surely as it had his first interest in the salvage money.

All right, *what*, then! He growled and cursed at his own stupidity. Here he was, and he didn't even know why. Here he was, being bludgeoned to death, being drowned, being torn apart by the wind. He was stuck out here now, and nobody could save him.

A wave roared over the highway and struck his car a blow that send a hubcap careening off into the darkness. The car tilted onto the gulf-side guardrail. The rail bellied outward, and the car hung halfway over the rocks on the other side. Successive waves smashed into it, exploding in spray, and the guardrail groaned in the lull after each strike. Dan Henry watched it dully in the violet light, with the water sluicing down over his head and shoulders for a moment before the wind found it and tore it away in horizontal strings of droplets.

The car's door panels had already been pushed in, and the windows were cracked and bulged. Now the exposed floorboards were being hammered. The muffler was wrenched out.

With the next smash of solid water, the horizontal rail broke its weld at one end and the car heeled forward to the right, impaling its radiator on an upright. It hung there, gradually tearing the radiator out of its brackets, spilling rusty water for one instant before a wave washed it clean, scraping its front axle down the sharp edge of the roadway, breaking loose pieces of the concrete and raising its left rear wheel higher and higher. The radiator came free with a snap like a breaking tooth, and the car dropped suddenly, its front end caught by the edge of the left wheel, kept from falling only by the straining uprights still jammed against it farther back on the right side. The hood flew back suddenly and was gone with a twang in one gust of wind.

Am I going to have to buy that cop a new gun, too? Dan Henry thought, and in that moment the wind began to die. The water hesitated. Three waves rolled across the road slowly, much higher than when the wind was flattening them, but almost gentle. The rain slackened. And then the eye of the storm had moved over him, and he had calm.

He pushed himself to his feet at last, after he sagged out of the hold the dungarees had on his chest. He leaned against the guardrail and stared woodenly at the ocean and the thing.

The beam went up out of sight, a clean, marvelously precise line. But down at the surface, the sea was finally hiding the thing, and making a new noise that had none of a storm-sea's clean power. It filled his ears and unnerved him.

With the wind and the pressure gone, the waves were leaping upward, clashing against each other, rebounding, colliding again, peaking sharply. Dan Henry could hear the highway over the water booming faintly as the waves slammed up against its underside. But he could actually see very little. It had grown sharply darker, and what he saw were mostly the tops of the exploding waves, glimmering pale violet.

The thing was buried deep where it lay at the foot of the key, and the arc that had diffused most of the light was visible only as a fitful glow that shifted and danced. The violet beam seemed to spring into life of itself at the plunging surface, and it kept most of its light compressed within itself.

Dan Henry swayed on the guardrail. It was stifling hot. The thick mugginess filled his lungs and choked him. He lolled his head back. The clouds were patchy overhead, and the stars shone through in places.

There was a sudden high-pitched chime, and a concentric circle of coruscating ice-blue flame came hurtling down the beam from the thing. It came out of the sky and shot into the water, and when it touched the glimmer of the arc there was another chime, this time from the thing, and this time the water quivered. The violet beam flickered once, and a red halo spat up with a crackle, traveling slowly. When it was a hundred feet over Dan Henry's head it split in two, leaving one thin ring moving at the old rate, and a larger one that suddenly doubled its speed until it split again, doubled its speed and split again, accelerated again, and so blazed upward along the violet beam's axis, leaving a spaced trail of slowly moving lesser rings behind it. They hung in the air, a ladder to the stars. Then they died out slowly, and before they had stopped glowing the violet beam was switched off.

The sky was abruptly empty, and the thing lay quiescent in the water once more. Dan Henry blinked at the flashes swimming across his eyes. It was pitch dark. He could barely see the white of swirling water as it dashed itself into the rocks at his feet.

Except that far up the highway, coming toward him, were two headlights with a swinging red beacon just above them.

The police car was plastered with wet leaves and broken palm fronds. The policeman slammed it to a halt beside him, and flung the door open. He stopped long enough to turn his head and say, "Jesus Christ! He's still here! He ain't gone!" to someone in the front seat with him, and then he jumped out. "What happened?" he asked Dan Henry. "What was that business with the lights?"

Dan Henry looked at him. "You made it," he mumbled.

"Yeah, I made it. Got to this Navy skywatch station. Phone was out, so I couldn't call in to headquarters. Found this Navy professor up there. Brought him down with me when the eye came over. He figures we got maybe twenty minutes more before the other side of the hurricane comes around."

The other man had slid out of the car. He was a thin, bony-faced man with rimless glasses. He was dressed in a badly fitted tropical suit that was pleated with dampness. He looked at Dan Henry's purpled chest, and asked, "Are you all right?"

"Sure."

The man twitched an eyebrow. "I'm assigned to the satellite tracking station north of here. Where is this thing?"

Dan Henry nodded toward it. "Down there. It got an answer to its signal, acknowledged, and switched off. That's what I think, anyhow."

"You do, eh? Well, you could be right. In any case, we don't have much time. I'll notify the naval district commandant's office as soon as the telephones are working again, but I want a quick look at it now, in case we lose it."

"We're not going to lose it," Dan Henry growled.

The professor looked at him sharply. "What makes you sure?"

"I wedged it," Dan Henry said with a tight note in his voice. "I almost ruined myself and I almost drowned, but I wedged it. I took a gun away from a cop to keep it from getting left here without anybody to watch it. And I stayed here and got almost drowned, and almost cut in half, and almost beat to death against this highway here, and *we're not going to lose it now.*"

"I . . . see," the professor said. He turned to the policeman. "If you happen to have some sedatives in your first-aid kit, they might be useful now," he murmured.

"Might have something. I'll look," the policeman said.

"And put your spotlight on the thing, please," the professor added, peering over the guardrail. "Though I don't suppose we'll see much."

The yellow beam of the spotlight slid over the top of the water. If it penetrated at all, it still did not reach any part of the thing. The policeman hunted for it, sweeping back and forth until Dan Henry made an impatient sound, went over to him, and pointed it straight. "Now, leave it there. That's where it is."

"Yeah? I don't see anythin' but water."

"That's where it is," Dan Henry said. "Haven't been here all this time for nothin'." He went back to the railing, but there was still nothing to see.

"You're sure that's where it is?" the professor asked.

"Yes. It's about ten feet down."

"All right," the professor sighed. "Tell me as much as you can about its activities."

"I think it's a sounding rocket," Dan Henry said. "I think somebody from some place sent that thing down here a while ago to find out things. I don't know what those things are. I don't know who that somebody is. But I'm pretty sure he lost it somehow, and didn't know where it was until it signaled him just now. I don't know why it worked out that way. I don't know why the rocket couldn't get its signal through before this, or why it didn't go home."

"You think it's of extraterrestrial origin, then?"

Dan Henry looked at the professor. "You don't think so?"

"If I did, I would be on my way to district headquarters at this moment, hurricane or no hurricane," the professor said testily.

"You don't believe it?" Dan Henry persisted.

The professor grew uneasy. "No."

"Wouldn't you *like* to believe it?"

The professor looked quickly out to sea.

"Here," the policeman said, handing Dan Henry a flat brown half-pint bottle. "Sedative." He winked.

Dan Henry knocked the bottle out of the cop's hand. It broke on the pavement.

"Look up!" the professor whispered.

They turned their heads. Something huge, flat, and multiwinged was shadowed faintly on the stars.

"Oh, Lord," the officer said.

There was a burst of chiming from the thing down in the water, and violet pulses of light came up through the water and burst on the underside of the thing up in the sky.

Answering darts of tawny gold came raining down. The thing in the water stirred, and they could see the rocks move. "Tractor rays," the professor said in a husky voice. "Theoretically impossible."

"What's it going to do?" the policeman asked.

"Pick it up," the professor answered. "And take it back to wherever it comes from."

Dan Henry began to curse.

The thing in the sky slipped down, and they could feel the air throb. After a moment, the sound came to them—a distant, rumbling purr, and a high metallic shrieking.

The thing in the water heaved itself upward. It struggled against the rocks.

"We'd better get back," the professor said.

The distant sound grew stronger and beat upon their ears. The professor and the policeman retreated to the car.

But Dan Henry did not. He straightened his back and gathered his muscles. As the tawny fire came down, he leaped over the guardrail into the water.

He swam with grim fury, thrown and sucked by the water, sputtering for breath, his feet pounding. Even so, he would not have reached the thing. But the water humped in the grip of the force that clutched at the thing, and the waves collapsed. Dan Henry's arms bit through the water with desperate precision, and just before the thing broke free, he was upon it.

"No, sir," hc grunted, closing his hand on one of the struts. "Not without me. We've been through too much together." He grinned coldly at the hovering ship as they rose to meet it.

# THE MARTIAN WAY

## by Isaac Asimov

*After science-fiction writers had been describing interplanetary voyages for twenty years or so, they grew jaded, and there were complaints that the crews of the fictional spaceships were as bored as the authors. Then Isaac Asimov, one of the great masters of science fiction, wrote this story. It magically combines the strict realism of modern science fiction with the pure wonder of the earliest space tales. For epic sweep and excitement, there is nothing quite like it; I only wish there were.*

### 1

FROM the doorway of the short corridor between the only two rooms in the travel-head of the spaceship, Mario Esteban Rioz watched sourly as Ted Long adjusted the video dials painstakingly. Long tried a touch clockwise, then a touch counter. The picture was lousy.

Rioz knew it would stay lousy. They were too far

from Earth and at a bad position facing the Sun. But then Long would not be expected to know that. Rioz remained standing in the doorway for an additional moment, head bent to clear the upper lintel, body turned half sidewise to fit the narrow opening. Then he jerked into the galley like a cork popping out of a bottle.

"What are you after?" he asked.

"I thought I'd get Hilder," said Long.

Rioz propped his rump on the corner of a table shelf. He lifted a conical can of milk from the companion shelf just above his head. Its point popped under pressure. He swirled it gently as he waited for it to warm.

"What for?" he said. He upended the cone and sucked noisily.

"Thought I'd listen."

"I think it's a waste of power."

Long looked up, frowning. "It's customary to allow free use of personal video sets."

"Within reason," retorted Rioz.

Their eyes met challengingly. Rioz had the rangy body, the gaunt, cheek-sunken face that was almost the hallmark of the Martian Scavenger, those Spacers who patiently haunted the space routes between Earth and Mars. Pale blue eyes were set keenly in the brown, lined face which, in turn, stood darkly out against the white surrounding synthо-fur that lined the upturned collar of his leathtic space jacket.

Long was altogether paler and softer. He bore some of the marks of the Grounder, although no second-generation Martian could be a Grounder in the sense that Earthmen were. His own collar was thrown back and his dark brown hair freely exposed.

"What do you call within reason?" demanded Long.

Rioz's thin lips grew thinner. He said, "Considering that we're not even going to make expenses this trip, the way it looks, any power drain at all is outside reason."

Long said, "If we're losing money, hadn't you better get back to your post? It's your watch."

Rioz grunted and ran a thumb and forefinger over the stubble on his chin. He got up and trudged to the door, his soft, heavy boots muting the sound of his steps. He paused to look at the thermostat, then turned with a flare of fury.

"I *thought* it was hot. Where do you think you are?"

Long said, "Forty degrees isn't excessive."

"For you it isn't, maybe. But this is space, not a heated office at the iron mines." Rioz swung the thermostat control down to minimum with a quick thumb movement. "Sun's warm enough."

"The galley isn't on Sunside."

"It'll percolate through, damn it."

Rioz stepped through the door and Long stared after him for a long moment, then turned back to the video. He did not turn up the thermostat.

The picture was still flickering badly, but it would have to do. Long folded a chair down out of the wall. He leaned forward, waiting through the formal announcement, the momentary pause before the slow dissolution of the curtain, the spotlight picking out the well-known bearded figure which grew as it was brought forward until it filled the screen.

The voice, impressive even through the flutings and croakings induced by the electron storms of twenty millions of miles, began, "Friends! My fellow citizens of Earth . . ."

## 2

Rioz's eye caught the flash of the radio signal as he stepped into the pilot room. For one moment, the palms of his hands grew clammy when it seemed to him that it was a radar pip; but that was only his guilt speaking. He should not have left the pilot room while on duty theoretically, though all Scavengers did it. Still, it was the standard nightmare, this business of a strike turning up during just those five minutes when one knocked off for a quick coffee because it seemed certain that space was clear. And the nightmare had been known to happen, too.

Rioz threw in the multiscanner. It was a waste of power, but while he was thinking about it, he might as well make sure.

Space was clear except for the far-distant echoes from the neighboring ships on the scavenging line.

He hooked up the radio circuit, and the blond, long-nosed head of Richard Swenson, copilot of the next ship on the Mars-ward side, filled it.

"Hey, Mario," said Swenson.

"Hi. What's new?"

There was a second and a fraction of pause between that and Swenson's next comment, since the speed of electromagnetic radiation is not infinite.

"What a day I've *had.*"

"Something happened?" Rioz asked.

"I had a strike."

"Well, good."

"Sure, if I'd roped it in," said Swenson morosely.

"What happened?"

"Damn it, I headed in the wrong direction."

Rioz knew better than to laugh. He said, "How did you do that?"

"It wasn't my fault. The trouble was the shell was moving way out of the ecliptic. Can you imagine the stupidity of a pilot who can't work the release maneuver decently? How was I to know? I got the distance of the shell and let it go at that. I just assumed its orbit was in the usual trajectory family. Wouldn't you? I started along what I thought was a good line of intersection and it was five minutes before I noticed the distance was still going up. The pips were taking their sweet time returning. So then I took the angular projections of the thing, and it was too late to catch up with it."

"Any of the other boys getting it?"

"No. It's 'way out of the ecliptic and'll keep on going forever. That's not what bothers me so much. It was only an inner shell. But I hate to tell you how many tons of propulsion I wasted getting up speed and then getting back to station. You should have heard Canute."

Canute was Richard Swenson's brother and partner.

"Mad, huh?" said Rioz.

"Mad? Like to have killed me! But then we've been out five months now and it's getting kind of sticky. You know."

"I know."

"How are you doing, Mario?"

Rioz made a spitting gesture. "About that much this trip. Two shells in the last two weeks and I had to chase each one for six hours."

"Big ones?"

"Are you kidding? I could have scaled them down to Phobos by hand. This is the worst trip I've ever had."

"How much longer are you staying?"

"For my part, we can quit tomorrow. We've only been out two months and it's got so I'm chewing Long out all the time."

There was a pause over and above the electromagnetic lag.

Swenson said, "What's he like, anyway? Long, I mean."

Rioz looked over his shoulder. He could hear the soft, crackly mutter of the video in the galley. "I can't make him out. He says to me about a week after the start of the trip, 'Mario, why are you a Scavenger?' I just look at him and say, 'To make a living. Why do you suppose?' I mean, what the hell kind of a question is that? Why is anyone a Scavenger?

"Anyway, he says, 'That's not it, Mario.' *He's* telling *me,* you see. He says, 'You're a Scavenger because this is part of the Martian way.' "

Swenson said, "And what did he mean by that?"

Rioz shrugged. "I never asked him. Right now he's sitting in there listening to the ultramicrowave from Earth. He's listening to some Grounder called Hilder."

"Hilder? A Grounder politician, an Assemblyman or something, isn't he?"

"That's right. At least, I think that's right. Long is always doing things like that. He brought about fifteen pounds of books with him, all about Earth. Just plain dead weight, you know."

"Well, he's your partner. And talking about partners, I think I'll get back on the job. If I miss another strike, there'll be murder around here."

He was gone and Rioz leaned back. He watched the even green line that was the pulse scanner. He tried the multiscanner a moment. Space was still clear.

He felt a little better. A bad spell is always worse if the Scavengers all about you are pulling in shell after shell, if the shells go spiraling down to the Phobos scrap forges with everyone's brand welded on except your own. Then, too, he had managed to work off some of his resentment toward Long.

It was a mistake teaming up with Long. It was always a mistake to team up with a tenderfoot. They thought what you wanted was conversation, especially Long, with his eternal theories about Mars and its great new role in human progress. That was the way he said it—Human Progress: the Martian Way; the New Creative Minority. And all the time what Rioz wanted wasn't talk, but a strike, a few shells to call their own.

At that, he hadn't any choice, really. Long was pretty well known down on Mars and made good pay as a mining engineer. He was a friend of Commissioner Sankov and he'd been out on one or two short scavenging missions before. You can't turn a fellow down flat before a tryout, even though it did look funny. Why should a mining engineer with a comfortable job and good money want to muck around in space?

Rioz never asked Long that question. Scavenger partners are forced too close together to make curiosity desirable, or sometimes even safe. But Long talked so much that he answered the question.

"I had to come out here, Mario," he said. "The future of Mars isn't in the mines; it's in space."

Rioz wondered how it would be to try a trip alone. Everyone said it was impossible. Even discounting lost opportunities when one man had to go off watch to sleep or attend to other things, it was well known that one man alone in space would become intolerably depressed in a relatively short while.

Taking a partner along made a six-month trip possible. A regular crew would be better, but no Scavenger could make money on a ship large enough to carry one. The capital it would take in propulsion alone!

Even two didn't find it exactly fun in space. Usually you had to change partners each trip and you could stay out longer with some than with others. Look at Richard and Canute Swenson. They teamed up every five or six trips because they were brothers. And yet whenever they did, it was a case of constantly mounting tension and antagonism after the first week.

Oh, well. Space was clear. Rioz would feel a little better if he went back in the galley and smoothed down some of the bickering with Long. He might as well show he was an old spacehand who took the irritations of space as they came.

He stood up, walked the three steps necessary to reach the short, narrow corridor that tied together the two rooms of the spaceship.

## 3

Once again Rioz stood in the doorway for a moment, watching. Long was intent on the flickering screen.

Rioz said gruffly, "I'm shoving up the thermostat. It's all right—we can spare the power."

Long nodded. "If you like."

Rioz took a hesitant step forward. Space was clear, so to hell with sitting and looking at a blank, green, pipless line. He said, "What's the Grounder been talking about?"

"History of space travel mostly. Old stuff, but he's doing it well. He's giving the whole works—color cartoons, trick photography, stills from old films, everything."

As if to illustrate Long's remarks, the bearded figure faded out of view, and a cross-sectional view of a spaceship flitted onto the screen. Hilder's voice continued, pointing out features of interest that appeared in schematic color. The communications system of the ship outlined itself in red as he talked about it, the storerooms, the proton micropile drive, the cybernetic circuits . . .

Then Hilder was back on the screen. "But this is only the travel-head of the ship. What moves it? What gets it off the Earth?"

Everyone knew what moved a spaceship, but Hilder's voice was like a drug. He made spaceship propulsion sound like the secret of the ages, like an ultimate revelation. Even Rioz felt a slight tingling of suspense, though he had spent the greater part of his life aboard ship.

Hilder went on. "Scientists call it different names. They call it the Law of Action and Reaction. Sometimes they call it Newton's Third Law. Sometimes they call it Conservation of Momentum. But we don't have to call it any name. We can just use our common sense. When we swim, we push water backward and move forward ourselves. When we walk, we push back against the ground and move forward. When we fly a gyro-flivver, we push air backward and move forward.

"Nothing can move forward unless something else moves backward. It's the old principle of 'You can't get something for nothing.'

"Now imagine a spaceship that weighs a hundred thousand tons lifting off Earth. To do that, something else must be moved downward. Since a spaceship is extremely heavy, a great deal of material must be moved downward. So much material, in fact, that there is no place to keep it all aboard ship. A special compartment must be built behind the ship to hold it."

Again Hilder faded out and the ship returned. It shrank and a truncated cone appeared behind it. In bright yellow, words appeared within it: MATERIAL TO BE THROWN AWAY.

"But now," said Hilder, "the total weight of the ship is much greater. You need still more propulsion and still more."

The ship shrank enormously to add on another larger shell and still another immense one. The ship proper, the travel-head, was a little dot on the screen, a glowing red dot.

Rioz said, "Hell, this is kindergarten stuff."

"Not to the people he's speaking to, Mario," replied Long. "Earth isn't Mars. There must be billions of Earth people who've never even seen a spaceship; don't know the first thing about it."

Hilder was saying, "When the material inside the biggest shell is used up, the shell is detached. It's thrown away, too."

The outermost shell came loose, wobbled about the screen.

"Then the second one goes," said Hilder, "and then, if the trip is a long one, the last is ejected."

The ship was just a red dot now, with three shells shifting and moving, lost in space.

Hilder said, "These shells represent a hundred thousand tons of tungsten, magnesium, aluminum, and steel. They are gone forever from Earth. Mars is ringed by Scavengers, waiting along the routes of space travel, waiting for the cast-off shells, netting and branding them, saving them for Mars. Not one cent of payment reaches Earth for them. They are salvage. They belong to the ship that finds them."

Rioz said, "We risk our investment and our lives. If we don't pick them up, no one gets them. What loss is that to Earth?"

"Look," said Long, "he's been talking about nothing but the drain that Mars, Venus, and the Moon put on Earth. This is just another item of loss."

"They'll get their return. We're mining more iron every year."

"And most of it goes right back into Mars. If you can believe his figures, Earth has invested two hundred billion dollars in Mars and received back about five billion dollars' worth of iron. It's put five hundred billion dollars into the Moon and gotten back a little over twenty-five billion dollars of magnesium, titanium, and assorted light metals. It's put fifty billion dollars into

Venus and gotten back nothing. And that's what the taxpayers of Earth are really interested in—tax money out; nothing in."

The screen was filled, as he spoke, with diagrams of the Scavengers on the route to Mars; little, grinning caricatures of ships, reaching out wiry, tenuous arms that groped for the tumbling, empty shells, seizing and snaking them in, branding them MARS PROPERTY in glowing letters, then scaling them down to Phobos.

Then it was Hilder again. "They tell us eventually they will return it all to us. Eventually! Once they are a going concern! We don't know when that will be. A century from now? A thousand years? A million? 'Eventually.' Let's take them at their word. Someday they will give us back all our metals. Someday they will grow their own food, use their own power, live their own lives.

"But one thing they can never return. Not in a hundred million years. *Water!*

"Mars has only a trickle of water because it is too small. Venus has no water at all because it is too hot. The Moon has none because it is too hot and too small. So Earth must supply not only drinking water and washing water for the Spacers, water to run their industries, water for the hydroponic factories they claim to be setting up—but even water to throw away by the millions of tons.

"What is the propulsive force that spaceships use? What is it they throw out behind so that they can accelerate forward? Once it was the gases generated from explosives. That was very expensive. Then the proton micropile was invented—a cheap power source that could heat up any liquid until it was a gas under tremendous pressure. What is the cheapest and most plentiful liquid available? Why, water, of course.

"Each spaceship leaves Earth carrying nearly a million tons—not pounds, *tons*—of water, for the sole purpose of driving it into space so that it may speed up or slow down.

"Our ancestors burned the oil of Earth madly and willfully. They destroyed its coal recklessly. We despise and condemn them for that, but at least they had this excuse—they thought that when the need arose, substitutes would be found. And they were right. We have our plankton farms and our proton micropiles.

"But there is no substitute for water. None! There never can be. And when our descendants view the desert we will have made of Earth, what excuse will they find for us? When the droughts come and grow—"

Long leaned forward and turned off the set. He said, "That bothers me. The damn fool is deliberately—What's the matter?"

Rioz had risen uneasily to his feet. "I ought to be watching the pips."

"The hell with the pips." Long got up likewise, followed Rioz through the narrow corridor, and stood just inside the pilot room. "If Hilder carries this through, if he's got the guts to make a real issue out of it—*Wow!*"

He had seen it too. The pip was a Class A, racing after the outgoing signal like a greyhound after a mechanical rabbit.

Rioz was babbling, "Space was clear, I tell you, *clear*. For Mars' sake, Ted, don't just freeze on me. See if you can spot it visually."

Rioz was working speedily and with an efficiency that was the result of nearly twenty years of scavenging. He had the distance in two minutes. Then, remembering Swenson's experience, he measured the angle of declination and the radial velocity as well.

He yelled at Long, "One point seven six radians. You can't miss it, man."

Long held his breath as he adjusted the vernier. "It's only half a radian off the Sun. It'll only be crescent-lit."

He increased magnification as rapidly as he dared, watching for the one "star" that changed position and grew to have a form, revealing itself to be no star.

"I'm starting, anyway," said Rioz. "We can't wait."

"I've got it. I've got it." Magnification was still too small to give it a definite shape, but the dot Long watched was brightening and dimming rhythmically as the shell rotated and caught sunlight on cross sections of different sizes.

"Hold on."

The first of many fine spurts of steam squirted out of the proper vents, leaving long trails of microcrystals of ice gleaming mistily in the pale beams of the distant Sun. They thinned out for a hundred miles or more. One spurt, then another, then another, as the Scavenger ship moved out of its stable trajectory and took up a course tangential to that of the shell.

"It's moving like a comet at perihelion!" yelled Rioz. "Those damned Grounder pilots knock the shells off that way on purpose. I'd like to—"

He swore his anger in a frustrated frenzy as he kicked steam backward and backward recklessly, till the hydraulic cushioning of his chair had soughed back a full foot and Long had found himself all but unable to maintain his grip on the guardrail.

"Have a heart," he begged.

But Rioz had his eye on the pips. "If you can't take it, man, stay on Mars!" The steam spurts continued to boom distantly.

The radio came to life. Long managed to leap forward through what seemed like molasses and closed contact. It was Swenson, eyes glaring.

Swenson yelled, "Where the hell are you guys going? You'll be in my sector in ten seconds."

Rioz said, "I'm chasing a shell."

"In *my* sector?"

"It started in mine and you're not in position to get it. Shut off that radio, Ted."

The ship thundered through space, a thunder that could be heard only within the hull. And then Rioz cut the engines in stages large enough to make Long flail forward. The sudden silence was more ear-shattering than the noise that had preceded it.

Rioz said, "All right. Let me have the 'scope."

They both watched. The shell was a definite truncated cone now, tumbling with slow solemnity as it passed along among the stars.

"It's a Class A shell, all right," said Rioz with satisfaction. A giant among shells, he thought. It would put them into the black.

Long said, "We've got another pip on the scanner. I think it's Swenson taking after us."

Rioz scarcely gave it a glance. "He won't catch us."

The shell grew larger still, filling the visiplate.

Rioz's hands were on the harpoon lever. He waited, adjusted the angle microscopically twice, played out the length allotment. Then he yanked, tripping the release.

For a moment, nothing happened. Then a metal mesh cable snaked out onto the visiplate, moving toward the shell like a striking cobra. It made contact, but it did not hold. If it had, it would have snapped instantly like a cobweb strand. The shell was turning with a rotational momentum amounting to thousands of tons. What the cable did do was to set up a powerful magnetic field that acted as a brake on the shell.

Another cable and another lashed out. Rioz sent them out in an almost heedless expenditure of energy.

"I'll get this one! By Mars, I'll get this one!"

With some two dozen cables stretching between ship and shell, he desisted. The shell's rotational energy, converted by braking into heat, had raised its temperature to a point where its radiation could be picked up by the ship's meters.

Long said, "Do you want me to put our brand on?"

"Suits me. But you don't have to if you don't want to. It's my watch."

"I don't mind."

Long clambered into his suit and went out the lock. It was the surest sign of his newness to the game that he could count the number of times he had been out in space in a suit. This was the fifth time.

He went out along the nearest cable, hand over hand, feeling the vibration of the mesh against the metal of his mitten.

He burned their serial number in the smooth metal of the shell. There was nothing to oxidize the steel in the emptiness of space. It simply melted and vaporized, condensing some feet away from the energy beam, turning the surface it touched into a gray, powdery dullness.

Long swung back toward the ship.

Inside again, he took off his helmet, white and thick with frost that collected as soon as he had entered.

The first thing he heard was Swenson's voice coming over the radio, almost unrecognizable in his rage: ". . . straight to the Commissioner. Damn it, there are rules to this game!"

Rioz sat back, unbothered. "Look, it hit my sector. I was late spotting it and I chased it into yours. You couldn't have gotten it with Mars for a backstop. That's all there is to it— You back, Long?"

He cut contact.

The signal button raged at him, but he paid no attention.

"He's going to the Commissioner?" Long asked.

"Not a chance. He just goes on like that because it breaks the monotony. He doesn't mean anything by it. He knows it's our shell. And how do you like that hunk of stuff, Ted?"

"Pretty good."

"Pretty good? It's terrific! Hold on. I'm setting it swinging."

The side jets spat steam and the ship started a slow rotation about the shell. The shell followed it. In thirty minutes, they were a gigantic bola spinning in emptiness. Long checked the *Ephemeris* for the position of Deimos.

At a precisely calculated moment, the cables released their magnetic field and the shell went streaking off tangentially in a trajectory that would, in a day or so, bring it within pronging distance of the shell stores on the Martian satellite.

Rioz watched it go. He felt good. He turned to Long. "This is one fine day for us."

"What about Hilder's speech?" asked Long.

"What? Who? Oh, that. Listen, if I had to worry about everything some damned Grounder said, I'd never get any sleep. Forget it."

"I don't think we should forget it."

"You're nuts. Don't bother me about it, will you? Get some sleep instead."

## 4

Ted Long found the breadth and height of the city's main thoroughfare exhilarating. It had been two months since the Commissioner had declared a moratorium on scavenging and had pulled all ships out of space, but this feeling of a stretched-out vista had not stopped thrilling Long. Even the thought that the moratorium was called pending a decision on the part of Earth to enforce its new insistence on water economy, by deciding upon a ration limit for scavenging, did not cast him entirely down.

The roof of the avenue was painted a luminous light blue, perhaps as an old-fashioned imitation of Earth's sky, Ted wasn't sure. The walls were lit with the store windows that pierced them.

Off in the distance, over the hum of traffic and the sloughing noise of people's feet passing him, he could hear the intermittent blasting as new channels were being bored into Mars' crust. All his life he remembered such blastings. The ground he walked on had been part of solid, unbroken rock when he was born. The city was growing and would keep on growing—if Earth would only let it.

He turned off at a cross street, narrower, not quite as brilliantly lit, shop windows giving way to apartment houses, each with its row of lights along the front façade. Shoppers and traffic gave way to slower-paced individuals and to squawling youngsters who had as yet evaded the maternal summons to the evening meal.

At the last minute, Long remembered the social amenities and stopped off at a corner water store.

He passed over his canteen. "Fill 'er up."

The plump storekeeper unscrewed the cap, cocked an eye into the opening. He shook it a little and let it gurgle. "Not much left," he said cheerfully.

"No," agreed Long.

The storekeeper trickled water in, holding the neck of the canteen close to the hose tip to avoid spillage. The volume gauge whirred. He screwed the cap back on.

Long passed over the coins and took his canteen. It clanked against his hip now with a pleasing heaviness. It would never do to visit a family without a full canteen. Among the boys, it didn't matter. Not as much, anyway.

He entered the hallway of No. 27, climbed a short flight of stairs, and paused with his thumb on the signal.

The sound of voices could be heard quite plainly.

One was a woman's voice, somewhat shrill. "It's all right for you to have your Scavenger friends here, isn't it? I'm supposed to be thankful you manage to get home two months a year. Oh, it's quite enough that you spend a day or two with me. After that, it's the Scavengers again."

"I've been home for a long time now," said a male voice, "and this is business. For Mars' sake, let up, Dora. They'll be here soon."

Long decided to wait a moment before signaling. It might give them a chance to hit a more neutral topic.

"What do I care if they come?" retorted Dora. "Let them hear me. And I'd just as soon the Commissioner kept the moratorium on permanently. You hear me?"

"And what would we live on?" came the male voice hotly. "You tell me that."

"I'll tell you. You can make a decent, honorable living right here on Mars, just like everybody else. I'm the only one in this apartment house that's a Scavenger widow. That's what I am—a widow. I'm worse than a widow, because if I were a widow, I'd at least have a chance to marry someone else— What did you say?"

"Nothing. Nothing at all."

"Oh, I know what you said. Now listen here, Dick Swenson—"

"I only said," cried Swenson, "that now I know why Scavengers usually don't marry."

"You shouldn't have either. I'm tired of having

every person in the neighborhood pity me and smirk and ask when you're coming home. Other people can be mining engineers and administrators and even tunnel borers. At least tunnel borers' wives have a decent homelife and their children don't grow up like vagabonds. Peter might as well not have a father—"

A thin boy-soprano voice made its way through the door. It was somewhat more distant, as though it were in another room. "Hey, Mom, what's a vagabond?"

Dora's voice rose a notch. "Peter! You keep your mind on your homework."

Swenson said in a low voice, "It's not right to talk this way in front of the kid. What kind of notions will he get about me?"

"Stay home then and teach him better notions."

Peter's voice called out again. "Hey, Mom, I'm going to be a Scavenger when I grow up."

Footsteps sounded rapidly. There was a momentary hiatus in the sounds, then a piercing, "Mom! Hey, Mom! Leggo my ear! What did I do?" and a snuffling silence.

Long seized the chance. He worked the signal vigorously.

Swenson opened the door, brushing down his hair with both hands.

"Hello, Ted," he said in a subdued voice. Then loudly, "Ted's here, Dora. Where's Mario, Ted?"

Long said, "He'll be here in a while."

Dora came bustling out of the next room, a small, dark woman with a pinched nose, and hair, just beginning to show touches of gray, combed off the forehead.

"Hello, Ted. Have you eaten?"

"Quite well, thanks. I haven't interrupted you, have I?"

"Not at all. We finished ages ago. Would you like some coffee?"

"I think so." Ted unslung his canteen and offered it.

"Oh, goodness, that's all right. We've plenty of water."

"I insist."

"Well, then—"

Back into the kitchen she went. Through the swinging door, Long caught a glimpse of dishes sitting in Secoterg, the "waterless cleaner that soaks up and absorbs grease and dirt in a twinkling. One ounce of water will rinse eight square feet of dish surface clean as clean. Buy Secoterg. Secoterg just cleans it right, makes your dishes shiny bright, does away with water waste—"

The tune started whining through his mind and Long crushed it with speech. He said, "How's Pete?"

"Fine, fine. The kid's in the fourth grade now. You know I don't get to see him much. Well, sir, when I came back last time, he looked at me and said . . ."

It went on for a while and wasn't too bad as bright sayings of bright children as told by dull parents go.

The door signal burped and Mario Rioz came in, frowning and red.

Swenson stepped to him quickly. "Listen, don't say anything about shell-snaring. Dora still remembers the time you fingered a Class A shell out of my territory and she's in one of her moods now."

"Who the hell wants to talk about shells?" Rioz slung off a fur-lined jacket, threw it over the back of the chair, and sat down.

Dora came through the swinging door, viewed the newcomer with a synthetic smile, and said, "Hello, Mario. Coffee for you, too?"

"Yeah," he said, reaching automatically for his canteen.

"Just use some more of my water, Dora," said Long quickly. "He'll owe it to me."

"Yeah," said Rioz.

"What's wrong, Mario?" asked Long.

Rioz said heavily, "Go on. Say you told me so. A year ago when Hilder made that speech, you told me so. Say it."

Long shrugged.

Rioz said, "They've set up the quota. Fifteen minutes ago the news came out."

"Well?"

"Fifty thousand tons of water per trip."

"What?" yelled Swenson, burning. "You can't get off Mars with fifty thousand!"

"That's the figure. It's a deliberate piece of gutting. No more scavenging."

Dora came out with the coffee and set it down all around.

"What's all this about no more scavenging?" She sat down very firmly and Swenson looked helpless.

"It seems," said Long, "that they're rationing us at fifty thousand tons and that means we can't make any more trips."

"Well, what of it?" Dora sipped her coffee and smiled gaily. "If you want my opinion, it's a good thing. It's time all you Scavengers found yourselves nice, steady jobs here on Mars. I mean it. It's no life to be running all over space—"

"Please, Dora," said Swenson.

Rioz came close to a snort.

Dora raised her eyebrows. "I'm just giving my opinions."

Long said, "Please feel free to do so. But I would like to say something. Fifty thousand is just a detail. We know that Earth—or at least Hilder's party—wants to make political capital out of a campaign for water economy, so we're in a bad hole. We've got to get water somehow or they'll shut us down altogether, right?"

"Well, sure," said Swenson.

"But the question is how, right?"

"If it's only getting water," said Rioz in a sudden gush of words, "there's only one thing to do and you know it. If the Grounders won't give us water, we'll take it. The water doesn't belong to them just because their fathers and grandfathers were too damned sick-yellow ever to leave their fat planet. Water belongs to people wherever they are. We're people and the water's ours, too. We have a right to it."

"How do you propose taking it?" asked Long.

"Easy! They've got oceans of water on Earth. They can't post a guard over every square mile. We can sink down on the night side of the planet any time we want, fill our shells, then get away. How can they stop us?"

"In half a dozen ways, Mario. How do you spot shells in space up to distances of a hundred thousand miles? One thin metal shell in all that space. How? By radar. Do you think there's no radar on Earth? Do you think that if Earth ever gets the notion we're engaged in waterlegging, it won't be simple for them to set up a radar network to spot ships coming in from space?"

Dora broke in indignantly. "I'll tell you one thing, Mario Rioz. My husband isn't going to be part of any raid to get water to keep up his scavenging with."

"It isn't just scavenging," said Mario. "Next they'll be cutting down on everything else. We've got to stop them now."

"But we don't need their water, anyway," said Dora. "We're not the Moon or Venus. We pipe enough water down from the polar caps for all we need. We have a water tap right in this apartment. There's one in every apartment on this block."

Long said, "Home use is the smallest part of it. The mines use water. And what do we do about the hydroponic tanks?"

"That's right," said Swenson. "What about the hydroponic tanks, Dora? They've got to have water and it's about time we arranged to grow our own fresh food instead of having to live on the condensed crud they ship us from Earth."

"Listen to him," said Dora scornfully. "What do you know about fresh food? You've never eaten any."

"I've eaten more than you think. Do you remember those carrots I picked up once?"

"Well, what was so wonderful about them? If you ask me, good baked protomeal is much better. And healthier, too. It just seems to be the fashion now to be talking fresh vegetables because they're increasing taxes for these hydroponics. Besides, all this will blow over."

Long said, "I don't think so. Not by itself, anyway. Hilder will probably be the next Coordinator, and then things may really get bad. If they cut down on food shipments, too—"

"Well, then," shouted Rioz, "what do we do? I still say take it! Take the water!"

"And I say we can't do that, Mario. Don't you see that what you're suggesting is the Earth way, the Grounder way? You're trying to hold on to the umbilical cord that ties Mars to Earth. Can't you get away from that? Can't you see the Martian way?"

"No, I can't. Suppose you tell me."

"I will, if you'll listen. When we think about the Solar System, what do we think about? Mercury, Venus, Earth, Moon, Mars, Phobos, and Deimos. There you are—seven bodies, that's all. But that doesn't represent one per cent of the Solar System. We Martians are right at the edge of the other ninety-nine per cent. Out there, farther from the Sun, there's unbelievable amounts of water!"

The others stared.

Swenson said uncertainly, "You mean the layers of ice on Jupiter and Saturn?"

"Not that specifically, but it is water, you'll admit. A thousand-mile-thick layer of water is a lot of water."

"But it's all covered up with layers of ammonia or —or something, isn't it?" asked Swenson. "Besides, we can't land on the major planets."

"I know that," said Long, "but I haven't said that was the answer. The major planets aren't the only objects out there. What about the asteroids and the satellites? Vesta is a two-hundred-mile-diameter asteroid that's hardly more than a chunk of ice. One of the moons of Saturn is mostly ice. How about that?"

Rioz said, "Haven't you ever been in space, Ted?"

"You know I have. Why do you ask?"

"Sure, I know you have, but you still talk like a Grounder. Have you thought of the distances involved? The average asteroid is a hundred twenty million miles from Mars at the closest. That's twice the Venus-Mars hop and you know that hardly any liners do even that in one jump. They usually stop off at Earth or the

Moon. After all, how long do you expect anyone to stay in space, man?"

"I don't know. What's your limit?"

"You know the limit. You don't have to ask me. It's six months. That's handbook data. After six months, if you're still in space you're psychotherapy meat. Right, Dick?"

Swenson nodded.

"And that's just the asteroids," Rioz went on. "From Mars to Jupiter is three hundred thirty million miles, and to Saturn it's seven hundred million. How can anyone handle that kind of distance? Suppose you hit standard velocity or, to make it even, say you get up to a good two hundred kilomiles an hour. It would take you—let's see, allowing time for acceleration and deceleration—about six or seven months to get to Jupiter and nearly a year to get to Saturn. Of course, you could hike the speed to a million miles an hour, theoretically, but where would you get the water to do that?"

"Gee," said a small voice attached to a smutty nose and round eyes. "Saturn!"

Dora whirled in her chair. "Peter, march right back into your room."

"Aw, Ma."

"Don't 'Aw, Ma' me." She began to get out of the chair, and Peter scuttled away.

Swenson said, "Say, Dora, why don't you keep him company for a while? It's hard to keep his mind on homework if we're all out here talking."

Dora sniffed obstinately and stayed put. "I'll sit right here until I find out what Ted Long is thinking of. I tell you right now I don't like the sound of it."

Swenson said nervously, "Well, never mind Jupiter and Saturn. I'm sure Ted isn't figuring on that. But what about Vesta? We could make it in ten or twelve weeks there and the same back. And two hundred miles in diameter. That's four million cubic miles of ice!"

"So what?" said Rioz. "What do we do on Vesta?

Quarry the ice? Set up mining machinery? Say, do you know how long that would take?"

Long said, "I'm talking about Saturn, not Vesta."

Rioz addressed an unseen audience. "I tell him seven hundred million miles and he keeps on talking."

"All right," said Long, "suppose you tell me how you know we can only stay in space six months, Mario?"

"It's common knowledge, damn it."

"Because it's in the *Handbook of Space Flight*. It's data compiled by Earth scientists from experience with Earth pilots and spacemen. You're still thinking Grounder style. You won't think the Martian way."

"A Martian may be a Martian, but he's still a man."

"But how can you be so blind? How many times have you fellows been out for over six months without a break?"

Rioz said, "That's different."

"Because you're Martians? Because you're professional Scavengers?"

"No. Because we're not on a flight. We can put back for Mars any time we want to."

"But you *don't* want to. That's my point. Earthmen have tremendous ships with libraries of films, with a crew of fifteen plus passengers. Still, they can only stay out six months maximum. Martian Scavengers have a two-room ship with only one partner. But we can stick it out more than six months."

Dora said, "I suppose you want to stay in a ship for a year and go to Saturn."

"Why not, Dora?" said Long. "We can do it. Don't you see we can? Earthmen can't. They've got a real world. They've got open sky and fresh food, all the air and water they want. Getting into a ship is a terrible change for them. More than six months is too much for them for that very reason. Martians are different. We've been living on a ship our entire lives.

"That's all Mars is—a ship. It's just a big ship forty-five hundred miles across with one tiny room in it occupied by fifty thousand people. It's closed in like a ship. We breathe packaged air and drink packaged water, which we repurify over and over. We eat the same food rations we eat aboard ship. When we get into a ship, it's the same thing we've known all our lives. We can stand it for a lot more than a year if we have to."

Dora said, "Dick, too?"

"We all can."

"Well, Dick can't. It's all very well for you, Ted Long, and this shell stealer here, this Mario, to talk about jaunting off for a year. You're not married. Dick is. He has a wife and he has a child and that's enough for him. He can just get a regular job right here on Mars. Why, my goodness, suppose you go to Saturn and find there's no water there. How'll you get back? Even if you had water left, you'd be out of food. It's the most ridiculous thing I ever heard of."

"No. Now listen," said Long tightly. "I've thought this thing out. I've talked to Commissioner Sankov and he'll help. But we've got to have ships and men. I can't get them. The men won't listen to me. I'm green. You two are known and respected. You're veterans. If you back me, even if you don't go yourselves, if you'll just help me sell this thing to the rest, get volunteers—"

"First," said Rioz grumpily, "you'll have to do a lot more explaining. Once we get to Saturn, where's the water?"

"That's the beauty of it," said Long. "That's why it's got to be Saturn. The water there is just floating around in space for the taking."

## 5

When Hamish Sankov had come to Mars, there was no such thing as a native Martian. Now there were two-hundred-odd babies whose grandfathers had been born on Mars—native in the third generation.

When he had come as a boy in his teens, Mars had been scarcely more than a huddle of grounded spaceships connected by sealed underground tunnels. Through the years, he had seen buildings grow and burrow widely, thrusting blunt snouts up into the thin, unbreathable atmosphere. He had seen huge storage depots spring up into which spaceships and their loads could be swallowed whole. He had seen the mines grow from nothing to a huge gouge in the Martian crust, while the population of Mars grew from fifty to fifty thousand.

It made him feel old, these long memories—they and the even dimmer memories induced by the presence of this Earthman before him. His visitor brought up those long-forgotten scraps of thought about a soft-warm world that was as kind and gentle to mankind as the mother's womb.

The Earthman seemed fresh from that womb. Not very tall, not very lean; in fact, distinctly plump. Dark hair with a neat little wave in it, a neat little mustache, and neatly scrubbed skin. His clothing was right in style and as fresh and neatly turned as plastek could be.

Sankov's own clothes were of Martian manufacture, serviceable and clean, but many years behind the times. His face was craggy and lined, his hair was pure white, and his Adam's apple wobbled when he talked.

The Earthman was Myron Digby, member of Earth's General Assembly. Sankov was Martian Commissioner.

Sankov said, "This all hits us hard, Assemblyman."

"It's hit most of us hard, too, Commissioner."

"Uh-huh. Can't honestly say then that I can make it out. Of course, you understand, I don't make out that I can understand Earth ways, for all that I was born there. Mars is a hard place to live, Assemblyman, and you have to understand that. It takes a lot of shipping space just to bring us food, water, and raw materials so we can live. There's not much room left for books and news films. Even video programs can't reach Mars, except for about a month when Earth is in conjunction, and even then nobody has much time to listen.

"My office gets a weekly summary film from Planetary Press. Generally, I don't have time to pay attention to it. Maybe you'd call us provincial, and you'd be right. When something like this happens, all we can do is kind of helplessly look at each other."

Digby said slowly, "You can't mean that your people on Mars haven't heard of Hilder's anti-Waster campaign."

"No, can't exactly say that. There's a young Scavenger, son of a good friend of mine who died in space—" Sankov scratched the side of his neck doubtfully—"who makes a hobby out of reading up on Earth history and things like that. He catches video broadcasts when he's out in space and he listened to this man Hilder. Near as I can make out, that was the first talk Hilder made about Wasters.

"The young fellow come to me with that. Naturally, I didn't take him very serious. I kept an eye on the Planetary Press films for a while after that, but there wasn't much mention of Hilder and what there was made him out to look pretty funny."

"Yes, Commissioner," said Digby, "it all seemed quite a joke when it started."

Sankov stretched out a pair of long legs to one side of his desk and crossed them at the ankles. "Seems to me it's still pretty much of a joke. What's his argument? We're using up water. Has he tried looking at some figures? I got them all here. Had them brought to me when this committee arrived.

"Seems that Earth has four hundred million cubic miles of water in its oceans and each cubic mile weighs four and a half billion tons. That's a lot of water. Now we use some of that heap in space flight. Most of the thrust is inside Earth's gravitational field, and that means the water thrown out finds its way back to the oceans. Hilder doesn't figure that in. When he says a million tons of water is used up per flight, he's a liar. It's less than a hundred thousand tons.

"Suppose, now, we have fifty thousand flights a year. We don't, of course; not even fifteen hundred. But let's say there are fifty thousand. I figure there's going to be considerable expansion as time goes on. With fifty thousand flights, one cubic mile of water would be lost to space each year. That means that in a million years, Earth would lose *one quarter of one per cent* of its total water supply!"

Digby spread his hands, palms upward, and let them drop. "Commissioner, Interplanetary Alloys has used figures like that in their campaign against Hilder, but you can't fight a tremendous, emotion-filled drive with cold mathematics. This man Hilder has invented a name, 'Wasters.' Slowly he has built this name up into a gigantic conspiracy; a gang of brutal, profit-seeking wretches raping Earth for their own immediate benefit.

"He has accused the government of being riddled with them, the Assembly of being dominated by them, the press of being owned by them. None of this, unfortunately, seems ridiculous to the average man. He knows all too well what selfish men can do to Earth's resources. He knows what happened to Earth's oil during the Time of Troubles, for instance, and the way topsoil was ruined.

"When a farmer experiences a drought, he doesn't care that the amount of water lost in space flight isn't a droplet in a fog as far as Earth's overall water supply is concerned. Hilder has given him something to blame and that's the strongest possible consolation for disaster. He isn't going to give that up for a diet of figures."

Sankov said, "That's where I get puzzled. Maybe it's because I don't know how things work on Earth, but it seems to me that there aren't just droughty farmers there. As near as I could make out from the news summaries, these Hilder people are a minority. Why is it Earth goes along with a few farmers and some crackpots that egg them on?"

"Because, Commissioner, there are such things as worried human beings. The steel industry sees that an era of space flight will stress increasingly the light, nonferrous alloys. The various miners' unions worry about extraterrestrial competition. Any Earthman who can't get aluminum to build a prefab is certain that it is because the aluminum is going to Mars. I know a professor of archaeology who's an anti-Waster because he can't get a government grant to cover his excavations.

He's convinced that all government money is going into rocketry research and space medicine, and he resents it."

Sankov said, "That doesn't sound like Earth people are much different from us here on Mars. But what about the General Assembly? Why do they have to go along with Hilder?"

Digby smiled sourly. "Politics isn't pleasant to explain. Hilder introduced this bill to set up a committee to investigate waste in space flight. Maybe three fourths or more of the General Assembly was against such an investigation as an intolerable and useless extension of bureaucracy—which it is. But then how could any legislator be against a mere investigation of waste? It would sound as though he had something to fear or to conceal. It would sound as though he were himself profiting from waste. Hilder is not in the least afraid of making such accusations, and whether true or not, they would be a powerful factor with the voters in the next election. The bill passed.

"And then there came the question of appointing the members of the committee. Those who were against Hilder shied away from membership, which would have meant decisions that would be continually embarrassing. Remaining on the sidelines would make one that much less a target for Hilder. The result is that I am the only member of the committee who is outspokenly anti-Hilder and it may cost me reelection."

Sankow said, "I'd be sorry to hear that, Assemblyman. It looks as though Mars didn't have as many friends as we thought we had. We wouldn't like to lose one. But if Hilder wins out—what's he after, anyway?"

"I should think," said Digby, "that that is obvious. He wants to be the next Global Coordinator."

"Think he'll make it?"

"If nothing happens to stop him, he will."

"And then what? Will he drop this Waster campaign then?"

"I can't say. I don't know if he's laid his plans past the Coordinacy. Still, if you want my guess, he couldn't abandon the campaign and maintain his popularity. It's gotten out of hand."

Sankov scratched the side of his neck. "All right. In that case, I'll ask you for some advice. What can we folks on Mars do? You know Earth. You know the situation. We don't. Tell us what to do."

Digby rose and stepped to the window. He looked out upon the low domes of other buildings; red, rocky, completely desolate plain in between; a purple sky and a shrunken sun.

He said, without turning, "Do you people really like it on Mars?"

Sankov smiled. "Most of us don't exactly know any other world, Assemblyman. Seems to me Earth would be something queer and uncomfortable to them."

"But wouldn't Martians get used to it? Earth isn't hard to take after this. Wouldn't your people learn to enjoy the privilege of breathing air under an open sky? You once lived on Earth. You remember what it was like."

"I sort of remember. Still, it doesn't seem to be easy to explain. Earth is just there. It fits people and people fit it. People take Earth the way they find it. Mars is different. It's sort of raw and doesn't fit people. People got to make something out of it. They got to *build* a world, and not take what they find. Mars isn't much yet, but we're building, and when we're finished, we're going to have just what we like. It's sort of a great feeling to know you're building a world. Earth would be kind of unexciting after that."

The Assemblyman said, "Surely the ordinary Martian isn't such a philosopher that he's content to live this terribly hard life for the sake of a future that must be hundreds of generations away."

"No-o, not just like that." Sankov put his right ankle on his left knee and cradled it as he spoke. "Like I said, Martians are a lot like Earthmen, which means they're sort of human beings, and human beings don't go in for philosophy much. Just the same, there's something to living in a growing world, whether you think about it much or not.

"My father used to send me letters when I first came to Mars. He was an accountant and he just sort of stayed an accountant. Earth wasn't much different when he died from what it was when he was born. He didn't see anything happen. Every day was like every other day, and living was just a way of passing time until he died.

"On Mars, it's different. Every day there's something new—the city's bigger, the ventilation system gets another kick, the water lines from the poles get slicked up. Right now, we're planning to set up a news-film association of our own. We're going to call it Mars Press. If you haven't lived when things are growing all about you, you'll never understand how wonderful it feels.

"No, Assemblyman, Mars is hard and tough and Earth is a lot more comfortable, but seems to me if you take our boys to Earth, they'll be unhappy. They probably wouldn't be able to figure out why, most of them, but they'd feel lost; lost and useless. Seems to me lots of them would never make the adjustment."

Digby turned away from the window and the smooth, pink skin of his forehead was creased into a frown. "In that case, Commissioner, I am sorry for you. For all of you."

"Why?"

"Because I don't think there's anything your people on Mars can do. Or the people on the Moon or Venus. It won't happen now; maybe it won't happen for a year or two, or even for five years. But pretty soon you'll all have to come back to Earth, unless—"

Sankov's white eyebrows bent low over his eyes. "Well?"

"Unless you can find another source of water besides the planet Earth."

Sankov shook his head. "Don't seem likely, does it?"

"Not very."

"And except for that, seems to you there's no chance?"

"None at all."

Digby said that and left, and Sankov stared for a

long time at nothing before he punched a combination of the local communiline.

After a while, Ted Long looked out at him.

Sankov said, "You were right, son. There's nothing they can do. Even the ones that mean well see no way out. How did you know?"

"Commissioner," said Long, "when you've read all you can about the Time of Troubles, particularly about the twentieth century, nothing political can come as a real surprise."

"Well, maybe. Anyway, son, Assemblyman Digby is sorry for us, quite a piece sorry, you might say, but that's all. He says we'll have to leave Mars—or else get water somewhere else. Only he thinks that we can't get water somewhere else."

"You know we can, don't you, Commissioner?"

"I know we *might*, son. It's a terrible risk."

"If I find enough volunteers, the risk is our business."

"How is it going?"

"Not bad. Some of the boys are on my side right now. I talked Mario Rioz into it, for instance, and you know he's one of the best."

"That's just it—the volunteers will be the best men we have. I hate to allow it."

"If we get back, it will be worth it."

"If! It's a big word, son."

"And a big thing we're trying to do."

"Well, I gave my word that if there was no help on Earth, I'll see that the Phobos water hole lets you have all the water you'll need. Good luck."

## 6

Halt a million miles above Saturn, Mario Rioz was cradled on nothing and sleep was delicious. He came out of it slowly and for a while, alone in his suit, he counted the stars and traced lines from one to another.

At first, as the weeks flew past, it was scavenging all over again, except for the gnawing feeling that every minute meant an additional number of thousands of miles away from all humanity. That made it worse.

They had aimed high to pass out of the ecliptic while moving through the Asteroid Belt. That had used up water and had probably been unnecessary. Although tens of thousands of worldlets look as thick as vermin in two-dimensional projection upon a photographic plate, they are nevertheless scattered so thinly through the quadrillions of cubic miles that make up their conglomerate orbit that only the most ridiculous of coincidences would have brought about a collision.

Still, they passed over the Belt and someone calculated the chances of collision with a fragment of matter large enough to do damage. The value was so low, so impossibly low, that it was perhaps inevitable that the notion of the "space-float" should occur to someone.

The days were long and many, space was empty, only one man was needed at the controls at any one time. The thought was a natural.

First, it was a particularly daring one who ventured out for fifteen minutes or so. Then another who tried half an hour. Eventually, before the asteroids were entirely behind, each ship regularly had its off-watch member suspended in space at the end of a cable.

It was easy enough. The cable, one of those intended for operations at the conclusion of their journey, was magnetically attached at both ends, one to the space suit to start with. Then you clambered out the lock onto the ship's hull and attached the other end there. You paused awhile, clinging to the metal skin by the electromagnets in your boots. Then you neutralized those and made the slightest muscular effort.

Slowly, ever so slowly, you lifted from the ship and even more slowly the ship's larger mass moved an equivalently shorter distance downward. You floated incredibly, weightlessly, in solid, speckled black. When the ship had moved far enough away from you, your gauntleted hand, which kept touch upon the cable, tightened its grip slightly. Too tightly, and you would begin moving back toward the ship and it toward you. Just tightly enough, and friction would halt you. Because your motion was equivalent to that of the ship, it seemed as motionless below you as though it had been painted against an impossible background while the cable between you hung in coils that had no reason to straighten out.

It was a half ship to your eye. One half was lit by the light of the feeble Sun, which was still too bright to look at directly without the heavy protection of the polarized space-suit visor. The other half was black on black, invisible.

Space closed in and it was like sleep. Your suit was warm, it renewed its air automatically, it had food and drink in special containers from which it could be sucked with a minimal motion of the head, it took care of wastes appropriately. Most of all, more than anything else, there was the delightful euphoria of weightlessness.

You never felt so well in your life. The days stopped being too long, they weren't long enough, and there weren't enough of them.

They had passed Jupiter's orbit at a spot some thirty degrees from its then position. For months, it was the brightest object in the sky, always excepting the glowing white pea that was the Sun. At its brightest, some of the Scavengers insisted they could make out Jupiter as a tiny sphere, one side squashed out of true by the night shadow.

Then over a period of additional months it faded, while another dot of light grew until it was brighter than Jupiter. It was Saturn, first as a dot of brilliance, then as an oval, glowing splotch.

("Why oval?" someone asked, and after a while, someone else said, "The rings, of course," and it was obvious.)

Everyone space-floated at all possible times toward the end, watching Saturn incessantly.

("Hey, you jerk, come on back in, damn it. You're on duty." "Who's on duty? I've got fifteen minutes more by my watch." "You set your watch back. Besides, I gave you twenty minutes yesterday." "You wouldn't give two minutes to your grandmother."

"Come on in, damn it, or I'm coming out anyway."
"All right, I'm coming. Holy howlers, what a racket over a lousy minute." But no quarrel could possibly be serious, not in space. It felt too good.)

Saturn grew until at last it rivaled and then surpassed the Sun. The rings, set at a broad angle to their trajectory of approach, swept grandly about the planet, only a small portion being eclipsed. Then, as they approached, the span of the rings grew still wider, yet narrower as the angle of approach constantly decreased.

The larger moons showed up in the surrounding sky like serene fireflies.

Mario Rioz was glad he was awake so that he could watch again.

Saturn filled half the sky, streaked with orange, the night shadow cutting it fuzzily nearly one quarter of the way in from the right. Two round little dots in the brightness were shadows of two of the moons. To the left and behind him (he could look over his left shoulder to see, and as he did so, the rest of his body inched slightly to the right to conserve angular momentum) was the white diamond of the Sun.

Most of all he liked to watch the rings. At the left, they emerged from behind Saturn, a tight, bright triple band of orange light. At the right, their beginnings were hidden in the night shadow, but showed up closer and broader. They widened as they came, like the flare of a horn, growing hazier as they approached, until, while the eye followed them, they seemed to fill the sky and lose themselves.

From the position of the Scavenger fleet just inside the outer rim of the outermost ring, the rings broke up and assumed their true identity as a phenomenal cluster of solid fragments rather than the tight, solid band of light they seemed.

Below him, or rather in the direction his feet pointed, some twenty miles away, was one of the ring fragments. It looked like a large, irregular splotch, marring the symmetry of space, three quarters in brightness and the night shadow cutting it like a knife.

Other fragments were farther off, sparkling like star dust, dimmer and thicker, until, as you followed them down, they became rings once more.

The fragments were motionless, but that was only because the ships had taken up an orbit about Saturn equivalent to that of the outer edge of the rings.

The day before, Rioz reflected, he had been on that nearest fragment, working along with more than a score of others to mold it into the desired shape. Tomorrow he would be at it again.

Today—today he was space-floating.

"Mario?" The voice that broke upon his earphones was questioning.

Momentarily Rioz was flooded with annoyance. Damn it, he wasn't in the mood for company.

"Speaking," he said.

"I thought I had your ship spotted. How are you?"

"Fine. That you, Ted?"

"That's right," said Long.

"Anything wrong on the fragment?"

"Nothing. I'm out here floating."

"You?"

"It gets me, too, occasionally. Beautiful, isn't it?"

"Nice," agreed Rioz.

"You know, I've read Earth books—"

"Grounder books, you mean." Rioz yawned and found it difficult under the circumstances to use the expression with the proper amount of resentment.

"—and sometimes I read descriptions of people lying on grass," continued Long. "You know that green stuff like thin, long pieces of paper they have all over the ground down there, and they look up at the blue sky with clouds in it. Did you ever see any films of that?"

"Sure. It didn't attract me. It looked cold."

"I suppose it isn't, though. After all, Earth is quite close to the Sun, and they say their atmosphere is thick enough to hold the heat. I must admit that personally I would hate to be caught under open sky with nothing on but clothes. Still, I imagine they like it."

"Grounders are nuts!"

"They talk about the trees, big brown stalks, and the winds, air movements, you know."

"You mean drafts. They can keep that, too."

"It doesn't matter. The point is they describe it beautifully, almost passionately. Many times I've wondered, 'What's it really like? Will I ever feel it or is this something only Earthmen can possibly feel?' I've felt so often that I was missing something vital. Now I know what it must be like. It's this. Complete peace in the middle of a beauty-drenched universe."

Rioz said, "They wouldn't like it. The Grounders, I mean. They're so used to their own lousy little world they wouldn't appreciate what it's like to float and look down on Saturn." He flipped his body slightly and began swaying back and forth about his center of mass, slowly, soothingly.

Long said, "Yes, I think so too. They're slaves to their planet. Even if they come to Mars, it will only be their children that are free. There'll be starships someday; great, huge things that can carry thousands of people and maintain their self-contained equilibrium for decades, maybe centuries. Mankind will spread through the whole Galaxy. But people will have to live their lives out on shipboard until new methods of interstellar travel are developed, so it will be Martians, not planet-bound Earthmen, who will colonize the Universe. That's inevitable. It's got to be. It's the Martian way."

But Rioz made no answer. He had dropped off to sleep again, rocking and swaying gently, half a million miles above Saturn.

## 7

The work shift of the ring fragment was the tail of the coin. The weightlessness, peace, and privacy of the space-float gave place to something that had neither peace nor privacy. Even the weightlessness, which continued, became more a purgatory than a paradise under the new conditions.

Try to manipulate an ordinarily nonportable heat

projector. It could be lifted despite the fact that it was six feet high and wide and almost solid metal, since it weighed only a fraction of an ounce. But its inertia was exactly what it had always been, which meant that if it wasn't moved into position very slowly, it would just keep on going, taking you with it. Then you would have to hike the pseudo-grav field of your suit and come down with a jar.

Keralski had hiked the field a little too high and he came down a little too roughly, with the projector coming down with him at a dangerous angle. His crushed ankle had been the first casualty of the expedition.

Rioz was swearing fluently and nearly continuously. He continued to have the impulse to drag the back of his hand across his forehead in order to wipe away the accumulating sweat. The few times that he had succumbed to the impulse, metal had met silicone with a clash that rang loudly inside his suit, but served no useful purpose. The desiccators within the suit were sucking at maximum and, of course, recovering the water and restoring ion-exchanged liquid, containing a careful proportion of salt, into the appropriate receptacle.

Rioz yelled, "Damn it, Dick, wait till I give the word, will you?"

And Swenson's voice rang in his ears, "Well, how long am I supposed to sit here?"

"Till I say," replied Rioz.

He strengthened pseudo-grav and lifted the projector a bit. He released pseudo-grav, ensuring that the projector would stay in place for minutes even if he withdrew support altogether. He kicked the cable out of the way (it stretched beyond the close "horizon" to a power source that was out of sight) and touched the release.

The material of which the fragment was composed bubbled and vanished under its touch. A section of the lip of the tremendous cavity he had already carved into its substance melted away and a roughness in its contour had disappeared.

"Try it now," called Rioz.

Swenson was in the ship that was hovering nearly over Rioz's head.

Swenson called, "All clear?"

"I told you to go ahead."

It was a feeble flicker of steam that issued from one of the ship's forward vents. The ship drifted down toward the ring fragment. Another flicker adjusted a tendency to drift sidewise. It came down straight.

A third flicker to the rear slowed it to a feather rate.

Rioz watched tensely. "Keep her coming. You'll make it. You'll make it."

The rear of the ship entered the hole, nearly filling it. The bellying walls came closer and closer to its rim. There was a grinding vibration as the ship's motion halted.

It was Swenson's turn to curse. "It doesn't fit," he said.

Rioz threw the projector groundward in a passion and went flailing up into space. The projector kicked up a white crystalline dust all about it, and when Rioz came down under pseudo-grav, he did the same.

He said, "You went in on the bias, you dumb Grounder."

"I hit it level, you dirt-eating farmer."

Backward-pointing side jets of the ship were blasting more strongly than before, and Rioz hopped to get out of the way.

The ship scraped up from the pit, then shot into space half a mile before forward jets could bring it to a halt.

Swenson said tensely, "We'll spring half a dozen plates if we do this once again. Get it right, will you?"

"I'll get it right. Don't worry about it. Just you come in right."

Rioz jumped upward and allowed himself to climb three hundred yards to get an overall look at the cavity. The gouge marks of the ship were plain enough. They were concentrated at one point halfway down the pit. He would get that.

It began to melt outward under the blaze of the projector.

Half an hour later the ship snuggled neatly into its cavity, and Swenson, wearing his space suit, emerged to join Rioz.

Swenson said, "If you want to step in and climb out of the suit I'll take care of the icing."

"It's all right," said Rioz. "I'd just as soon sit here and watch Saturn."

He sat down at the lip of the pit. There was a six-foot gap between it and the ship. In some places about the circle, it was two feet; in a few places, even merely a matter of inches. You couldn't expect a better fit out of handwork. The final adjustment would be made by steaming ice gently and letting it freeze into the cavity between the lip and the ship.

Saturn moved visibly across the sky, its vast bulk inching below the horizon.

Rioz said, "How many ships are left to put in place?"

Swenson said, "Last I heard, it was eleven. We're in now, so that means only ten. Seven of the ones that are placed are iced in. Two or three are dismantled."

"We're coming along fine."

"There's plenty to do yet. Don't forget the main jets at the other end. And the cables and the power lines. Sometimes I wonder if we'll make it. On the way out, it didn't bother me so much, but just now I was sitting at the controls and I was saying, 'We won't make it. We'll sit out here and starve and die with nothing but Saturn over us.' It makes me feel—"

He didn't explain how it made him feel. He just sat there.

Rioz said, "You think too damn much."

"It's different with you," said Swenson. "I keep thinking of Pete—and Dora."

"What for? She said you could go, didn't she? The Commissioner gave her that talk on patriotism and how you'd be a hero and set for life once you got back, and she said you could go. You didn't sneak out the way Adams did."

"Adams is different. That wife of his should have been shot when she was born. Some women can make hell for a guy, can't they? She didn't want him to go—but she'd probably rather he didn't come back if she can get his settlement pay."

"What's your kick, then? Dora wants you back, doesn't she?"

Swenson sighed. "I never treated her right."

"You turned over your pay, it seems to me. I wouldn't do that for any woman. Money for value received, not a cent more."

"Money isn't it. I get to thinking out here. A woman likes company. A kid needs his father. What am I doing 'way out here?"

"Getting set to go home."

"Ah-h, you don't understand."

## 8

Ted Long wandered over the ridged surface of the ring fragment with his spirits as icy as the ground he walked on. It had all seemed perfectly logical back on Mars, but that was Mars. He had worked it out carefully in his mind in perfectly reasonable steps. He could still remember exactly how it went.

It didn't take a ton of water to move a ton of ship. It was not mass equals mass, but mass times velocity equals mass times velocity. It didn't matter, in other words, whether you shot out a ton of water at a mile a second or a hundred pounds of water at twenty miles a second. You got the same final velocity out of the ship.

That meant the jet nozzles had to be made narrower and the steam hotter. But then drawbacks appeared. The narrower the nozzle, the more energy was lost in friction and turbulence. The hotter the steam, the more refractory the nozzle had to be and the shorter its life. The limit in that direction was quickly reached.

Then, since a given weight of water could move considerably more than its own weight under the narrow-nozzle conditions, it paid to be big. The bigger the water-storage space, the larger the size of the actual travel-head, even in proportion. So they started to make liners heavier and bigger. But then the larger the shell, the heavier the bracings, the more difficult the weldings, the more exacting the engineering requirements. At the moment, the limit in that direction had been reached also.

And then he had put his finger on what had seemed to him to be the basic flaw—the original unswervable conception that the fuel had to be placed *inside* the ship; the metal had to be built to encircle a million tons of water.

Why? Water did not have to be water. It could be ice, and ice could be shaped. Holes could be melted into it. Travel-heads and jets could be fitted into it. Cables could hold travel-heads and jets stiffly together under the influence of magnetic field-force grips.

Long felt the trembling of the ground he walked on. He was at the head of the fragment. A dozen ships were blasting in and out of sheaths carved in its substance, and the fragment shuddered under the continuing impact.

The ice didn't have to be quarried. It existed in proper chunks in the rings of Saturn. That's all the rings were—pieces of nearly pure ice, circling Saturn. So spectroscopy stated and so it had turned out to be. He was standing on one such piece now, over two miles long, nearly one mile thick. It was almost half a billion tons of water, all in one piece, and he was standing on it.

But now he was face to face with the realities of life. He had never told the men just how quickly he had expected to set up the fragment as a ship, but in his heart, he had imagined it would be two days. It was a week now and he didn't dare to estimate the remaining time. He no longer even had any confidence that the task was a possible one. Would they be able to control jets with enough delicacy through leads slung across two miles of ice to manipulate out of Saturn's dragging gravity?

Drinking water was low, though they could always

distill more out of the ice. Still, the food stores were not in a good way either.

He paused, looked up into the sky, eyes straining. *Was* the object growing larger? He ought to measure its distance. Actually, he lacked the spirit to add that trouble to the others. His mind slid back to greater immediacies.

Morale, at least, was high. The men seemed to enjoy being out Saturn-way. They were the first humans to penetrate this far, the first to pass the asteroids, the first to see Jupiter like a glowing pebble to the naked eye, the first to see Saturn—like that.

He didn't think fifty practical, case-hardened, shell-snatching Scavengers would take time to feel that sort of emotion. But they did. And they were proud.

Two men and a half-buried ship slid up the moving horizon as he walked.

He called crisply, "Hello, there!"

Rioz answered, "That you, Ted?"

"You bet. Is that Dick with you?"

"Sure. Come on, sit down. We were just getting ready to ice in and we were looking for an excuse to delay."

"I'm not," said Swenson promptly. "When will we be leaving, Ted?"

"As soon as we get through. That's no answer, is it?"

Swenson said dispiritedly, "I suppose there isn't any other answer."

Long looked up, staring at the irregular bright splotch in the sky.

Rioz followed his glance. "What's the matter?"

For a moment, Long did not reply. The sky was black otherwise and the ring fragments were an orange dust against it. Saturn was more than three fourths below the horizon and the rings were going with it. Half a mile away a ship bounded past the icy rim of the planetoid into the sky, was orange-lit by Saturn-light, and sank down again.

The ground trembled gently.

Rioz said, "Something bothering you about the Shadow?"

They called it that. It was the nearest fragment of the rings, quite close considering that they were at the outer rim of the rings, where the pieces spread themselves relatively thin. It was perhaps twenty miles off, a jagged mountain, its shape clearly visible.

"How does it look to you?" asked Long.

Rioz shrugged. "Okay, I guess. I don't see anything wrong."

"Doesn't it seem to be getting larger?"

"Why should it?"

"Well, doesn't it?" Long insisted.

Rioz and Swenson stared at it thoughtfully.

"It does look bigger," said Swenson.

"You're just putting the notion into our minds," Rioz argued. "If it were getting bigger, it would be coming closer."

"What's impossible about that?"

"These things are on stable orbits."

"They were when we came here," said Long. "There, did you feel that?"

The ground had trembled again.

Long said, "We've been blasting this thing for a week now. First, twenty-five ships landed on it, which changed its momentum right there. Not much, of course. Then we've been melting parts of it away and our ships have been blasting in and out of it—all at one end, too. In a week, we may have changed its orbit just a bit. The two fragments, this one and the Shadow, might be converging."

"It's got plenty of room to miss us in." Rioz watched it thoughtfully. "Besides, if we can't even tell for sure that it's getting bigger, how quickly can it be moving? Relative to us, I mean."

"It doesn't have to be moving quickly. Its momentum is as large as ours, so that, however gently it hits, we'll be nudged completely out of our orbit, maybe in toward Saturn, where we don't want to go. As a matter of fact, ice has a very low tensile strength, so that both planetoids might break up into gravel."

Swenson rose to his feet. "Damn it, if I can tell how a shell is moving a thousand miles away, I can tell what a mountain is doing twenty miles away." He turned toward the ship.

Long didn't stop him.

Rioz said, "There's a nervous guy."

The neighboring planetoid rose to zenith, passed overhead, began sinking. Twenty minutes later, the horizon opposite that portion behind which Saturn had disappeared burst into orange flame as its bulk began lifting again.

Rioz called into his radio, "Hey, Dick, are you dead in there?"

"I'm checking," came the muffled response.

"Is it moving?" asked Long.

"Yes."

"Toward us?"

There was a pause. Swenson's voice was a sick one. "On the nose, Ted. Intersection of orbits will take place in three days."

"You're crazy!" yelled Rioz.

"I checked four times," said Swenson.

Long thought blankly, What do *we* do now?

## 9

Some of the men were having trouble with the cables. They had to be laid precisely; their geometry had to be very nearly perfect for the magnetic field to attain maximum strength. In space, or even in air, it wouldn't have mattered. The cables would have lined up automatically once the juice went on.

Here it was different. A gouge had to be plowed along the planetoid's surface and into it the cable had to be laid. If it were not lined up within a few minutes of arc of the calculated direction, a torque would be applied to the entire planetoid, with consequent loss of energy, none of which could be spared. The gouges then had to be redriven, the cables shifted and iced into the new positions.

The men plodded wearily through the routine.

And then the word reached them:

"All hands to the jets!"

Scavengers could not be said to be the type that took kindly to discipline. It was a grumbling, growling, muttering group that set about disassembling the jets of the ships that yet remained intact, carrying them to the tail end of the planetoid, grubbing them into position, and stringing the leads along the surface.

It was almost twenty-four hours before one of them looked into the sky and said, "Holy jeepers!" followed by something less printable.

His neighbor looked and said, "I'll be damned!"

Once they noticed, all did. It became the most astonishing fact in the Universe.

"Look at the Shadow!"

It was spreading across the sky like an infected wound. Men looked at it, found it had doubled its size, wondered why they hadn't noticed that sooner.

Work came to a virtual halt. They besieged Ted Long.

He said, "We can't leave. We don't have the fuel to see us back to Mars and we don't have the equipment to capture another planetoid. So we've got to stay. Now the Shadow is creeping in on us because our blasting has thrown us out of orbit. We've got to change that by continuing the blasting. Since we can't blast the front end any more without endangering the ship we're building, let's try another way."

They went back to work on the jets with a furious energy that received impetus every half hour when the Shadow rose again over the horizon, bigger and more menacing than before.

Long had no assurance that it would work. Even if the jets would respond to the distant controls, even if the supply of water, which depended upon a storage chamber opening directly into the icy body of the planetoid, with built-in heat projectors steaming the propulsive fluid directly into the driving cells, were adequate, there was still no certainty that the body of the planetoid without a magnetic cable sheathing would hold together under the enormously disruptive stresses.

"Ready!" came the signal in Long's receiver.

Long called, "Ready!" and depressed the contact.

The vibration grew about him. The star field in the visiplate trembled.

In the rearview, there was a distant gleaming spume of swiftly moving ice crystals.

"It's blowing!" was the cry.

It kept on blowing. Long dared not stop. For six hours, it blew, hissing, bubbling, steaming into space; the body of the planetoid converted to vapor and hurled away.

The Shadow came closer until men did nothing but stare at the mountain in the sky, surpassing Saturn itself in spectacularity. Its every groove and valley was a plain scar upon its face. But when it passed through the planetoid's orbit, it crossed more than half a mile behind its then position.

The steam jet ceased.

Long bent in his seat and covered his eyes. He hadn't eaten in two days. He could eat now, though. Not another planetoid was close enough to interrupt them, even if it began an approach that very moment.

Back on the planetoid's surface, Swenson said, "All the time I watched that damned rock coming down, I kept saying to myself, 'This can't happen. We can't let it happen.' "

"Hell," said Rioz, "we were all nervous. Did you see Jim Davis? He was green. I was a little jumpy myself."

"That's not it. It wasn't just—dying, you know. I was thinking—I know it's funny, but I can't help it—I was thinking that Dora warned me I'd get myself killed, she'll never let me hear the last of it. Isn't that a crummy sort of attitude at a time like that?"

"Listen," said Rioz, "you wanted to get married, so you got married. Why come to me with your troubles?"

## 10

The flotilla, welded into a single unit, was returning over its mighty course from Saturn to Mars. Each day it flashed over a length of space that had taken nine days outward.

Ted Long had put the entire crew on emergency. With twenty-five ships embedded in the planetoid taken out of Saturn's rings and unable to move or maneuver independently, the coordination of their power sources into unified blasts was a ticklish problem. The jarring that took place on the first day of travel nearly shook them out from under their hair.

That, at least, smoothed itself out as the velocity raced upward under the steady thrust from behind. They passed the one-hundred-thousand-mile-an-hour mark late on the second day, and climbed steadily toward the million-mile mark and beyond.

Long's ship, which formed the needle point of the frozen fleet, was the only one which possessed a five-way view of space. It was an uncomfortable position under the circumstances. Long found himself watching tensely, imagining somehow that the stars would slowly begin to slip backward, to whizz past them, under the influence of the multiship's tremendous rate of travel.

They didn't, of course. They remained nailed to the black backdrop, their distance scorning with patient immobility any speed mere man could achieve.

The men complained bitterly after the first few days. It was not only that they were deprived of the spacefloat. They were burdened by much more than the ordinary pseudo-gravity field of the ships, by the effects of the fierce acceleration under which they were living. Long himself was weary to death of the relentless pressure against hydraulic cushions.

They took to shutting off the jet thrusts one hour out of every four and Long fretted.

It had been just over a year that he had last seen Mars shrinking in an observation window from this ship, which had then been an independent entity. What had happened since then? Was the colony still there?

In something like a growing panic, Long sent out radio pulses toward Mars daily, with the combined power of twenty-five ships behind it. There was no answer. He expected none. Mars and Saturn were on opposite sides of the Sun now, and until he mounted high enough above the ecliptic to get the Sun well beyond the line connecting himself and Mars, solar interference would prevent any signal from getting through.

High above the outer rim of the Asteroid Belt, they reached maximum velocity. With short spurts of power from first one side jet, then another, the huge vessel reversed itself. The composite jet in the rear began its mighty roaring once again, but now the result was deceleration.

They passed a hundred million miles over the Sun, curving down to intersect the orbit of Mars.

A week out of Mars, answering signals were heard for the first time, fragmentary, ether-torn, and incomprehensible, but they were coming from Mars. Earth and Venus were at angles sufficiently different to leave no doubt of that.

Long relaxed. There were still humans on Mars, at any rate.

Two days out of Mars, the signal was strong and clear and Sankov was at the other end.

Sankov said, "Hello, son. It's three in the morning here. Seems like people have no consideration for an old man. Dragged me right out of bed."

"I'm sorry, sir."

"Don't be. They were following orders. I'm afraid to ask, son. Anyone hurt? Maybe dead?"

"No deaths, sir. Not one."

"And—and the water? Any left?"

Long said, with an effort at nonchalance, "Enough."

"In that case, get home as fast as you can. Don't take any chances, of course."

"There's trouble, then."

"Fair to middling. When will you come down?"

"Two days. Can you hold out that long?"

"I'll hold out."

Forty hours later Mars had grown to a ruddy-orange ball that filled the ports and they were in the final planet-landing spiral.

"Slowly," Long said to himself, "slowly." Under these conditions, even the thin atmosphere of Mars could do dreadful damage if they moved through it too quickly.

Since they came in from well above the ecliptic, their spiral passed from north to south. A polar cap shot whitely below them, then the much smaller one of the summer hemisphere, the large one again, the small one, at longer and longer intervals. The planet approached closer, the landscape began to show features.

"Prepare for landing!" called Long.

## 11

Sankov did his best to look placid, which was difficult considering how closely the boys had shaved their return. But it had worked out well enough.

Until a few days ago, he had no sure knowledge that they had survived. It seemed more likely—inevitable, almost—that they were nothing but frozen corpses somewhere in the trackless stretches from Mars to Saturn, new planetoids that had once been alive.

The Committee had been dickering with him for weeks before the news had come. They had insisted on his signature to the paper for the sake of appearances. It would look like an agreement, voluntarily and mutually arrived at. But Sankov knew well that, given complete obstinacy on his part, they would act unilaterally and be damned with appearances. It seemed fairly certain that Hilder's election was secure now and they would take the chance of arousing a reaction of sympathy for Mars.

So he dragged out the negotiations, dangling before them always the possibility of surrender.

And then he heard from Long and concluded the deal quickly.

The papers had lain before him and he had made a last statement for the benefit of the reporters who were present.

He said, "Total imports of water from Earth are twenty million tons a year. This is declining as we develop our own piping system. If I sign this paper agreeing to an embargo, our industry will be paralyzed, any possibilities of expansion will halt. It looks to me as if that can't be what's in Earth's mind, can it?"

Their eyes met his and held only a hard glitter. Assemblyman Digby had already been replaced and they were unanimous against him.

The Committee Chairman impatiently pointed out, "You have said all this before."

"I know, but right now I'm kind of getting ready to sign and I want it clear in my head. Is Earth set and determined to bring us to an end here?"

"Of course not. Earth is interested in conserving its irreplaceable water supply, nothing else."

"You have one and a half quintillion tons of water on Earth."

The Committee Chairman said, "We cannot spare water."

And Sankov had signed.

That had been the final note he wanted. Earth had one and a half quintillion tons of water and could spare none of it.

Now, a day and a half later, the Committee and the reporters waited in the spaceport dome. Through thick, curving windows, they could see the bare and empty grounds of Mars Spaceport.

The Committee Chairman asked with annoyance, "How much longer do we have to wait? And, if you don't mind, what are we waiting for?"

Sankov said, "Some of our boys have been out in space, out past the asteroids."

The Committee Chairman removed a pair of spectacles and cleaned them with a snowy-white handkerchief. "And they're returning?"

"They are."

The Chairman shrugged, lifted his eyebrows in the direction of the reporters.

In the smaller room adjoining, a knot of women and children clustered about another window. Sankov stepped back a bit to cast a glance toward them. He would much rather have been with them, been part of their excitement and tension. He, like them, had waited over a year now. He, like them, had thought, over and over again, that the men must be dead.

"You see that?" said Sankov, pointing.

"Hey!" cried a reporter. "It's a ship!"

A confused shouting came from the adjoining room.

It wasn't a ship so much as a bright dot obscured by a drifting white cloud. The cloud grew larger and began to have form. It was a double streak against the sky, the lower ends billowing out and upward again. As it dropped still closer, the bright dot at the upper end took on a crudely cylindrical form.

It was rough and craggy, but where the sunlight hit, brilliant highlights bounced back.

The cylinder dropped toward the ground with the ponderous slowness characteristic of space vessels. It hung suspended on those blasting jets and settled down upon the recoil of tons of matter hurling downward like a tired man dropping into his easy chair.

And as it did so, a silence fell upon all within the dome. The women and children in one room, the politicians and reporters in the other remained frozen, heads craned incredulously upward.

The cylinder's landing flanges, extending far below the two rear jets, touched ground and sank into the pebbly morass. And then the ship was motionless and the jet action ceased.

But the silence continued in the dome. It continued for a long time.

Men came clambering down the sides of the immense vessel, inching down, down the two-mile trek to the ground, with spikes on their shoes and ice axes in their hands. They were gnats against the blinding surface.

One of the reporters croaked, "What is it?"

"That," said Sankov calmly, "happens to be a chunk of matter that spent its time scooting around Saturn as part of its rings. Our boys fitted it out with travel-head and jets and ferried it home. It just turns out the fragments in Saturn's rings are made up out of ice."

He spoke into a continuing deathlike silence. "That

thing that looks like a spaceship is just a mountain of hard water. If it were standing like that on Earth, it would be melting into a puddle and maybe it would break under its own weight. Mars is colder and has less gravity, so there's no such danger.

"Of course, once we get this thing really organized, we can have water stations on the moons of Saturn and Jupiter and on the asteroids. We can scale in chunks of Saturn's rings and pick them up and send them on at the various stations. Our Scavengers are good at that sort of thing.

"We'll have all the water we need. That one chunk you see is just under a cubic mile—or about what Earth would send us in two hundred years. The boys used quite a bit of it coming back from Saturn. They made it in five weeks, they tell me, and used up about a hundred million tons. But, Lord, that didn't make any dent at all in that mountain. Are you getting all this, boys?"

He turned to the reporters. There was no doubt they were getting it.

He said, "Then get this, too. Earth is worried about its water supply. It only has one and a half quintillion tons. It can't spare us a single ton out of it. Write down that we folks on Mars are worried about Earth and don't want anything to happen to Earth people. Write down that we'll sell water to Earth. Write down that we'll let them have million-ton lots for a reasonable fee. Write down that in ten years, we figure we can sell it in cubic-mile lots. Write down that Earth can quit worrying because Mars can sell it all the water it needs and wants."

The Committee Chairman was past hearing. He was feeling the future rushing in. Dimly he could see the reporters grinning as they wrote furiously.

*Grinning.*

He could hear the grin become laughter on Earth as Mars turned the tables so neatly on the anti-Wasters. He could hear the laughter thunder from every continent when word of the fiasco spread. And he could see the abyss, deep and black as space, into which would drop forever the political hopes of John Hilder and of every opponent of space flight left on Earth—his own included, of course.

In the adjoining room, Dora Swenson screamed with joy, and Peter, grown two inches, jumped up and down, calling, "Daddy! Daddy!"

Richard Swenson had just stepped off the extremity of the flange and, face showing clearly through the clear silicone of the headpiece, marched toward the dome.

"Did you ever see a guy look so happy?" asked Ted Long. "Maybe there's something in this marriage business."

"Ah, you've just been out in space too long," Rioz said.

# THE BIG CONTEST

## by John D. MacDonald

*In 1950, when this story was first published in an obscure magazine, John D. MacDonald was just beginning the career which has since made him one of the most widely read and most successful writers in the world.*

*Now he seldom has time to write a short story, and when he does, it is published in* The Saturday Evening Post *or* Cosmopolitan. *Then, when he wrote "The Big Contest," he was serving a planned apprenticeship in the pulps: He wrote sports fiction, detective stories, and science fiction, all at a penny a word; but in all of it, even then, a major talent was clearly at work. This warm, surprising, and funny story is a favorite of mine—and now, I hope, it is about to become one of yours.*

THERE was a blueness in the sharp-edged shadow cast by the Fire House, a blueness that hinted of dusk. There had been a piece in the *Cardon Gazette* about the man over in Chamber County who claimed to have seen a flying saucer. Through the heat of the long Saturday the front of the Fire House had been the focal point for the saucer discussion. Men came and went all afternoon and the talk at times grew as hot as the sun against the pavement and store fronts across the way.

Hobe Traik had been in the same faded blue kitchen chair all afternoon, tipped back against the weathered wood, his belly resting comfortably against his beer-keg thighs, his store teeth clamped into the deep grooves of the pipestem, a mist of sweat gleaming on his bald head. He had taken no part in the discussion, a fact which was so unusual as to be remarked upon many times that Saturday. But each time Hobe merely smiled with enigmatic amusement.

Now the group was down to five, if you don't count the small boy. There are always small boys around fire houses. This one had a brown face, pale blue eyes, taffy hair, and a pair of jeans so big for him the cuffs were rolled up. The five were Hobe Traik, Stu Ganser—the only other old-timer in the group, a grizzled, indestructible man much given to belching—young Harry Darian from the bank, prissy Arthur LeBlanc trying hard, as usual, to be one of the boys, and Brad Sedwell, the cattle buyer.

Brad and Harry were hunkered down against the wall. Hobe Traik, Stu Ganser and Arthur LeBlanc were tipped back in the three kitchen chairs from the card room and bunk room over the Fire House.

Harry's argument with Brad Sedwell about the saucers being mass hypnosis had petered out, as arguments will, when dusk began to spread layers of stillness over the town.

Hobe took his pipe out of his mouth and spat toward the road. It was a very respectable effort, carrying across the sidewalk and curb out onto the pavement. He cleared his throat. "Now I've heard a lot of fool talk today about these here saucers. Might be I'm a little tired of it. Me, I've been a-waitin' on them for just about forty years. Ever since Woolmutt left town. You remember Woolmutt, Stu?"

"Can't say as I do," Stu Ganser said, applying the usual terminal belch.

"That spitter."

"Oh! *That* Woolmutt."

"You're a damned old fool, Stu Ganser. There was only the one Woolmutt in this town, ever. You're gettin' so damn old, that head of yours . . ."

"What's a spitter got to do with saucers?" Arthur LeBlanc demanded in that voice of his, just a little bit lispy.

"Now you just settle back there," Hobe said, "and listen to it the way I want to tell it. It was nineteen eleven, the year we built this here Fire House so we wouldn't have to keep the pumper over in Holly's barn. Good thing we got it built when we did. The next week that barn burned to the ground. I was a sprout then. Full of sass. Seems like every minute I wasn't courtin' them Loomis sisters, I was right here at the Fire House. Both of 'em finally said no to me. Mary Alice married Clarence French from over Dellville way. Had nine kids afore Clarence fell the hell off the silo, but that's neither here nor there.

"That was the year we had the spittin'. Crown Street wasn't paved then, of course, and in a dry spell it was just plain dust. Yalla dust. Choke you to death when somebody stirred it up. Now I don't rightly remember just who it was started it. You could say we all started it one hot day when there wasn't a breath of wind. Somebody just up and spit and in that dust you could see where they hit and just how much roll they got. So somebody else, he spits a little further. First thing you know we got us a line drawed and rules made and we're takin' turns.

"You take a town like this in the summer forty years ago, there wasn't so much for people to do. Surprisin' how spittin' contests caught on that year. I've always been a right fair spitter myself, but there was a couple boys I just couldn't beat. Fred Tunnison was one. Fred got killed in the first war. Luke Amery was the other one. Luke later went over to Youngstown and got in the banking business. Built a big house and sired four kids off that Junior Leaguer he married and then jumped the hell out of his office window in nineteen thirty.

"Well, Fred would win one contest and the next one Luke would win. The way we had it set up, each contestant got three spits. Took turns to give each man time to work up something to spit in between. Why, we had boys coming over from Lake Valley and far away as Dunstan to try against Fred and Luke. Sort of swept the county you might say.

"It must have been after the spittin' had been going on for a month that this Woolmutt fella started comin' around to watch. One of those fellas, he was, you don't even think once about. You don't see him come and you don't notice him leave. Little chunky fella with washed-out eyes, sort of a stupid look, and a big mouth. He was workin' as hired man over to old Cable Fisher's place on the east side of Perry Woods.

"Now you know how these contests go. Some of the boys Luke and Fred out-spit went back and practiced up and the first thing you know we got ourselves a big Fourth of July contest all lined up. I kind of took charge of it, me havin' no urge to do any spittin' against Luke and Fred. These boys could stand right at the near edge of that walk right there and let one go that would carry out as far as that white line down the middle of the road. Everybody that wanted to get in the contest had to put twenty-five cents in the hat for every time they tried a string of three spits. We roped off the street to keep traffic off it, and I made up some blocks of wood painted bright colors so we could get 'em out to mark the best spits.

"In those days Marty Loofer's Saloon was right around the corner on Chestnut and it being so handy to bring the buckets of beer around, we figured that nobody'd get too dry to spit, anyway. Well, the start-off time was two o'clock and I collected six dollars and a quarter in the hat. You got to remember, you young fellows, that six dollars was a good week's pay in this town in nineteen eleven. Those boys had something to spit for.

"Just as we were gettin' started, this Woolmutt fella comes up to me, shy like, and drops a quarter in the hat. I knew he'd been watching a lot, but I knew, too, how tight old Cable Fisher was with money, so I tried to talk Woolmutt out of entering. No sir, he wouldn't have a chance, I told him. He had a funny accent and he didn't talk much, but he sure was stubborn. So I kept his quarter and told him that because he was the last one to enter, he could spit last.

"With so much at stake, everybody was taking their time, believe me. Old Fred, he strutted up to the line and got himself balanced nice on the balls of his feet, his mouth working. There wasn't a breath of wind. Sure was a hot day. When he was all ready and everybody quieted down, Fred sort of hunched back and then shot his head up and out like a blacksnake hitting a horsefly. He got a good explosion and a nice arc on that first spit. It was one of the best he ever did. A big cheer went up, because Fred was a pretty popular fella around this town in those days. He swaggered back from the line trying to look meek, but you could see he was pretty proud of that effort. The next few boys did pretty well, as far as spittin's concerned, but the best of them was a good four foot eight inches back of the red block we set out to mark where Fred hit. Then Luke came up. His style was a little different, but just as good as Fred's I'd say. Luke made himself just as high on his toes as he could get, and he stuck his head up just as far as he could get it, balanced there and let fly. You should have heard the yell when he got a good inch beyond Fred's mark. Fred turned red and then white. You could see him setting his jaw for the next effort.

"One fella from out of town got within six inches of Fred, but the rest of them were almost pitiful. Woolmutt was the last one up to toe the mark. All those people standing around seemed to scare him. I was off to the side because it was part of my job to see that nobody fouled by stepping across the line. So from there I could see how Woolmutt worked himself up to it.

"First thing I see, he sticks his tongue out. Now I tell you, boys, that was the biggest tongue I ever did see on anybody. He sticks it straight out, flat like, and then he curls it up from the sides to make a sort of tube. That tube is a good four inches out beyond the end of his stubby little nose. I see him take a breath. Big chest on the little fella.

"He goes whih-THOO! And something goes bang across the street. Now afterward there were some claimed they could see that line of flight, right from the tip of his tongue over to the hole in the plate glass in the front of Winkelhauer's Merchandise Mart. Wilbur Winkelhauer is a spectator, and when he sees what happens to his front window, he lets out a scream of mortal agony. Then the yell of the crowd drowns out Wilbur. Fred and Luke, they look badly shaken. Little Woolmutt is sort of dazed by all the commotion.

"Fred and Luke, they try to get me to rule Woolmutt out of the competition. First they say he isn't spittin' at all and that he's got a friend hid somewhere with a gun. Then Woolmutt has to prove that he is spitting. He does so. Next Fred and Luke say that the little fella has some sort of a thing in his mouth like a blow gun. They make him stick out his tongue. It sure is big. Fred even reaches out slow like and pinches the end of it. He yanks his hand back quick and wipes it on his shirt and says, 'Yep, it sure is a tongue.' Then they say he didn't hit the road.

"Fred and Luke don't do so well the next turn around. A lot of the others have dropped out. Woolmutt steps up and hits the road. Where he hits there is a long line in the dust and a big cloud of dust comes up. It ricochets up and smacks the front of Winkelhauer's again, this time just under the busted window.

"On the third try, Fred and Luke are weaker than ever. The heart is gone out of them. Woolmutt takes a long time aiming. He hits that red block that marks Fred's best shot and knocks it clean over onto the walk on the other side of the road. I kept that block around for years. Soft pine. Had a half-inch dent in the side of it. Never did know where it disappeared to finally.

"Well, I'm here to tell you that the rest of that Fourth of July was one of the gol-damnedest days I ever did see. How about it, Stu?"

Stu belched softly, reminiscently. "Sure was," he sighed.

"You see," said Hobe, "the crowd sort of took Woolmutt to its heart. He was a kind of likable little guy. And we knew that in him we had the best spitter in the state, if not the world at large. I announced him the winner and he shoved the money in his pants and they carried him on their shoulders around to Loofer's. I guess the little guy wasn't used to drinking. They loaded him up, and I do mean they loaded him up. The better element went home. Along about midafternoon, Woolmutt, sort of loosened up at every joint, led what you might call a triumphant procession through town.

"You could hear him coming a block away. First all you'd hear would be the bang, bang, bang, as he hit the wooden buildings. After each bang all those fellas following him would let out a yell, Fred and Luke yelling louder than anybody. When he got closer you could hear the whole works. 'Whih-THOO BANG YELL. Whih-THOO BANG YELL.' It was something terrible. I was with him when Mrs. Thomas' cat, big yella devil named Wheedlekins, made the mistake of runnin' across the road in front of Woolmutt. Little Woolmutt really threw up the dust around that cat. Wheedlekins run up a tree, panting and yelling, and made the mistake of leaving a little bit exposed around the edge of the top limb. Woolmutt nailed Wheedlekins again and that cat dropped out of the tree and raced across town like its tail was afire.

"Judge Proctor's bay team caught it next. You might say Woolmutt sort of encouraged those horses. It's said that the Judge got them stopped just short of the county line. The good citizens who wanted no part of all this locked their doors and they didn't get in line with the windows either. Woolmutt proved himself a gentleman, though, even when he was the most carried away with it all. You gentlemen know Mrs. Iverson. Well, she was about eighteen then, and the way she dressed there were some ready and willing to say she'd come to no good end. A handsome filly always looking as though she'd bust right out of her clothes.

"When they came around the corner of Market and Crown, there was Hazel fifty feet away, bent over tying her shoe. They all pleaded, but Woolmutt refused. He said it wasn't right and proper. And . . ."

"I don't see what this has got to do with flying saucers," Brad Sedwell complained.

"You young folks are always too damn impatient," Hobe said. "You're hurrying me. Well, on that day Harry Chase's son, John, was in town, taking a vacation from the hospital down east where he was doing his interning. Smart boy, John Chase. Of course, he's no boy now. It surprised me to find him following around after Woolmutt and then I noticed that he wasn't yelling the way the others were. He just kept his eyes glued to Woolmutt as though he couldn't look away.

"When the whole mob stopped back here in front of the Fire House, John got right up next to Woolmutt, staring at him hard. The first thing we knew, he grabbed one of Woolmutt's hands and looked at it close, front and back. Woolmutt tried to pull away. Then John got his fingers on Woolmutt's pulse. He looked deep into Woolmutt's eyes and I could see him turn white. Woolmutt yanked free, plunged through the crowd, and ran out of town. Nobody ever saw him again. And John Chase wouldn't say a word about what he saw—but he didn't seem too surprised when he found out that Woolmutt had left the country for good. That's how it ties in with them saucers, Brad."

Brad snorted. "Oh, sure. Woolmutt came in a flying saucer."

"Use the brains God gave squirrels, Brad," Hobe said angrily. "It stands to reason that whoever flies around in them saucers has been watching us for a long time, maybe hundreds of years. I say they're making a study of us mortals. You ever read Charles Fort's stuff? He says right out that we're nothing but property. The more I pondered on Woolmutt and his accent and the funny way he looked, the more I began to think that Woolmutt was a spy from someplace. Someplace off this earth. They made him look like a man and they stuck him here on us to make out his reports.

"But the little bugger got lonesome. You know how it is. Here he was among strangers, maybe for most of his life, getting lonesomer every day. They didn't do a good job of making him look like a man maybe because they didn't know enough about us, forty years ago. But when he saw the spittin' he knew that it was something he could do, something he could get in on. Just like the time that drummer told Nancy Carrwell she had a good singing voice. She like to drove the whole town crazy for three years until she got over it.

"Now John Chase was a trained doctor and he could see things about Woolmutt that we wouldn't notice. Woolmutt, with his spittin', attracted too much attention and he knew it when John started examining him. So Woolmutt had to go back where he came from. Now they've had spies here long enough so that they know about the fix this world's gettin' into, and they're coming around in their saucers and keep us from killing each other off—the same way you divide up a chicken run when they start peckin' each other to death."

The street lights came on with startling suddenness, turning the blue dusk to night. Stu sighed and shuffled off into the darkness. Arthur LeBlanc stood up and laughed nervously and said, "Well, this has all been very interesting." His lisp seemed more pronounced. Hobe's closing comments had seemed to put some restraint on the group. Brad and Harry mumbled something about getting home and went off together.

Only the boy was left. "You better be gettin' on home to your Ma," Hobe suggested gently.

The boy sighed as though awakening from a dream. "Sure, mister. Sure. G'night, mister."

He went off up the street. He walked down Crown to the tracks and turned east. When he got beyond the street lights the countryside seemed brighter, as though there were a last legitimate bit of the day left.

He cut across lots toward Perry Woods. When he neared the tangle of impenetrable brush he took a small iridescent cube out of the pocket of the jeans and held it to his ear. He spoke, listened a few moments, and then spoke again, his tone firm and brisk.

He put the cube back in his pocket. A small tawny rabbit, barely visible in the dusk, stood atop a knoll sixty yards away.

The rabbit suddenly tumbled over and over, jumped up and scurried away. The small boy flattened the long tongue out again, smiled almost sadly, and rose straight up, with increasing speed, toward the navy-blue sky of night.

# ORDEAL IN SPACE

## by Robert A. Heinlein

*This story takes place on earth; nevertheless, as you will see, the title is not deceptive. A man's hardest struggles may be those he wages against himself, and the moment of truth for a spaceman may come on a narrow ledge outside a hotel room in Great New York.*

MAYBE we should never have ventured out into space. Our race has but two basic, innate fears; noise and the fear of falling. Those terrible heights—Why should any man in his right mind let himself be placed where he could fall. . . . and fall. . . . and fall—But all spacemen are crazy. Everybody knows that.

The medicos had been very kind, he supposed. "You're lucky. You want to remember that, old fellow. You're still young and your retired pay relieves you of all worry about your future. You've got both arms and legs and are in fine shape."

"Fine shape!" His voice was unintentionally contemptuous.

"No, I mean it," the chief psychiatrist had persisted gently. "The little quirk you have does you no harm at all—except that you can't go out into space again. I can't honestly call acrophobia a neurosis; fear of falling is normal and sane. You've just got it a little more strongly than most—but that is not abnormal, in view of what you have been through."

The reminder set him to shaking again. He closed his eyes and saw the stars wheeling below him again. He was falling . . . falling endlessly. The psychiatrist's voice came through to him and pulled him back. "Steady, old man! Look around you."

"Sorry."

"Not at all. Now tell me, what do you plan to do?"

"I don't know. Get a job, I suppose."

"The Company will give you a job, you know."

He shook his head. "I don't want to hang around a spaceport." Wear a little button in his shirt to show that he was once a man, be addressed by a courtesy title of captain, claim the privileges of the pilots' lounge on the basis of what he used to be, hear the shoptalk die down whenever he approached a group, wonder what they were saying behind his back—no, thank you!

"I think you're wise. Best to make a clean break, for a while at least, until you are feeling better."

"You think I'll get over it?"

The psychiatrist pursed his lips. "Possible. It's functional, you know. No trauma."

"But you don't think so?"

"I didn't say that. I honestly don't know. We still know very little about what makes a man tick."

"I see. Well, I might as well be leaving."

The psychiatrist stood up and shoved out his hand. "Holler if you want anything. And come back to see us in any case."

"Thanks."

"You're going to be all right. I know it."

But the psychiatrist shook his head as his patient walked out. The man did not walk like a spaceman; the easy, animal self-confidence was gone.

Only a small part of Great New York was roofed

over in those days; he stayed underground until he was in that section, then sought out a passageway lined with bachelor rooms. He stuck a coin in the slot of the first one which displayed a lighted "vacant" sign, chucked his jump bag inside, and left. The monitor at the intersection gave him the address of the nearest placement office. He went there, seated himself at an interview desk, stamped in his finger-prints, and started filling out forms. It gave him a curious back-to-the-beginning feeling; he had not looked for a job since precadet days.

He left filling in his name to the last and hesitated even then. He had had more than his bellyfull of publicity; he did not want to be recognized; he certainly did not want to be throbbed over—and most of all he did not want anyone telling him he was a hero. Presently he printed in the name "William Saunders" and dropped the forms in the slot.

He was well into his third cigarette and getting ready to strike another when the screen in front of him at last lighted up. He found himself staring at a nice-looking brunette. "Mr. Saunders," the image said, "will you come inside, please? Door seventeen."

The brunette in person was there to offer him a seat and a cigarette. "Make yourself comfortable, Mr. Saunders. I'm Miss Joyce. I'd like to talk with you about your application."

He settled himself and waited, without speaking.

When she saw that he did not intend to speak, she added, "Now take this name 'William Saunders' which you have given us—we know who you are, of course, from your prints."

"I suppose so."

"Of course I know what everybody knows about you, but your action in calling yourself 'William Saunders,' Mr.—"

"Saunders."

"—Mr. Saunders, caused me to query the files." She held up a microfilm spool, turned so that he might read his own name on it. "I know quite a lot about you—now—more than the public knows and more than you saw fit to put into your application. It's a good record, Mr. Saunders."

"Thank you."

"But I can't use it in placing you in a job. I can't even refer to it if you insist on designating yourself as 'Saunders.'"

"The name is Saunders." His voice was flat, rather than emphatic.

"Don't be hasty, Mr. Saunders. There are many positions in which the factor of prestige can be used quite legitimately to obtain for a client a much higher beginning rate of pay than—"

"I'm not interested."

She looked at him and decided not to insist. "As you wish. If you will go to reception room B, you can start your classification and skill tests."

"Thank you."

"*If* you should change your mind later, Mr. Saunders, we will be glad to reopen the case. Through that door, please."

Three days later found him at work for a small firm specializing in custom-built communication systems. His job was calibrating electronic equipment. It was soothing work, demanding enough to occupy his mind, yet easy for a man of his training and experience. At the end of his three months probation he was promoted out of the helper category.

He was building himself a well-insulated rut, working, sleeping, eating, spending an occasional evening at the public library or working out at the YMCA—and never, under any circumstances, going out under the open sky nor up to any height, not even a theater balcony.

He tried to keep his past life shut out of his mind, but his memory of it was still fresh; he would find himself daydreaming—the star-sharp, frozen sky of Mars, or the roaring night life of Venusburg. He would see again the swollen, ruddy bulk of Jupiter hanging over the port on Ganymede, its oblate bloated shape impossibly huge and crowding the sky.

Or he might, for a time, feel again the sweet quiet of

the long watches on the lonely reaches between the planets. But such reveries were dangerous; they cut close to the edge of his new peace of mind. It was easy to slide over and find himself clinging for life to his last handhold on the steel sides of the *Valkyrie,* fingers numb and failing, and nothing below him but the well of space.

Then he would come back to Earth, shaking uncontrollably and gripping his chair or the workbench.

The first time it had happened at work he had found one of his benchmates, Joe Tully, staring at him curiously. "What's the trouble, Bill?" he had asked. "Hangover?"

"Nothing," he had managed to say. "Just a chill."

"You better take a pill. Come on—let's go to lunch."

Tully led the way to the elevator; they crowded in. Most of the employees—even the women—preferred to go down via the drop chute, but Tully always used the elevator. "Saunders," of course, never used the drop chute; this had eased them into the habit of lunching together. He knew that the chute was safe, that even if the power should fail, safety nets would snap across at each floor level—but he could not force himself to step off the edge.

Tully said publicly that a drop-chute landing hurt his arches, but he confided privately to Saunders that he did not trust automatic machinery. Saunders nodded understandingly but said nothing. It warmed him toward Tully. He began feeling friendly and not on the defensive with another human being for the first time since the start of his new life. He began to want to tell Tully the truth about himself. If he could be sure that Joe would not insist on treating him as a hero—not that he really objected to the role of hero. As a kid, hanging around spaceports, trying to wangle chances to go inside the ships, cutting classes to watch takeoffs, he had dreamed of being a "hero" someday, a hero of the spaceways, returning in triumph from some incredible and dangerous piece of exploration. But he was troubled by the fact that he still had the same picture of what a hero should look like and how he should behave; it did not include shying away from open windows, being fearful of walking across an open square, and growing too upset to speak at the mere thought of boundless depths of space.

Tully invited him home for dinner. He wanted to go, but fended off the invitation while he inquired where Tully lived. The Shelton Homes, Tully told him, naming one of those great, boxlike warrens that used to disfigure the Jersey flats. "It's a long way to come back," Saunders said doubtfully, while turning over in his mind ways to get there without exposing himself to the things he feared.

"You won't have to come back," Tully assured him. "We've got a spare room. Come on. My old lady does her own cooking—that's why I keep her."

"Well, all right," he conceded. "Thanks, Joe." The La Guardia Tube would take him within a quarter of a mile; if he could not find a covered way he would take a ground cab and close the shades.

Tully met him in the hall and apologized in a whisper. "Meant to have a young lady for you, Bill. Instead we've got my brother-in-law. He's a louse. Sorry."

"Forget it, Joe. I'm glad to be here." He was indeed. The discovery that Bill's flat was on the thirty-fifth floor had dismayed him at first, but he was delighted to find that he had no feeling of height. The lights were on, the windows occulted, the floor under him was rock solid; he felt warm and safe. Mrs. Tully turned out in fact to be a good cook, to his surprise—he had the bachelor's usual distrust of amateur cooking. He let himself go to the pleasure of feeling at home and safe and wanted; he managed not even to hear most of the aggressive and opinionated remarks of Joe's in-law.

After dinner he relaxed in an easy chair, glass of beer in hand, and watched the video screen. It was a musical comedy; he laughed more heartily than he had in months. Presently the comedy gave way to a religious program, the National Cathedral Choir; he let it be, listening with one ear and giving some attention to the conversation with the other.

The choir was more than half way through "Prayer for Travelers" before he became fully aware of what they were singing:

*—hear us when we pray to Thee*
*For those in peril on the sea.*

*Almighty Ruler of the all*
*Whose power extends to great and small,*
*Who guides the stars with steadfast law,*
*Whose least creation fills with awe;*
*Oh, grant Thy mercy and Thy grace*
*To those who venture into space.*

He wanted to switch it off, but he had to hear it out, he could not stop listening to it, though it hurt him in his heart with the unbearable homesickness of the hopelessly exiled. Even when he was a cadet this one hymn could fill his eyes with tears; now he kept his face turned away from the others to try to hide from them the drops wetting his cheeks.

When the choir's "amen" let him do so he switched quickly to some other—any other—program and remained bent over the instrument, pretending to fiddle with it, while he composed his features. Then he turned back to the company, outwardly serene, though it seemed to him that anyone could see the hard, aching knot in his middle.

The brother-in-law was still sounding off.

"We ought to annex 'em," he was saying. "That's what we ought to do. Three-Planets Treaty—what a lot of ruddy rot! What right have they got to tell us what we can and can't do on Mars?"

"Well, Ed," Tully said mildly, "it's their planet, isn't it? They were there first."

Ed brushed it aside. "Did we ask the Indians whether or not they wanted us in North America? Nobody has any right to hang on to something he doesn't know how to use. With proper exploitation—"

"You been speculating, Ed?"

"Huh? It wouldn't be speculation if the government wasn't made up of a bunch of weak-spined old women. 'Rights of Natives,' indeed! What rights do a bunch of degenerates have?"

Saunders found himself contrasting Ed Schultz with Knath Sooth, the only Martian he himself had ever known well. Gentle Knath, who had been old before Ed was born, and yet was rated as young among his own kind. Knath . . . why, Knath could sit for hours with a friend or trusted acquaintance, saying nothing, needing to say nothing. "Growing together" they called it—his entire race had so grown together that they had needed no government, until the Earthman came.

Saunders had once asked his friend why he exerted himself so little, was satisfied with so little. More than an hour passed and Saunders was beginning to regret his inquisitiveness when Knath replied, "My fathers have labored and I am weary."

Saunders sat up and faced the brother-in-law. "They are not degenerate."

"Huh? I suppose *you* are an expert!"

"The Martians aren't degenerate, they're just tired," Saunders persisted.

Tully grinned. His brother-in-law saw it and became surly. "What gives you the right to an opinion? Have you ever been to Mars?"

Saunders realized suddenly that he had let his censors down. "Have you?" he answered cautiously.

"That's beside the point. The best minds all agree . . ." Bill let him go on and did not contradict him again. It was a relief when Tully suggested that, since they all had to be up early, maybe it was about time to think about beginning to get ready to go to bed.

He said good-night to Mrs. Tully and thanked her for a wonderful dinner, then followed Tully into the guest room. "Only way to get rid of that family curse we're saddled with, Bill," he apologized. "Stay up as long as you like." Tully stepped to the window and opened it. "You'll sleep well here. We're up high enough to get honest-to-goodness fresh air." He stuck his head out and took a couple of big breaths. "Nothing like the real article," he continued as he withdrew from the window. "I'm a country boy at heart. What's the matter, Bill?"

"Nothing. Nothing at all."

"I thought you looked a little pale. Well, sleep tight. I've already set your bed for seven; that'll give us plenty of time."

"Thanks, Joe. Good-night." As soon as Tully was out of the room he braced himself, then went over and closed the window. Sweating, he turned away and switched the ventilation back on. That done, he sank down on the edge of the bed.

He sat there for a long time, striking one cigarette after another. He knew too well that the peace of mind he thought he had regained was unreal. There was nothing left to him but shame and a long, long hurt. To have reached the point where he had to knuckle under to a tenth-rate knothead like Ed Schultz—it would have been better if he had never come out of the *Valkyrie* business.

Presently he took five grains of Fly-Rite from his pouch, swallowed them, and went to bed. He got up almost at once, forced himself to open the window a trifle, then compromised by changing the setting of the bed so that it would not turn out the lights after he got to sleep.

He had been asleep and dreaming for an indefinitely long time. He was back in space again—indeed, he had never been away from it. He was happy, with the full happiness of a man who has awakened to find it was only a bad dream.

The crying disturbed his serenity. At first it made him only vaguely uneasy, then he began to feel in some way responsible—he must do something about it. The transition to falling had only dream logic behind it, but it was real to him. He was grasping, his hands were slipping, had slipped—and there was nothing under him but the black emptiness of space—

He was awake and gasping, on Joe Tully's guest-room bed; the lights burned bright around him.

But the crying persisted.

He shook his head, then listened. It was real all right. Now he had it identified—a cat, a kitten by the sound of it.

He sat up. Even if he had not had the spaceman's traditional fondness for cats, he would have investigated. However, he liked cats for themselves, quite aside from their neat shipboard habits, their ready adaptability to changing accelerations, and their usefulness in keeping the ship free of those other creatures that go wherever man goes. So he got up at once and looked for this one.

A quick look around showed him that the kitten was not in the room, and his ear led him to the correct spot; the sound came in through the slightly opened window. He shied off, stopped, and tried to collect his thoughts.

He told himself that it was unnecessary to do anything more; if the sound came in through his window, then it must be because it came out of some nearby window. But he knew that he was lying to himself; the sound was close by. In some impossible way the cat was just outside his window, thirty-five stories above the street.

He sat down and tried to strike a cigarette, but the tube broke in his fingers. He let the fragments fall to the floor, got up, and took six nervous steps toward the window, as if he were being jerked along. He sank down to his knees, grasped the window, and threw it wide open, then clung to the windowsill, his eyes tight shut.

After a time the sill seemed to steady a bit. He opened his eyes, gasped, and shut them again. Finally he opened them again, being very careful not to look out at the stars, not to look down at the street. He had half expected to find the cat on a balcony outside his room—it seemed the only reasonable explanation. But there was no balcony, no place at all where a cat could reasonably be.

However, the mewing was louder than ever. It seemed to come from directly under him. Slowly he forced his head out, still clinging to the sill, and made himself look down. Under him, about four feet lower than the edge of the window, a narrow ledge ran around the side of the building. Seated on it was a woebegone ratty-looking kitten. It stared up at him and meowed again.

It was barely possible that by clinging to the sill with one hand and making a long arm with the other, he could reach it without actually going out the window, he thought—if he could bring himself to do it. He considered calling Tully, then thought better of it. Tully was shorter than he was, had less reach. And the kitten had to be rescued now, before the fluff-brained idiot jumped or fell.

He tried for it. He shoved his shoulders out, clung with his left arm and reached down with his right. Then he opened his eyes and saw that he was a foot or ten inches away from the kitten still. It sniffed curiously in the direction of his hand.

He stretched till his bones cracked. The kitten promptly skittered away from his clutching fingers, stopping a good six feet down the ledge. There it settled down and commenced washing its face.

He inched back inside and collapsed, sobbing, on the floor underneath the window. "I can't do it," he whispered. "I can't do it. Not again—"

The Rocket Ship *Valkyrie* was two hundred and forty-nine days out from Earth-Luna Space Terminal and approaching Mars Terminal on Deimos, outer Martian satellite. William Cole, Chief Communications Officer and relief pilot, was sleeping sweetly when his assistant shook him. "Hey! Bill! Wake up—we're in a jam."

"Huh? Wazzat?" But he was already reaching for his socks. "What's the trouble, Tom?"

Fifteen minues later he knew that his junior officer had not exaggerated; he was reporting the facts to the Old Man—the primary piloting radar was out of whack. Tom Sandburg had discovered it during a routine check, made as soon as Mars was inside the maximum range of the radar pilot. The captain had shrugged. "Fix it, Mister—and be quick about it. We need it."

Bill Cole shook his head. "There's nothing wrong with it, Captain—inside. She acts as if the antenna were gone completely."

"That's impossible. We haven't even had a meteor alarm."

"Might be anything, Captain. Might be metal fatigue and it just fell off. But we've got to replace that antenna. Stop the spin on the ship and I'll go out and fix it. I can jury-rig a replacement while she loses her spin."

The *Valkyrie* was a luxury ship, of her day. She was assembled long before anyone had any idea of how to produce an artificial gravity field. Nevertheless she had pseudo-gravity for the comfort of her passengers. She spun endlessly around her main axis, like a shell from a rifled gun; the resulting angular acceleration—miscalled centrifugal force—kept her passengers firm in their beds, or steady on their feet. The spin was started as soon as her rockets stopped blasting at the beginning of a trip and was stopped only when it was necessary to maneuver into a landing. It was accomplished, not by magic, but by reaction against the contrary spin of a flywheel located on her centerline.

The captain looked annoyed, "I've started to take the spin off, but I can't wait that long. Jury-rig the astrogational radar for piloting."

Cole started to explain why the astrogational radar could not be adapted to short-range work, then decided not to try. "It can't be done, sir. It's a technical impossibility."

"When I was your age I could jury-rig anything! Well, find me an answer, Mister. I can't take this ship down blind. Not even for the Harriman Medal."

Bill Cole hesitated for a moment before replying, "I'll have to go out while she's still got spin on her, Captain, and make the replacement. There isn't any other way to do it."

The captain looked away from him, his jaw muscles

flexed. "Get the replacement ready. Hurry up about it."

Cole found the captain already at the airlock when he arrived with the gear he needed for the repair. To his surprise the Old Man was suited up. "Explain to me what I'm to do," he ordered Bill.

"You're not going out, sir?"

The captain simply nodded.

Bill took a look at his captain's waistline, or where his waistline used to be. Why, the Old Man must be thirty-five if he were a day! "I'm afraid I can't explain too clearly. I had expected to make the repair myself."

"I've never asked a man to do a job I wouldn't do myself. Explain it to me."

"Excuse me, sir—but can you chin yourself with one hand?"

"What's that got to do with it?"

"Well, we've got forty-eight passengers, sir, and—"

"Shut up!"

Sandburg and he, both in space suits, helped the Old Man down the hole after the inner door of the lock was closed and the air exhausted. The space beyond the lock was a vast, star-flecked emptiness. With spin still on the ship, every direction outward was down, down for millions of uncounted miles. They put a safety line on him, of course—nevertheless it gave him a sinking feeling to see the captain's head disappear in the bottomless, black hole.

The line paid out steadily for several feet, then stopped. When it had been stopped for several minutes, Bill leaned over and touched his helmet against Sandburg's. "Hang on to my feet. I'm going to take a look."

He hung head down out the lock and looked around. The captain was stopped, hanging by both hands, nowhere near the antenna fixture. He scrambled back up and reversed himself. "I'm going out."

It was no great trick, he found, to hang by his hands and swing himself along to where the captain was stalled. The *Valkyrie* was a space-to-space ship, not like the sleek-sided jobs we see around earthports; she was covered with handholds for the convenience of repairmen at the terminals. Once he reached him, it was possible, by grasping the same steel rung that the captain clung to, to aid him in swinging back to the last one he had quitted. Five minutes later Sandburg was pulling the Old Man up through the hole and Bill was scrambling after him.

He began at once to unbuckle the repair gear from the captain's suit and transfer it to his own. He lowered himself back down the hole and was on his way before the older man had recovered enough to object, if he still intended to.

Swinging out to where the antenna must be replaced was not too hard, though he had all eternity under his toes. The suit impeded him a little—the gloves were clumsy—but he was used to space suits. He was a little winded from helping the captain, but he could not stop to think about that. The increased spin bothered him somewhat; the airlock was nearer the axis of spin than was the antenna—he felt heavier as he moved out.

Getting the replacement antenna shipped was another matter. It was neither large nor heavy, but he found it impossible to fasten it into place. He needed one hand to cling by, one to hold the antenna, and one to handle the wrench. That left him shy one hand, no matter how he tried it.

Finally he jerked his safety line to signal Sandburg for more slack. Then he unshackled it from his waist, working with one hand, passed the end twice through a handhold and knotted it; he left about six feet of it hanging free. The shackle on the free end he fastened to another handhold. The result was a loop, a bight, an improvised bosun's chair which would support his weight while he manhandled the antenna into place. The job went fairly quickly then.

He was almost through. There remained one bolt to fasten on the far side, away from where he swung. The antenna was already secured at two points and its circuit connection made. He decided he could manage it with one hand. He left his perch and swung over, monkey fashion.

The wrench slipped as he finished tightening the

bolt; it slipped from his grasp, fell free. He watched it go, out and out and out, down and down and down, until it was so small he could no longer see it. It made him dizzy to watch it, bright in the sunlight against the deep black of space. He had been too busy to look down, up to now.

He shivered. "Good thing I was through with it," he said. "It would be a long walk to fetch it." He started to make his way back.

He found that he could not.

He had swung past the antenna to reach his present position, using a grip on his safety-line swing to give him a few inches more reach. Now the loop of line hung quietly, just out of reach. There was no way to reverse the process.

He hung by both hands and told himself not to get panicky—he must think his way out. Around the other side? No, the steel skin of the *Valkyrie* was smooth there—no handhold for more than six feet. Even if he were not tired—and he had to admit that he was, tired and getting a little cold—even if he were fresh, it was an impossible swing for anyone not a chimpanzee.

He looked down—and regretted it.

There was nothing below him but stars, down and down, endlessly. Stars, swinging past as the ship spun with him. Emptiness of all time and blackness and cold.

He found himself trying to hoist himself bodily onto the single narrow rung he clung to, trying to reach it with his toes. It was a futile, strength-wasting excess. He quieted his panic sufficiently to stop it, then hung limp.

It was easier if he kept his eyes closed. But after a while he always had to open them and look. The Big Dipper would swing past and then, presently, Orion. He tried to compute the passing minutes in terms of the number of rotations the ship made, but his mind would not work clearly, and, after a while. he would have to shut his eyes.

His hands were becoming stiff—and cold. He tried to rest them by hanging by one hand at a time. He let go with his left hand, felt pins and needles course through it, and beat it against his side. Presently it seemed time to spell his right hand.

He could no longer reach up to the rung with his left hand. He did not have the power left in him to make the extra pull; he was fully extended and could not shorten himself enough to get his left hand up.

He could no longer feel his right hand at all.

He could see it slip. It was slipping—

The sudden release in tension let him know that he was falling . . . falling. The ship dropped away from him.

He came to with the captain bending over him. "Just keep quiet, Bill."

"Where—"

"Take it easy. The patrol from Deimos was already close by when you let go. They tracked you on the 'scope, matched orbits with you, and picked you up. First time in history, I guess. Now keep quiet. You're a sick man—you hung there more than two hours, Bill."

The meowing started up again, louder than ever. He got up on his knees and looked out over the window-sill. The kitten was still away to the left on the ledge. He thrust his head cautiously out a little farther, remembering not to look at anything but the kitten and the ledge. "Here, kitty!" he called. "Here, kit-kit-kitty! Here, kitty, come kitty!"

The kitten stopped washing and managed to look puzzled.

"Come, kitty," he repeated softly. He let go the windowsill with his right hand and gestured toward it invitingly. The kitten approached about three inches, then sat down. "Here, kitty," he pleaded and stretched his arm as far as possible.

The fluff ball promptly backed away again.

He withdrew his arm and thought about it. This was getting nowhere, he decided. If he were to slide over the edge and stand on the ledge, he could hang on with one arm and be perfectly safe. He knew that, he knew it would be safe—he needn't look down!

He drew himself back inside, reversed himself, and, with great caution, gripping the sill with both arms, let his legs slide down the face of the building. He focused his eyes carefully on the corner of the bed.

The ledge seemed to have been moved. He could not find it, and was beginning to be sure that he had reached past it, when he touched it with one toe—then he had both feet firmly planted on it. It seemed about six inches wide. He took a deep breath.

Letting go with his right arm, he turned and faced the kitten. It seemed interested in the procedure but not disposed to investigate more closely. If he were to creep along the ledge, holding on with his left hand, he could just about reach it from the corner of the window—

He moved his feet one at a time, baby fashion, rather than pass one past the other. By bending his knees a trifle, and leaning, he could just manage to reach it. The kitten sniffed his groping fingers, then leaped backward. One tiny paw missed the edge; it scrambled and regained its footing. "You little idiot!" he said indignantly. "Do you want to bash your brains out?

"If any," he added. The situation looked hopeless now; the baby cat was too far away to be reached from his anchorage at the window, no matter how he stretched. He called "Kitty, kitty" rather hopelessly, then stopped to consider the matter.

He could give it up.

He could prepare himself to wait all night in the hope that the kitten would decide to come closer. Or he could go get it.

The ledge was wide enough to take his weight. If he made himself small, flat to the wall, no weight rested on his left arm. He moved slowly forward, retaining the grip on the window as long as possible, inching so gradually that he hardly seemed to move. When the window frame was finally out of reach, when his left hand was flat to smooth wall, he made the mistake of looking down, down, past the sheer wall at the glowing pavement far below.

He pulled his eyes back and fastened them on a spot on the wall, level with his eyes and only a few feet away. He was still there!

And so was the kitten. Slowly he separated his feet, moving his right foot forward, and bent his knees. He stretched his right hand along the wall, until it was over and a little beyond the kitten.

He brought it down in a sudden swipe, as if to swat a fly. He found himself with a handful of scratching, biting fur.

He held perfectly still then, and made no attempt to check the minor outrages the kitten was giving him. Arms still outstretched, body flat to the wall, he started his return. He could not see where he was going and could not turn his head without losing some little of his margin of balance. It seemed a long way back, longer than he had come, when at last the fingertips of his left hand slipped into the window opening.

He backed up the rest of the way in a matter of seconds, slid both arms over the sill, then got his right knee over. He rested himself on the sill and took a deep breath. "Man!" he said aloud. "That was a tight squeeze. You're a menace to traffic, little cat."

He glanced down at the pavement. It was certainly a long way down—looked hard, too.

He looked up at the stars. Mighty nice they looked and mighty bright. He braced himself in the window frame, back against one side, foot pushed against the other, and looked at them. The kitten settled down in the cradle of his stomach and began to buzz. He stroked it absent-mindedly and reached for a cigarette. He would go out to the port and take his physical and his psycho tomorrow, he decided. He scratched the kitten's ears. "Little fluff head," he said, "how would you like to take a long, long ride with me?"

# THAT SHARE OF GLORY

## by C. M. Kornbluth

*Now we move on a little—past the first tentative explorations of our own family of planets, into the universe beyond. The conquest of the stars will bring our descendants new problems, new dangers. And the virtues demanded of these men may not be the ones you would expect.*

YOUNG Alen, one of a thousand in the huge refectory, ate absent-mindedly as the reader droned into the perfect silence of the hall. Today's lesson happened to be a word list of the Thetis VIII planet's seagoing folk.

"*Tlon*—a ship," droned the reader.

"*Rtlo*—some ships, number unknown.

"*Long*—some ships, number known, always modified by cardinal.

"*Ongr*—a ship in a collection of ships, always modified by ordinal.

"*Ngrt*—first ship in a collection of ships; an exception to *ongr*."

A lay brother tiptoed to Alen's side. "The Rector summons you," he whispered.

Alen had no time for panic, though that was the usual reaction to a summons from the Rector to a novice. He slipped from the refectory, stepped onto the northbound corridor and stepped off at his cell, a minute later and a quarter mile farther on. Hastily, but meticulously, he changed from his drab habit to the heraldic robes in the cubicle with its simple stool, washstand, desk, and paperweight or two. Alen, a levelheaded young fellow, was not aware that he had broken any section of the Order's complicated Rule, but he was aware that he could have done so without knowing it. It might, he thought, be the last time he would see the cell.

He cast a glance which he hoped would not be the final one over it; a glance which lingered a little fondly on the reel rack where were stowed: *Nicholson on Martian Verbs, The New Oxford Venusian Dictionary,* the ponderous six-reeler *Deutsche-Ganymedische Konversasionslexikon* published long ago and far away in Leipzig. The later works were there, too: *The Tongues of the Galaxy—an Essay in Classification, A Concise Grammar of Cephean, The Self-Pronouncing Vegan II Dictionary*—scores of them, and, of course, the worn reel of old Machiavelli's *The Prince.*

Enough of that! Alen combed out his small, neat beard and stepped onto the southbound corridor. He transferred to an eastbound at the next intersection and minutes later was before the Rector's lay secretary.

"You better review your Lyran irregulars," said the secretary disrespectfully. "There's a trader in there who's looking for a cheap herald on a swindling trip to Lyra VI." Thus unceremoniously did Alen learn that he was not to be ejected from the Order but that he was to be elevated to Journeyman. But as a herald should, he betrayed no sign of his immense relief. He did, however, take the secretary's advice and sensibly reviewed his Lyran.

While he was in the midst of a declension which applied only to inanimate objects, the voice of the Rector —and what a mellow voice it was!—floated through the secretary's intercom.

"Admit the novice, Alen," said the Master Herald.

A final settling of his robes and the youth walked into the Rector's huge office, with the seal of the Order blazing in diamonds above his desk. There was a stranger present; presumably the trader—a black-bearded fellow whose rugged frame didn't carry his Vegan cloak with ease.

Said the Rector: "Novice, this is to be the crown of your toil if you are acceptable to—?" He courteously turned to the trader, who shrugged irritably.

"It's all one to me," growled the blackbeard. "Somebody cheap, somebody who knows the cant of the thievish Lyran gem peddlers, above all, somebody *at once*. Overhead is devouring my flesh day by day as the ship waits at the field. And when we are space-borne, my imbecile crew will doubtless waste liter after priceless liter of my fuel. And when we land the swindling Lyrans will without doubt make my ruin complete by tricking me even out of the minute profit I hope to realize. Good Master Herald, let me have the infant cheap and I'll bid you good day."

The Rector's shaggy eyebrows drew down in a frown. "Trader," he said sonorously, "our mission of galactic utilitarian culture is not concerned with your margin of profit. I ask you to test this youth and, if you find him able, to take him as your Herald on your voyage. He will serve you well, for he has been taught that commerce and words, its medium, are the unifying bonds which will one day unite the cosmos into a single humankind. Do not conceive that the College and Order of Heralds is a mere aid to you in your commercial adventure."

"Very well," growled the trader. He addressed Alen in broken Lyran: "Boy, how you make up Vegan stones of three fires so Lyran women like, come buy, buy again?"

Alen smoothly replied: "The Vegan triple-fire gem finds most favor on Lyra and especially among its women when set in a wide glass anklet if large, and when arranged in the Lyran 'lucky five' pattern in a glass thumb ring if small." He was glad, very glad, he had come across—and as a matter of course memorized, in the relentless fashion of the Order—a novel which touched briefly on the Lyran jewel trade.

The trader glowered and switched to Cephean—apparently his native tongue. "That was well-enough said, Herald. Now tell me whether you've got guts to man a squirt in case we're intercepted by the thieving so-called Customs collectors of Eyolf's Realm between here and Lyra?"

Alen knew the Rector's eyes were on him. "The noble mission of our Order," he said, "forbids me to use any weapon but the truth in furthering cosmic utilitarian civilization. No, master trader, I shall not man one of your weapons."

The trader shrugged. "So I must take what I get. Good Master Herald, make me a price."

The Rector said casually: "I regard this chiefly as a training mission for our novice; the fee will be nominal. Let us say twenty-five per cent of your net as of blastoff from Lyra, to be audited by Journeyman-Herald Alen."

The trader's howl of rage echoed in the dome of the huge room. "It's not fair!" he roared. "Who but you thievish villains with your Order and your catch-'em-young and your years of training can learn the tongues of the galaxy? What chance has a decent merchant busy with profit and loss got to learn the cant of every race between Sirius and the Coalsack? It's not fair! It's not fair and I'll say so until my dying breath!"

"Die outside if you find our terms unacceptable," said the Rector. "The Order does not haggle."

"Well I know it," sighed the trader brokenly. "I should have stuck to my own system and my good father's pump-flange factory. But no! I had to pick up a bargain in gems on Vega! Enough of this—bring me your contract and I'll sign it."

The Rector's shaggy eyebrows went up. "There is no contract," he said. "A mutual trust between Herald and trader is the cornerstone upon which cosmos-wide amity and understanding will be built."

"At twenty-five per cent for an unlicked pup," muttered blackbeard to himself in Cephean.

None of his instructors had played Polonius as Alen, with the seal of the Journeyman-Herald on his brow, packed for blastoff and vacated his cell. He supposed they knew that twenty years of training either had done their work or had not.

The trader taking Alen to the field where his ship waited was less wise. "The secret of successful negotiation," he weightily told his Herald, "is to yield willingly. This may strike you as a paradox, but it is the veritable key to my success in maintaining the profits of my good father's pump-flange trade. The secret is to yield with rueful admiration of your opponent—but *only in unimportant details*. Put up a little battle about delivery date or about terms of credit and then let him have his way. But you never give way a hair's breadth on your asking price unless—"

Alen let him drivel on as they drove through the outer works of the College. He was glad the car was open. For the first time he was being accorded the doffed hat that is the due of Heralds from their inferiors in the Order, and the grave nod of salutation from equals. Five-year-old postulants seeing his brow seal tugged off their headgear with comical celerity; fellow novices, equals a few hours before, uncovered as though he were the Rector himself.

The ceremonial began to reach the trader. When, with a final salutation, a lay warder let them through the great gate of the curtain wall, he said with some irritation, "They appear to hold you in high regard, boy."

"I am better addressed as Herald," said Alen composedly.

"A plague descend on the College and Order! Do you think I don't know my manners? Of course, I call a Herald 'Herald,' but we're going to be cooped up together and you'll be working for me. What'll happen to ship's discipline if I have to kowtow to you?"

"There will be no problem," said Alen.

Blackbeard grunted and trod fiercely on the accelerator.

"That's my ship," he said at length. "*Starsong*.

Vegan registry—it may help passing through Eyolf's Realm, though it cost me overmuch in bribes. A crew of eight, lazy, good-for-nothing wastrels—Agh! Can I believe my eyes?" The car jammed to a halt before the looming ship, and blackbeard was up the ladder and through the port in a second. Settling his robes, Alen followed.

He found the trader fiercely denouncing his chief engineer for using space drive to heat the ship; he had seen the faint haze of a minimum exhaust from the stern tubes.

"For that, dolt," screamed blackbeard, "we have a thing known as electricity. Have you by chance ever heard of it? Are you aware that a chief engineer's responsibility is the efficient and *economical* operation of his ship's drive mechanism?"

The chief, a cowed-looking Cephean, saw Alen with relief and swept off his battered cap. The Herald nodded gravely and the trader broke off in irritation. "We need none of that bowing and scraping for the rest of the voyage," he declared.

"Of course not, sir," said the chief. "O'course not. I was just welcoming the Herald aboard. Welcome aboard, Herald. I'm Chief Elwon, Herald. And I'm glad to have a Herald with us." A covert glance at the trader. *"I've* voyaged with Heralds and without, and I don't mind saying I feel safer indeed with you aboard."

"May I be taken to my quarters?" asked Alen.

"Your—" began the trader, stupefied.

The chief broke in, "I'll fix you a cabin, Herald. We've got some bulkheads I can rig aft for a snug little space, not roomy, but the best a little ship like this can afford."

The trader collapsed into a bucket seat as the chief bustled aft and Alen followed.

"Herald," the chief said with some embarrassment after he had collared two crewmen and set them to work, "you'll have to excuse our good master trader. He's new to the interstar lanes and he doesn't exactly know the jets yet. Between us we'll get him squared away."

Alen inspected the cubicle run up for him—a satisfactory enclosure affording him the decent privacy he rated. He dismissed the chief and the crewmen with a nod and settled himself on the cot.

Beneath the iron composure in which he had been trained, he felt scared and alone. Not even old Machiavelli seemed to offer comfort or council: "There is nothing more difficult to take in hand, more perilous to conduct, or more uncertain in its success, than to take the lead in the introduction of a new order of things," said Chapter Six.

But what said Chapter Twenty-Six? "Where the willingness is great, the difficulties cannot be great."

*Starsong* was not a happy ship. Blackbeard's nagging stinginess hung over the crew like a thundercloud, but Alen professed not to notice. He walked regularly fore and aft for two hours a day greeting the crew members in their various native tongues and then wrapping himself in the reserve the Order demanded—though he longed to salute them man-to-man, eat with them, gossip about their native planets, the past misdeeds that had brought them to their berths aboard the miserly *Starsong,* their hopes for the future. The Rule of the College and Order of Heralds decreed otherwise. He accepted the uncoverings of the crew with a nod and tried to be pleased because they stood in growing awe of him that ranged from Chief Elwon's lively appreciation of a Herald's skill to Wiper Jukkl's superstitious reverence. Jukkl was a low-browed specimen from a planet of the decadent Sirius system. He outdid the normal slovenliness of an all-male crew on a freighter—a slovenliness in which Alen could not share. Many of his waking hours were spent in his locked cubicle burnishing his metal and cleaning and pressing his robes. A Herald was never supposed to suggest by his appearance that he shared mortal frailties.

Blackbeard himself yielded a little, to the point of touching his cap sullenly. This probably was not so much awe at Alen's studied manner as respect for the incisive, lightning-fast job of auditing the Herald did on the books of the trading venture—absurdly complicated books with scores of accounts to record a simple matter of buying gems cheap on Vega and chartering a ship in the hope of selling them dearly on Lyra. The complicated books and overlapping accounts did tell the story, but they made it very easy for an auditor to erroneously read a number of costs as far higher than they actually were. Alen did not fall into the trap.

On the fifth day after blastoff, Chief Elwon rapped, respectfully but urgently, on the door of Alen's cubicle.

"If you please, Herald," he urged, "could you come to the bridge?"

Alen's heart bounded in his chest, but he gravely said, "My meditation must not be interrupted. I shall join you on the bridge in ten minutes." And for ten minutes he methodically polished a murky link in the massive gold chain that fastened his boat-cloak—the "meditation." He donned the cloak before stepping out; the summons sounded like a full-dress affair in the offing.

The trader was stamping and fuming. Chief Elwon was riffling through his spec book unhappily. Astrogator Hufner was at the plot computer running up trajectories and knocking them down again. A quick glance showed Alen that they were all high-speed trajectories in the evasive-action class.

"Herald," said the trader grimly, "we have broken somebody's detector bubble." He jerked his thumb at a red-lit signal. "I expect we'll be overhauled shortly. Are you ready to earn your twenty-five per cent of the net?"

Alen overlooked the crudity. "Are you rigged for color video, merchant?" he asked.

"We are."

"Then I am ready to do what I can for my client."

He took the communicator's seat, stealing a glance in the still-blank screen. The reflection of his face was reassuring, though he wished he had thought to comb his small beard.

Another light flashed on, and Hufner quit the operator to study the detector board. "Big, powerful, and getting closer," he said tersely. "Scanning for us with directionals now. Putting out plenty of energy—"

The loudspeaker of the ship-to-ship audio came to life.

"What ship are you?" it demanded in Vegan. "We are a Customs cruiser of the Realm of Eyolf. What ship are you?"

"Have the crew man the squirts," said the trader softly to the chief.

Elwon looked at Alen, who shook his head. "Sorry, sir," said the engineer apologetically. "The Herald—"

"We are the freighter *Starsong,* Vegan registry," said Alen into the audio mike as the trader choked. "We are carrying Vegan gems to Lyra."

"They're on us," said the astrogator despairingly, reading his instruments. The ship-to-ship video flashed on, showing an arrogant, square-jawed face topped by a battered naval cap.

"Lyra indeed? We have plans of our own for Lyra. You will heave to—" began the officer in the screen, before he noted Alen. "My pardon, Herald," he said sardonically. "Herald, will you please request the ship's master to heave to for boarding and search? We wish to assess and collect Customs duties. You are aware, of course, that your vessel is passing through the Realm."

The man's accented Vegan reeked of Algol IV. Alen switched to that obscure language to say, "We were not aware of that. Are you aware that there is a reciprocal trade treaty in effect between the Vegan system and the Realm which specifies that freight in Vegan bottoms is dutiable only when consigned to ports in the Realm?"

"You speak Algolian, do you? You Heralds have not been underrated, but don't plan to lie your way out of this. Yes, I am aware of some such agreement as you mentioned. We shall board you, as I said, and assess and collect duty in kind. If, regrettably, there has been any mistake, you are of course free to apply to the Realm for reimbursement. Now, heave to!"

"I have no intentions of lying. I speak the solemn truth when I say that we shall fight to the last man any attempt of yours to board and loot us."

Alen's mind was racing furiously through the catalog of planetary folkways the Rule had decreed that he master. Algol IV—some ancestor worship; veneration of mother; hand-to-hand combat with knives; complimentary greeting, "May you never strike down a weaker foe"; folk-hero Gaarek unjustly accused of slaying a cripple and exiled but it was an enemy's plot—

A disconcerted shadow was crossing the face of the officer as Alen improvised: "You will, of course, kill us all. But before this happens I shall have messaged back to the College and Order of Heralds the facts in the case, with a particular request that your family be informed. Your name, I think, will be remembered as long as Gaarek's—though not in the same way, of course; the Algolian whose hundred-man battle cruiser wiped out a virtually unarmed freighter with a crew of eight."

The officer's face was dark with rage. "You devil!" he snarled. "Leave my family out of this! I'll come aboard and fight you man-to-man if you have the stomach for it!"

Alen shook his head regretfully. "The Rule of my Order forbids recourse to violence," he said. "Our only permissible weapon is the truth."

"We're coming aboard," said the officer grimly. "I'll order my men not to harm your people. We'll just be collecting customs. If your people shoot first, my men will be under orders to do nothing more than disable them."

Alen smiled and uttered a sentence or two in Algolian.

The officer's jaw dropped and he croaked, after a pause, "I'll cut you to ribbons. You can't say that about my mother, you—" and he spewed back some of the words Alen had spoken.

"Calm yourself," said the Herald gravely. "I apologize for my disgusting and unheraldic remarks. But I wished to prove a point. You would have killed me if you could; I touched off a reaction which had been planted in you by your culture. I will be able to do the same with the men of yours who come aboard. For every race of man there is the intolerable insult that must be avenged in blood.

"Send your men aboard under orders not to kill if you wish; I shall goad them into a killing rage. We shall be massacred, yours will be the blame and you will be disgraced and disowned by your entire planet." Alen hoped desperately that the naval crews of the Realm were, as reputed, a barbarous and undisciplined lot—

Evidently they were, and the proud Algolian dared not risk it. In his native language he spat again, "You devil!" and switched back into Vegan. "Freighter *Starsong,*" he said bleakly, "I find that my space fix was in error and that you are not in Realm territory. You may proceed."

The astrogator said from the detector board, incredulously, "He's disengaging. He's off us. He's accelerating. Herald, *what* did you say to him?"

But the reaction from blackbeard was more gratifying. Speechless, the trader took off his cap. Alen acknowledged the salute with a grave nod before he started back to his cubicle. It was just as well, he reflected, that the trader didn't know his life and his ship had been unconditionally pledged in a finish fight against a hundred-man battle cruiser.

Lyra's principal spaceport was pocked and broken, but they made a fair-enough landing. Alen, in full heraldic robes, descended from *Starsong* to greet a handful of port officials.

"Any metals aboard?" demanded one of them.

"None for sale," said the Herald. "We have Vegan gems, chiefly triple-fire." He knew that the dull little planet was short of metals and, having made a virtue of necessity, was somehow prejudiced against their import.

"Have your crew transfer the cargo to the Customs

shed," said the port official studying *Starsong*'s papers. "And all of you wait there."

All of them—except Alen—lugged numbered sacks and boxes of gems to the low brick building designated. The trader was allowed to pocket a handful for samples before the shed was sealed—a complicated business. A brick was mortared over the simple ironwood latch that closed the ironwood door, a pat of clay was slapped over the brick, and the port seal stamped in it. A mechanic with what looked like a pottery blowtorch fed by powdered coal played a flame on the clay seal until it glowed orange-red and that was that.

"Herald," said the port official, "tell the merchant to sign here and make his fingerprints."

Alen studied the document; it was a simple identification form. Blackbeard signed with the reed pen provided and fingerprinted the document. After two weeks in space he scarcely needed to ink his fingers first.

"Now tell him that we'll release the gems on his written fingerprinted order to whatever Lyran citizens he sells to. And explain that this roundabout system is necessary to avoid metal smuggling. Please remove *all* metal from your clothes and stow it on your ship. Then we will seal that, too, and put it under guard until you are ready to take off. We regret that we will have to search you before we turn you loose, but we can't afford to have our economy disrupted by irresponsible introduction of metals." Alen had not realized it was that bad.

After the thorough search that extended to the confiscation of forgotten watches and pins, the port officials changed a sheaf of the trader's uranium-backed Vegan currency into Lyran legal tender based on man-hours. Blackbeard made a partial payment to the crew, told them to have a good liberty and check in at the port at sunset the next day for probable takeoff.

Alen and the trader were driven to town in an unlikely vehicle whose power plant was a pottery turbine.

The driver, when they were safely out on the open road, furtively asked whether they had any metal they wanted to discard.

. The trader asked sharply in his broken Lyran: "What you do you get metal? Where sell, how use?"

The driver, following a universal tendency, raised his voice and lapsed into broken Lyran himself to tell the strangers: "Black market science men pay much, much for little bit metal. Study, use build. Politicians make law no metal, what I care politicians? But you no tell, gentlemen?"

"We won't tell," said Alen. "But we have no metal for you."

The driver shrugged.

"Herald," said the trader, "what do you make of it?"

"I didn't know it was a political issue. We concern ourselves with the basic patterns of a people's behavior, not the day-to-day expressions of the patterns. The planet's got no heavy metals, which means there were no metals available to the primitive Lyrans. The lighter metals don't occur in native form or in easily split compounds. They proceeded along the ceramic line instead of the metallic line and appear to have done quite well for themselves up to a point. No electricity, of course, no aviation and no space flight."

"And," said the trader, "naturally the people who make these buggies and that blowtorch we saw are scared witless that metals will be imported and put them out of business. So naturally they have laws passed prohibiting it."

"Naturally," said the Herald, looking sharply at the trader. But blackbeard was back in character a moment later. "An outrage," he growled. "Trying to tell a man what he can and can't import when he sees a decent chance to make a bit of profit."

The driver dropped them at a boardinghouse. It was half-timbered construction, which appeared to be swankier than the more common brick. The floors were plate glass, roughened for traction. Alen got them a double room with a view.

"What's that thing?" demanded the trader, inspecting the view.

The thing was a structure looming above the slate and tile roofs of the town—a round brick tower for its first twenty-five meters and then wood for another fifteen. As they studied it, it pricked up a pair of ears at the top and began to flop them wildly.

"Semaphore," said Alen.

A minute later blackbeard piteously demanded from the bathroom, "*How* do you make water come out of the tap? I touched it all over but nothing happened."

"You have to turn it," said Alen, demonstrating. "And that thing—you pull it sharply down, hold it, and then release."

"Barbarous," muttered the trader. "Barbarous."

An elderly maid came in to show them how to string their hammocks and ask if they happened to have a bit of metal to give her for a souvenir. They sent her away and, rather than face the public dining room, made a meal from their own stores and turned in for the night.

It's going well, thought Alen drowsily; going very well indeed.

He awoke abruptly, but made no move. It was dark in the double room, and there were stealthy, furtive little noises nearby. A hundred thoughts flashed through his head of Lyran treachery and double-dealing. He lifted his eyelids a trifle and saw a figure silhouetted against the faint light of the big window. If a burglar, he was a clumsy one.

There was a stirring from the other hammock, the trader's. With a subdued roar that sounded like "Thieving villains!" blackbeard launched himself from the hammock at the intruder. But his feet tangled in the hammock cords and he belly-flopped on the floor.

The burglar, if it was one, didn't dash smoothly and efficiently for the door. He straightened himself against the window and said resignedly, "You need not fear. I will make no resistance."

Alen rolled from the hammock and helped the

trader to his feet. "He said he doesn't want to fight," he told the trader.

Blackbeard seized the intruder and shook him like a rat. "So the rogue is a coward too!" he boomed. "Give us a light, Herald."

Alen uncovered the slow-match, blew it to a flame, squeakily pumped up a pressure torch until a jet of pulverized coal sprayed from its nozzle and ignited it. A dozen strokes more and there was enough heat feeding back from the jet to maintain the pressure cycle.

Through all of this the trader was demanding in his broken Lyran, "What make here, thief? What reason thief us room?"

The Herald brought the hissing pressure lamp to the window. The intruder's face was not the unhealthy, neurotic face of a criminal. Its thin lines told of discipline and thought.

"What did you want here?" asked Alen.

"Metal," said the intruder simply. "I thought you might have a bit of iron."

It was the first time a specific metal had been named by any Lyran. He used, of course, the Vegan word for iron.

"You are particular," remarked the Herald. "Why iron?"

"I have heard that it possesses certain properties—perhaps you can tell me before you turn me over to the police. Is it true, as we hear, that a mass of iron whose crystals have been aligned by a sharp blow will strongly attract another piece of iron with a force related to the distance between them?"

"It is true," said the Herald, studying the man's face. It was lit with excitement. Deliberately Alen added, "This alignment is more easily and uniformly ejected by placing the mass of iron in an electric field—that is, a space surrounding the passage of an electron stream through a conductor." Many of the words he used had to be Vegan; there were no Lyran words for "electric," "electron," or "conductor."

The intruder's face fell. "I have tried to master the concept you refer to," he admitted. "But it is beyond me. I have questioned other interstar voyagers and they have touched on it, but I cannot grasp it— But thank you, sir; you have been very courteous. I will trouble you no further while you summon the watch."

"You give up too easily," said Alen. "For a scientist, much too easily. If we turn you over to the watch, there will be hearings and testimony and whatnot. Our time is limited here on your planet; I doubt that we can spare any for your legal processes."

The trader let go of the intruder's shoulder and grumbled, "Why you no ask we have iron, I tell you no. Search, search, take all metal away. We no police you. I sorry hurted you arms. Here for you." Blackbeard brought out a palmful of his sample gems and picked out a large triple-fire stone. "You not be angry me," he said, putting it in the Lyran's hand.

"I can't—" said the scientist.

Blackbeard closed his fingers over the stone and growled, "I give, you take. Maybe buy iron with, eh?"

"That's so," said the Lyran. "Thank you both, gentlemen. Thank you—"

"You go," said the trader. "You go, we sleep again."

The scientist bowed with dignity and left their room.

"Gods of space," swore the trader. "To think that Jukkl, the *Starsong*'s wiper, knows more about electricity and magnetism than a brainy fellow like that."

"And they are the key to physics," mused Alen. "A scientist here is dead-ended forever, because their materials are all insulators! Glass, clay, glaze, wood."

"Funny, all right," yawned blackbeard. "Did you see me collar him once I got on my feet? Sharp, eh? Good night, Herald." He gruntingly hauled himself into the hammock again, leaving Alen to turn off the hissing light and cover the slow-match with its perforated lid.

They had roast fowl of some sort or other for breakfast in the public dining room. Alen was required by his Rule to refuse the red wine that went with it. The trader gulped it approvingly. "A sensible, though backward people," he said. "And now if you'll inquire of the management where the thievish jewel buyers congregate, we can get on with our business and perhaps be off by dawn tomorrow."

"So quickly?" asked Alen, almost forgetting himself enough to show surprise.

"My charter on *Starsong,* good Herald—thirty days to go, but what might not go wrong in space? And then there would be penalties to mulct me of whatever minute profit I may realize."

Alen learned that Gromeg's Tavern was the gem mart and they took another of the turbine-engined cabs through the brick-paved streets.

Gromeg's was a dismal, small-windowed brick barn with heavyset men lounging about, an open kitchen at one end and tables at the other. A score of smaller, sharp-faced men were at the tables, sipping wine and chatting.

"I am Journeyman-Herald Alen," announced Alen clearly, "with Vegan gems to dispose of."

There was a silence of elaborate unconcern, and then one of the dealers spat and grunted, "Vegan gems. A drug on the market. Take them away, Herald."

"Come, master trader," said Alen in the Lyran tongue. "The gem dealers of Lyra do not want your wares." He started for the door.

One of the dealers called languidly, "Well, wait a moment. I have nothing better to do; since you've come all this way, I'll have a look at your stuff."

"You honor us," said Alen. He and blackbeard sat at the man's table. The trader took out a palmful of samples, counted them meaningfully, and laid them on the boards.

"Well," said the gem dealer, "I don't know whether to be amused or insulted. I am Garthkint, the gem dealer—not a retailer of *beads*. However, I have no hard feelings. A drink for your frowning friend, Herald? I know you gentry don't indulge." The drink was already on the table, brought by one of the hulking guards.

Alen passed Garthkint's own mug of wine to the trader, explaining politely: "In my master trader's native Cepheus it is considered honorable for the guest to sip the drink his host laid down and none other. A charming custom, is it not?"

"Charming, though unsanitary," muttered the gem dealer—and he did not touch the drink he had ordered for blackbeard.

"I can't understand a word either of you is saying —too flowery. Was this little rat trying to drug me?" demanded the trader in Cephean.

"No," said Alen. "Just trying to get you drunk." To Garthkint in Lyran, he explained, "The good trader was saying that he wishes to leave at once. I was agreeing with him."

"Well," said Garthkint, "perhaps I can take a couple of your gauds. For some youngster who wishes a cheap ring."

"He's getting to it," Alen told the trader.

"High time," grunted blackbeard.

"The trader asks me to inform you," said Alen, switching back to Lyran, "that he is unable to sell in lots smaller than five hundred gems."

"A compact language, Cephean," said Garthkint, narrowing his eyes.

"Is it not?" Alen blandly agreed.

The gem dealer's forefinger rolled an especially fine three-fire stone from the little pool of gems on the table. "I suppose," he said grudgingly, "that this is what I must call the best of the lot. What, I am curious to know, is the price you would set for five hundred equal in quality and size to this poor thing?"

"This," said Alen, "is the good trader's first venture to your delightful planet. He wishes to be remembered and welcomed all of the many times he anticipates returning. Because of this he has set an absurdly low price, counting good will as more important than a prosperous voyage. Two thousand Lyran credits."

"Absurd," snorted Garthkint. "I cannot do business with you. Either you are insanely rapacious or you have been pitifully misguided as to the value of your wares. I am well known for my charity; I will assume that the latter is the case. I trust you will not be too downcast when I tell you that five hundred of these muddy, undersized out-of-round objects are worth no more than two hundred credits."

"If you are serious," said Alen with marked amazement, "we would not dream of imposing on you. At the figure you mention, we might as well not sell at all but return with our wares to Cepheus and give these gems to children in the streets for marbles. Good gem trader, excuse us for taking up so much of your time and many thanks for your warm hospitality in the matter of the wine." He switched to Cephean and said: "We're dickering now. Two thousand and two hundred. Get up; we're going to start to walk out."

"What if he lets us go?" grumbled blackbeard, but he did heave himself to his feet and turn to the door as Alen rose.

"My trader echoes my regrets," the Herald said in Lyran. "Farewell."

"Well, stay a moment," said Garthkint. "I am well known for my soft heart toward strangers. A charitable man might go as high as five hundred and absorb the inevitable loss. If you should return some day with a passable lot of *real* gems, it would be worth my while for you to remember who treated you with such benevolence and give me fair choice."

"Noble Lyran," said Alen, apparently almost overcome. "I shall not easily forget your combination of acumen and charity. It is a lesson to traders. It is a lesson to me. I shall *not* insist on two thousand. I shall cut the throat of my trader's venture by reducing his price to eighteen hundred credits, though I wonder how I shall dare tell him of it."

"What's going on now?" demanded blackbeard.

"Five hundred and eighteen hundred," said Alen. "We can sit down again."

"Up, down—up, down," muttered the trader.

They sat, and Alen said in Lyran: "My trader unexpectedly endorses the reduction. He says, 'Better to lose some than all'—an old proverb in the Cephean tongue. And he forbids any further reduction."

"Come, now," wheedled the gem dealer. "Let us be men of the world about this. One must give a little and take a little. Everybody knows he can't have his own way forever. I shall offer a good, round eight hundred credits and we'll close on it, eh? Pilquis, fetch us a pen and ink!" One of the burly guards was right there with an inkpot and a reed pen. Garthkint had a Customs form out of his tunic and was busily filling it in to specify the size, number, and fire of gems to be released to him.

"What's it now?" asked blackbeard.

"Eight hundred."

"Take it!"

"Garthkint," said Alen regretfully, "you heard the firmness and decision in my trader's voice? What can I do? I am only speaking for him. He is a hard man but perhaps I can talk him around later. I offer you the gems at a ruinous fifteen hundred credits."

"Split the difference," said Garthkint resignedly.

"Done at eleven-fifty," said Alen.

That blackbeard understood. "Well done!" he boomed at Alen and took a swig at Garthkint's wine cup. "Have him fill in 'Sack eighteen' on his paper. It's five hundred of that grade."

The gem dealer counted out twenty-three fifty-credit notes and blackbeard signed and fingerprinted the release.

"Now," said Garthkint, "you will please remain here while I take a trip to the spaceport for my property." Three or four of the guards were suddenly quite close.

"You will find," said Alen dryly, "that our standard of commercial morality is no lower than yours."

The dealer smiled politely and left.

"Who will be the next?" asked Alen of the room at large.

"I'll look at your gems," said another dealer, sitting at the table.

With the ice breaking down, the transactions went

quicker. Alen had disposed of a dozen lots by the time their first buyer returned.

"It's all right," he said. "We've been tricked before, but your gems are as represented. I congratulate you, Herald, on driving a hard, fair bargain."

"That means," said Alen regretfully, "that I should have asked for more." The guards were once more lounging in corners and no longer seemed so menacing.

They had a midday meal and continued to dispose of their wares. At sunset Alen held a final auction to clean up the odd lots that remained over and was urged to stay to dinner.

The trader, counting a huge wad of the Lyran manpower-based notes, shook his head. "We should be off before dawn, Herald," he told Alen. "Time is money, time is money."

"They are very insistent."

"And I am very stubborn. Thank them and let us be on our way before anything else is done to increase my overhead."

Something did turn up—a city watchman with a bloody nose and split lip.

He demanded of the Herald, "Are you responsible for the Cephean maniac known as Elwon?"

Garthkint glided up to mutter in Alen's ear, "Beware how you answer!"

Alen needed no warning. His grounding included Lyran legal concepts—and on the backward little planet touched with many relics of feudalism, "responsible" covered much territory.

"What has Chief Elwon done?" he parried.

"As you see," the watchman glumly replied, pointing to his wounds. "And the same to three others before we got him out of the wrecked wine shop and into the castle. Are you responsible for him?"

"Let me speak with my trader for a moment. Will you have some wine meantime?" He signaled and one of the guards brought a mug.

"Don't mind if I do. I can use it," sighed the watchman.

"We are in trouble," said Alen to blackbeard. "Chief Elwon is in the castle—prison—for drunk and disorderly conduct. You as his master are considered responsible for his conduct under Lyran law. You must pay his fines or serve his penalties. Or you can disown him, which is considered dishonorable but sometimes necessary. For paying his fine or serving his time you have a prior lien on his services, without pay—but of course that's unenforceable off Lyra."

Blackbeard was sweating a little. "Find out from the policeman how long all this is likely to take. I don't want to leave Elwon here and I do want us to get off as soon as possible. Keep him occupied, now, while I go about some business."

The trader retreated to a corner of the darkening barnlike tavern, beckoning Garthkint and a guard with him as Alen returned to the watchman.

"Good keeper of the peace," he said, "will you have another?"

He would.

"My trader wishes to know what penalties are likely to be levied against the unfortunate Chief Elwon."

"Going to leave him in the lurch, eh?" asked the watchman a little belligerently. "A fine master you have!"

One of the dealers at the table indignantly corroborated him. "If you foreigners aren't prepared to live up to your obligations, why did you come here in the first place? What happens to business if a master can send his man to steal and cheat and then say, 'Don't blame *me*—it was *his* doing!' "

Alen patiently explained, "On other planets, good Lyrans, the tie of master and man is not so strong that a man would obey if he were ordered to go and steal or cheat."

They shook their heads and muttered. It was unheard of.

"Good watchman," pressed the Herald, "my trader does not *want* to disown Chief Elwon. Can you tell me what recompense would be necessary—and how long it would take to manage the business?"

The watchman started on a third cup which Alen had unostentatiously signaled for. "It's hard to say," he told the Herald weightily. "For my damages, I would demand a hundred credits at least. The three other members of the watch battered by your lunatic could ask no less. The wine shop suffered easily five hundred credits' damage. The owner of it was beaten, but that doesn't matter, of course."

"No imprisonment?"

"Oh, a flogging, of course." Alen started before he recalled that the "flogging" was a few half-hearted symbolic strokes on the covered shoulders with a light cane. "But no imprisonment. His Honor, Judge Krarl, does not sit on the night bench. Judge Krarl is a new-fangled reformer, stranger. He professes to believe that mulcting is unjust—that it makes it easy for the rich to commit crime and go scot-free."

"But doesn't it?" asked Alen, drawn off course in spite of himself. There was pitying laughter around him.

"Look you," a dealer explained kindly. "The good watchman suffers battery, the mad Cephean or his master is mulcted for damages, the watchman is repaid for his injuries. What kind of justice is it to the watchman if the mad Cephean is locked away in a cell, unfined?"

The watchman nodded approvingly. "Well said," he told the dealer. "Luckily we have on the night bench a justice of the old school, His Honor, Judge Treel. Stern, but fair. You should hear him! 'Fifty credits! A hundred credits and the lash! Robbed a ship, eh? Two thousand credits!' " He returned to his own voice and said with awe, "For a murder, he never assesses less than *ten thousand credits!*"

And if the murderer couldn't pay, Alen knew, he became a "public charge," "responsible to the state" —that is, a slave. If he could pay, of course, he was turned loose.

"And His Honor, Judge Treel," he pressed, "is sitting tonight? Can we possibly appear before him, pay the fines, and be off?"

"To be sure, stranger. I'd be a fool if I waited until morning, wouldn't I?" The wine had loosened his tongue a little too far and he evidently realized it. "Enough of this," he said. "Does your master honorably accept responsibility of the Cephean? If so, come along with me, the two of you, and we'll get this over with."

"Thanks, good watchman. We are coming."

He went to blackbeard, now alone in his corner, and said, "It's all right. We can pay off—about a thousand credits—and be on our way."

The trader muttered darkly, "Lyran jurisdiction or not, it's coming out of Elwon's pay. The bloody fool!"

They rattled through the darkening streets of the town in one of the turbine-powered wagons, the watchman sitting up front with the driver and the trader and the Herald behind.

"Something's burning," said Alen to the trader, sniffing the air.

"This stinking buggy—" began blackbeard. "Oops," he said, interrupting himself and slapping at his cloak.

"Let me, trader," said Alen. He turned back the cloak, licked his thumb, and rubbed out a crawling ring of sparks spreading across a few centimeters of the cloak's silk lining. And he looked fixedly at what had started the little fire. It was an improperly covered slow-match protruding from a holstered device that was unquestionably a hand weapon.

"I bought it from one of their guards while you were parleying with the policeman," explained blackbeard embarrassedly. "I had a time making him understand. That Garthkint fellow helped." He fiddled with the perforated cover of the slow-match, screwing it on more firmly.

"A pitiful excuse for a weapon," he went on, carefully arranging his cloak over it. "The trigger isn't a trigger and the thumb safety isn't a safety. You pump the trigger a few times to build up pressure, and a little air squirts out to blow the match to life. Then you uncover the match and pull back the cocking piece. This levers a dart into the barrel. *Then* you push the thumb safety which puffs coal dust into the firing chamber and also swivels down the slow-match onto a touch-hole. *Poof,* and away goes the dart if you didn't forget any of the steps or do them in the wrong order. Luckily, I also got a knife."

He patted the nape of his neck and said, "That's where they carry 'em here. A little sheath between the shoulder blades—wonderful for a fast draw-and-throw, though it exposes you a little more than I like when you reach. The knife's black glass. Splendid edge and good balance.

"And the thieving Lyrans knew they had me where it hurt. Seven thousand, five hundred credits for the knife and gun—if you can call it that—and the holsters. By rights I should dock Elwon for them, the bloody fool. Still, it's better to buy his way out and leave no hard feelings behind us, eh, Herald?"

"Incomparably better," said Alen. "And I am amazed that you even entertain the idea of an armed jail-delivery. What if Chief Elwon had to serve a few days in a prison? Would that be worse than forever barring yourself from the planet and blackening the names of all traders with Lyra? Trader, do not hope to put down the credits that your weapons cost you as a legitimate expense of the voyage. I will not allow it when I audit your books. It was a piece of folly on which you spent personal funds, as far as the College and Order of Heralds is concerned."

"Look here," protested blackbeard. "You're supposed to be spreading utilitarian civilization, aren't you? What's utilitarian about leaving one of my crewmen here?"

Alen ignored the childish argument and wrapped himself in angry silence. As to civilization, he wondered darkly whether such a trading voyage and his part in it were relevant at all. Were the slanders true? Was the College and Order simply a collection of dupes headed by cynical oldsters greedy for luxury and power?

Such thoughts hadn't crossed his mind in a long time. He'd been too busy to entertain them, cramming his head with languages, folkways, mores, customs, underlying patterns of culture, of hundreds of galactic peoples—and for what? So that this fellow could make a profit and the College and Order take a quarter of that profit. If civilization was to come to Lyra, it would have to come in the form of metal. If the Lyrans didn't want metal, *make* them take it.

What did Machiavelli say? "The chief foundations of all states are good laws and good arms; and as there cannot be good laws where the state is not well-armed, it follows that where they are well-armed, they have good laws." It was odd that the teachers had slurred over such a seminal idea, emphasizing instead the spiritual integrity of the weaponless College and Order—or was it?

The disenchantment he felt creeping over him was terrifying.

"The castle," said the watchman over his shoulder, and their wagon stopped with a rattle before a large but unimpressive brick structure of five stories.

"You wait," the trader told the driver after they got out. He handed him two of his fifty-credit bills. "You wait, you get many, many more money. You understand, wait?"

"I wait plenty much," shouted the driver delightedly. "I wait all night, all day. You wonderful master. You great, great master, I wait—"

"All right," growled the trader, shutting him off. "You wait."

The watchman took them through an entrance hall lit by hissing pressure lamps and casually guarded by a few liveried men with truncheons. He threw open the door of a medium-sized, well-lit room with a score of people in it, looked in, and uttered a despairing groan.

A personage on a chair that looked like a throne said sharply, "Are those the star travelers? Well, don't just stand there. Bring them in!"

"Yes, Your Honor, Judge Krarl," said the watchman unhappily.

*"It's the wrong judge!"* Alen hissed at the trader. "This one gives out jail sentences!"

"Do what you can," said blackbeard grimly.

The watchman guided them to the personage in the chair and indicated a couple of low stools, bowed to the chair, and retired to stand at the back of the room.

"Your Honor," said Alen, "I am Journeyman-Herald Alen, Herald for the trading voyage—"

"Speak when you're spoken to," said the judge sharply. "Sir, with the usual insolence of wealth you have chosen to keep us waiting. I do not take this personally; it might have happened to Judge Treel, whom —to your evident dismay—I am replacing because of a sudden illness, or to any other member of the bench. But as an insult to our justice, we cannot overlook it. Sir, consider yourself reprimanded. Take your seats. Watchman, bring in the Cephean."

"Sit down," Alen murmured to the trader. "This is going to be bad."

A watchman brought in Chief Elwon, bleary-eyed, tousled, and sporting a few bruises. He gave Alen and the trader a shamefaced grin as his guard sat him on a stool beside them. The trader glared back.

Judge Krarl mumbled perfunctorily: "Let battle be joined among the several parties in this dispute let no man question our impartial awarding of the victory speak now if you yield instead to our judgment. *Well?* Speak up, you watchmen!"

The watchman who had brought the Herald and the trader started and said from the back of the room, "I yield instead to Your Honor's judgment."

Three other watchmen and a battered citizen, the wine-shop keeper, mumbled in turn, "I yield instead to Your Honor's judgment."

"Herald, speak for the accused," snapped the judge.

Well, thought Alen, I can try. "Your Honor," he said, "Chief Elwon's master does not yield to Your Honor's judgment. He is ready to battle the other parties in the dispute or their masters."

"What insolence is this?" screamed the judge, leaping from his throne. "The barbarous customs of other worlds do not prevail in this court! Who spoke of battle—" He shut his mouth with a snap, evidently abruptly realizing that *he* had spoken of battle, in an archaic phrase that harked back to the origins of justice on the planet. The judge sat down again and told Alen, more calmly, "You have mistaken a mere formality. The offer was not made in earnest." Obviously, he didn't like the sound of that himself, but he proceeded, "Now say 'I yield instead to Your Honor's judgment,' and we can get on with it. For your information, trial by combat has not been practiced for many generations on our enlightened planet."

Alen said politely, "Your Honor, I am a stranger to many of the ways of Lyra, but our excellent College and Order of Heralds instructed me well in the underlying principles of your law. I recall that one of your most revered legal maxims declares: 'The highest crime against man is murder; the highest crime against man's society is breach of promise.' "

Purpling, the judge snarled, "Are you presuming to bandy law with me, you slippery-tongued foreigner? Are you presuming to accuse me of the high crime of breaking my promise? For your information, a promise consists of an offer to do, or refrain from doing, a thing in return for a consideration. There must be the five elements of promiser, promisee, offer, substance, and consideration."

"If you will forgive a foreigner," said Alen, suddenly feeling the ground again under his feet, "I maintain that you offered the parties in the dispute your services in awarding the victory."

"An empty argument," snorted the judge. "Just as an offer with substance from somebody to nobody for a consideration is no promise, or an offer without substance from somebody to somebody for a consideration is no promise, so my offer was no promise, for there was no consideration involved."

"Your Honor, must the consideration be from the promisee to the promiser?"

"Of course not. A third party may provide the consideration."

"Then I respectfully maintain that your offer was a promise, since a third party, the government, provided you with the considerations of salary and position in return for offering your services to the disputants."

"Watchmen, clear the room of disinterested persons," said the judge hoarsely. While it was being done, Alen swiftly filled in the trader and Chief Elwon. Blackbeard grinned at the mention of a five-against-one battle royal, and the engineer looked alarmed.

When the doors closed leaving the nine of them in privacy, the judge said bitterly, "Herald, where did you learn such devilish tricks?"

Alen told him: "My College and Order instructed me well. A similar situation existed on a planet called England during an age known as the Victorious. Trial by combat had long been obsolete, there as here, but had never been declared so—there as here. A litigant won a hopeless lawsuit by publishing a challenge to his opponent and appearing at the appointed place in full armor. His opponent ignored the challenge and so lost the suit by default. The English dictator, one Disraeli, hastily summoned his parliament to abolish trial by combat."

"And so," mused the judge, "I find myself accused in my own chamber of high crime if I do not permit you five to slash away at each other and decide who won."

The wine-shop keeper began to blubber that he was a peaceable man and didn't intend to be carved up by that blackbearded, bloodthirsty star traveler. All he wanted was his money.

"Silence!" snapped the judge. "Of course there will be no combat. Will you, shopkeeper, and you, watchmen, withdraw if you receive satisfactory financial settlements?"

They would.

"Herald, you may dicker with them."

The four watchmen stood fast by their demand for a

hundred credits apiece, and got it. The terrified shopkeeper regained his balance and demanded a thousand. Alen explained that his black-bearded master from a rude and impetuous world might be unable to restrain his rage when he, Alen, interpreted the demand and, ignoring the consequences, might beat him, the shopkeeper, to a pulp. The asking price plunged to a reasonable five hundred, which was paid over. The shopkeeper got the judge's permission to leave and backed out, bowing.

"You see, trader," Alen told blackbeard, "that it was needless to buy weapons when the spoken word—"

"And now," said the judge with a sneer, "we are easily out of *that* dilemma. Watchmen, arrest the three star travelers and take them to the cages."

"Your Honor!" cried Alen, outraged.

"Money won't get you out of *this* one. I charge you with treason."

"The charge is obsolete—" began the Herald hotly, but he broke off as he realized the vindictive strategy.

"Yes, it is. And one of its obsolete provisions is that treason charges must be tried by the parliament at a regular session, which isn't due for two hundred days. You'll be freed and I may be reprimanded, but by my head, for two hundred days you'll regret that you made a fool of *me*. Take them away."

"A trumped-up charge against us. Prison for two hundred days," said Alen swiftly to the trader as the watchmen closed in.

"Why buy weapons?" mocked the blackbeard, showing his teeth. His left arm whipped up and down, there was a black streak through the air—and the judge was pinned to his throne with a black glass knife through his throat and the sneer of triumph still on his lips.

The trader, before the knife struck, had the clumsy pistol out, with the cover off the glowing match and the cocking piece back. He must have pumped and cocked it under his cloak, thought Alen numbly as he told the watchmen, without prompting, "Get back against the wall and turn around." They did. They wanted to live, and the grinning blackbeard who had made meat of the judge with a flick of the arm was a terrifying figure.

"Well done, Alen," said the trader. "Take their clubs, Elwon. Two for you, two for the Herald. Alen, don't argue! I had to kill the judge before he raised an alarm—nothing but death will silence his breed. You may have to kill too before we're out of this. Take the clubs." He passed the clumsy pistol to Chief Elwon and said, "Keep it on their backs. The thing that looks like a thumb safety is a trigger. Put a dart through the first one who tries to make a break. Alen, tell the fellow on the end to turn around and come to me slowly."

Alen did. Blackbeard swiftly stripped him, tore and knotted his clothes into ropes and bound and gagged him. The others got the same treatment in less than ten minutes.

The trader holstered the gun and rolled the watchmen out of the line of sight from the door of the chamber. He recovered his knife and wiped it on the judge's shirt. Alen had to help him prop the body behind the throne's high back.

"Hide those clubs," blackbeard said. "Straight faces. Here we go."

They went out, single file, opening the door only enough to pass. Alen, last in line, told one of the liveried guards nearby, "His honor, Judge Krarl, does not wish to be disturbed."

"That's news?" asked the tipstaff sardonically. He put his hand on the Herald's arm. "Only yesterday he gimme a blast when I brought him a mug of water he asked me for himself. An outrageous interruption, he called me, and he asked for the water himself. What do you think of that?"

"Terrible," said Alen hastily. He broke away and caught up with the trader and the engineer at the entrance hall. Idlers and loungers were staring at them as they headed for the waiting wagon.

"I wait!" the driver told them loudly. "I wait long, much. You pay more, more?"

"We pay more," said the trader. "You start."

The driver brought out a smoldering piece of punk, lit a pressure torch, lifted the barn-door section of the wagon's floor to expose the pottery turbine and preheated it with the torch. He pumped squeakily for minutes, spinning a flywheel with his other hand, before the rotor began to turn on its own. Down went the hatch, up onto the seats went the passengers.

"The spaceport," said Alen. With a slate-pencil screech the driver engaged his planetary gear and they were off.

Through it all, blackbeard had ignored frantic muttered questions from Chief Elwon, who had wanted nothing to do with murder, especially of a judge. "You sit up there," growled the trader, "and every so often you look around and see if we're being followed. Don't alarm the driver. And if we get to the spaceport and blast off without any trouble, keep your story to yourself." He settled down in the back seat with Alen and maintained a gloomy silence. The young Herald was too much in awe of this stranger, so suddenly competent in assorted forms of violence, to question him.

They did get to the spaceport without trouble, and found the crew in the Customs shed, emptied of the gems by dealers with releases. They had built a fire for warmth.

"We wish to leave immediately," said the trader to the port officer. "Can you change my Lyran currency?"

The officer began to sputter apologetically that it was late and the vault was sealed for the night—

"That's all right. We'll change it on Vega. It'll get back to you. Call off your guards and unseal our ship."

They followed the port officer to *Starsong*'s dim bulk out on the field. The officer cracked the seal on her with his club in the light of a flaring pressure lamp held by one of the guards.

Alen was sweating hard through it all. As they started across the field he had seen what looked like two closely spaced green stars low on the horizon toward town suddenly each jerk up and toward each other in minute arcs. The semaphore!

The signal officer in the port administration building would be watching too—but nobody on the field, preoccupied with the routine of departure, seemed to have noticed.

The lights flipped this way and that. Alen didn't know the code and bitterly regretted the lack. After some twenty signals the lights flipped to the "rest" position again as the port officer was droning out a set of takeoff regulations: bearing, height above settled areas, permissible atomic fuels while in atmosphere—Alen saw somebody start across the field toward them from the administration building. The guards were leaning on their long, competent looking weapons.

Alen inconspicuously detached himself from the group around *Starsong* and headed across the dark field to meet the approaching figure. Nearing it, he called out a low greeting in Lyran, using the noncom-to-officer military form.

"Sergeant," said the signal officer quietly, "go and draw off the men a few meters from the star travelers. Tell them the ship mustn't leave, that they're to cover the foreigners, and shoot if—"

Alen stood dazedly over the limp body of the signal officer. And then he quickly hid the bludgeon again and strolled back to the ship, wondering whether he'd cracked the Lyran's skull.

The port was open by then and the crew filing in. He was last. "Close it fast," he told the trader. "I had to—"

"I saw you," grunted blackbeard. "A semaphore message?" He was working as he spoke, and the metal port closed.

"Astrogator and engineer, take over," he told them.

"All hands to their bunks," ordered Astrogator Hufner. "Blast off immediate."

Alen took to his cubicle and strapped himself in. Blastoff deafened him, rattled his bones, and made him thoroughly sick as usual. After what seemed like several wretched hours, they were definitely space-borne under smooth acceleration, and his nausea subsided.

Blackbeard knocked, came in, and unbuckled him.

"Ready to audit the books of the voyage?" asked the trader.

"No," said Alen feebly.

"It can wait," said the trader. "The books are the least important part, anyway. We have headed off a frightful war."

"War? We have?"

"War between Eyolf's Realm and Vega. It is the common gossip of chancellories and trade missions that both governments have cast longing eyes on Lyrane, that they have plans to penetrate its economy by supplying metals to the planet without metals—by force, if need be. Alen, we have removed the pretext by which Eyolf's Realm and Vega would have attempted to snap up Lyrane and inevitably have come into conflict. Lyra is getting its metal now, and without imperialist entanglements."

"I saw none," the Herald said blankly.

"You wondered why I was in such haste to get off Lyra, and why I wouldn't leave Elwon there. It is because our Vegan gems were most unusual gems. I am not a technical man, but I understand they are actual gems which were treated to produce a certain effect at just about this time."

Blackbeard glanced at his wrist chronometer and said dreamily, "Lyra is getting metal. Wherever there is one of our gems, pottery is decomposing into its constituent aluminum, silicon, and oxygen. Fluxes and glazes are decomposing into calcium, zinc, barium, potassium, chromium, *and iron.* Buildings are crumbling, pants are dropping as ceramic belt-buckles disintegrate—"

"It means chaos!" protested Alen.

"It means civilization and peace. An ugly clash was in the making." Blackbeard paused and added deliberately, "Where neither their property nor their honor is touched, most men live content."

"*The Prince,* Chapter Nineteen. You are—"

"There was another important purpose to the voyage," said the trader, grinning. "You will be interested in this." He handed Alen a document which, unfolded, had the seal of the College and Order at its head.

Alen read in a daze, "Examiner Nineteen to the Rector—final clearance of Novice—"

He lingered pridefully over the paragraph that described how he had "with coolness and great resource" foxed the battle cruiser of the Realm, "adapting himself readily in a delicate situation requiring not only physical courage but swift recall, evaluation, and application of a minor planetary culture."

Not so pridefully he read, ". . . inclined toward pomposity of manner somewhat ludicrous in one of his years, though not unsuccessful in dominating the crew by his bearing—"

And, ". . . highly profitable disposal of our gems; a feat of no mean importance since the College and Order must, after all, maintain itself."

And, ". . . cleared the final and crucial hurdle with some mental turmoil if I am any judge, but did clear it. After some twenty years of indoctrination in unrealistic nonviolence, the youth was confronted with a situation where nothing but violence would serve, correctly evaluated this, and applied violence in the form of a truncheon to the head of a Lyran signal officer, thereby demonstrating an ability to learn and common sense as precious as it is rare."

And, finally, simply, "Recommended for training."

"Training?" gasped Alen. "You mean there's more?"

"Not for most, boy. Not for most. The bulk of us are what we seem to be: oily, gun-shy, indispensable adjuncts to trade who feather our nest with percentages. We need those percentages and we need gun-shy Heralds."

Alen recited slowly, "Among other evils which being unarmed brings you, it causes you to be despised."

"Chapter Fourteen," said blackbeard mechanically. "We leave such clues lying by their bedsides for twenty years, and they never notice them. For the few of us who do—more training."

"Will I learn to throw a knife like you?" asked Alen, repelled and fascinated at once by the idea.

"On your own time, if you wish. Mostly it's ethics and morals so you'll be able to weigh the values of such things as knife-throwing."

"Ethics! Morals!"

"We started as missionaries, you know."

"Everybody knows that. But the Great Utilitarian Reform—"

"Some of us," said blackbeard dryly, "think it was neither great, nor utilitarian, nor a reform."

It was a staggering idea. "But we're spreading utilitarian civilization!" protested Alen. "Or if we're not, what's the sense of it all?"

Blackbeard told him, "We have our different motives. One is a sincere utilitarian; another is a gambler—happy when he's in danger and his pulses are pounding. Another is proud and likes to trick people. More than a few conceive themselves as servants of mankind. I'll let you rest for a bit now." He rose.

"But you?" asked Alen hesitantly.

"Me? You will find me in Chapter Twenty-Six," grinned blackbeard. "And perhaps you'll find someone else." He closed the door behind him.

Alen ran through the chapter in his mind, puzzled, until—that was it.

It had a strange and inevitable familiarity to it as if he had always known that he would be saying it aloud, welcomingly, in this cramped cubicle aboard a battered starship:

"God is not willing to do everything, and thus take away our free will and that share of glory which belongs to us."

# SUNKEN UNIVERSE

## by James Blish

*Nearly every famous science-fiction writer has one story which continues to fascinate his readers long after he is thoroughly tired of it. This one is Blish's; he does not understand its continuing popularity, but I do, and I think you will too, when I tell you what it's about.*

*A sky of ice, a microscopic enemy, and two hundred naked men struggling to survive in a puddle of water . . .*

*In a forgotten corner of the galaxy, the watery world of Hydrot hurtles endlessly around the red star, Tau Ceti. For many months its single small continent has been snowbound, and the many pools and lakes which dot the continent have been locked in the grip of the ice. Now, however, the red sun swings closer and closer to the zenith in Hydrot's sky; the snow rushes in torrents toward the eternal ocean, and the ice recedes toward the shores of the lakes and ponds . . .*

## 1

THE first thing to reach the consciousness of the sleeping Lavon was a small, intermittent scratching sound. This was followed by a disquieting sensation in his body, as if the world—and Lavon with it—were being rocked back and forth. He stirred uneasily, without opening his eyes. His vastly slowed metabolism made him feel inert and queasy, and the rocking did not help. At his slight motion, however, both the sound and the motion became more insistent.

It seemed to take days for the fog over his brain to clear, but whatever was causing the disturbance would not let him rest. With a groan he forced his eyelids open and made an abrupt gesture with one webbed hand. By the waves of phosphorescence which echoed away from his fingers at the motion, he could see that the smooth amber walls of his spherical shell were unbroken. He tried to peer through them, but he could see nothing but darkness outside. Well, that was natural; the amnionic fluid inside the spore would generate light, but ordinary water did not, no matter how vigorously it was stirred.

Whatever was outside the sphere was rocking it again, with the same whispering friction against its shell. Probably some nosey diatom, Lavon thought sleepily, trying to butt its way through an object it was too stupid to go around. Or some early hunter, yearning for a taste of the morsel inside the spore. Well, let it worry itself; Lavon had no intention of breaking the shell just yet. The fluid in which he had slept for so many months had held his body processes static, and had slowed his mind. Once out into the water, he would have to start breathing and looking for food again, and he could tell by the unrelieved darkness outside that it was too early in the spring to begin thinking about that.

He flexed his fingers reflectively, in the disharmonic motion from little finger to thumb that no animal but man can copy, and watched the widening wavefronts of greenish light rebound in larger arcs from the curved spore walls. Here he was, curled up quite comfortably in a little amber ball, where he could stay until even the depths were warm and light. At this moment there was probably still some ice on the sky, and certainly there would not be much to eat as yet. Not that there was ever much, what with the voracious rotifers coming awake too with the first gust of warm water—

The rotifers! That was it. There was a plan afoot to drive them out. Memory returned in an unwelcome rush. As if to help it, the spore rocked again. That was probably one of the Protos, trying to awaken him; nothing man-eating ever came to the Bottom this early. He had left an early call with the Paras, and now the time had come, as cold and early and dark as he had thought he wanted it.

Reluctantly, Lavon uncurled, planting his webbed toes and arching his backbone as hard as he could, pressing with his whole body against his amber prison. With small, sharp, crepitating sounds, a network of cracks raced through the translucent shell.

Then the spore wall dissolved into a thousand brittle shards, and he was shivering violently with the onslaught of the icy water. The warmer fluid of his winter cell dissipated silently, a faint glowing fog. In the brief light he saw, not far from him, a familiar shape: a transparent, bubble-filled cylinder, a colorless slipper of jelly, spirally grooved, almost as long as he was tall. Its surface was furred with gently vibrating fine hairs, thickened at the base.

The light went out. The Proto said nothing; it waited while Lavon choked and coughed, expelling the last remnants of the spore fluid from his book-lungs and sucking in the pure, ice-cold water.

"Para?" Lavon said at last. "Already?"

"Already," the invisible cilia vibrated in even, emotionless tones. Each separate hairlike process buzzed at an independent, changing rate; the resulting sound waves spread through the water, intermodulating, reinforcing, or canceling each other. The aggregate wavefront, by the time it reached human ears, was rather eerie, but nevertheless recognizable human speech. "This is the time, Lavon."

"Time and more than time," another voice said from the returned darkness, "if we are to drive Flosc from his castles."

"Who's that?" Lavon said, turning futilely toward the new voice.

"I am Para also, Lavon. We are sixteen since the awakening. If you could reproduce as rapidly as we—"

"Brains are better than numbers," Lavon said, "as the Eaters will find out soon enough."

"What shall we do, Lavon?"

The man drew up his knees and sank to the cold mud of the Bottom to think. Something wriggled under his buttocks and a tiny spirillum corkscrewed away, identifiable only by feel. He let it go; he was not hungry yet, and he had the Eaters—the rotifers—to think about. Before long they would be swarming in the upper reaches of the sky, devouring everything, even men when they could catch them, even their natural enemies the Protos now and then. And whether or not the Protos could be organized to battle them was a question still to be tested.

Brains are better than numbers; even that, as a proposition, was still to be tested. The Protos, after all, were intelligent after their fashion and they knew their world, as the men did not. Lavon could still remember how hard it had been for him to get straight in his head the various clans of beings in this world, and to make sense of their confused names; his tutor Shar had drilled him unmercifully until it had begun to penetrate.

When you said "Man," you meant creatures that, generally speaking, looked alike. The bacteria were of three kinds, the rods and the globes and the spirals, but they were all tiny and edible, so he had learned to differentiate them quickly. When it came to the Protos, identification became a real problem. Para here was a Proto, but he certainly looked very different from Stent and his family, and the family of Didin was unlike both. Anything, as it turned out, that was not green and had a visible nucleus was a Proto, no matter how strange its shape might be. The Eaters were all different, too, and some of them were as beautiful as the fruiting crowns of water plants; but all of them were deadly, and all had the whirling crown of cilia which could suck you into the incessantly grinding mastax in a moment. Everything which was green and had an engraved shell of glass, Shar had called a diatom, dredging the strange word as he dredged them all from some bottom in his skull which none of the rest of them could reach, and even Shar could not explain.

Lavon arose quickly. "We need Shar," he said. "Where is his spore?"

"On a plant frond, far up near the sky."

Idiot! The old man would never think of safety. To sleep near the sky, where he might be snatched up and borne off by any Eater to chance by when he emerged, sluggish with winter's long sleep? How could a wise man be so foolish?

"We'll have to hurry. Show me the way."

"Soon; wait," one of the Paras said. "You cannot see. Noc is foraging nearby." There was a small stir in the texture of the darkness as the swift cylinder shot away.

"Why do we need Shar?" the other Para said.

"For his brains, Para. He is a thinker."

"But his thoughts are water. Since he taught the Protos man's language, he has forgotten to think of the Eaters. He thinks forever of the mystery of how man came here. It is a mystery—even the Eaters are not like man. But understanding it will not help us to live."

Lavon turned blindly toward the creature. "Para, tell me something. Why do the Protos side with us? With man, I mean? Why do you need us? The Eaters fear you."

There was a short silence. When the Para spoke again, the vibrations of its voice were more blurred than before, more even, more devoid of any understandable feeling.

"We live in this world," the Para said. "We are of it. We rule it. We came to that state long before the coming of men, in long warfare with the Eaters. But we think as the Eaters do, we do not plan, we share our knowledge and we exist. Men plan; men lead; men are different from each other; men want to remake the world. And they hate the Eaters, as we do. We will help."

"And give up your rule?"

"And give it up, if the rule of men is better. That is reason. Now we can go; Noc is coming back with light."

Lavon looked up. Sure enough, there was a brief flash of cold light far overhead, and then another. In a moment the spherical Proto had dropped into view, its body flaring regularly with blue-green pulses. Beside it darted the second Para.

"Noc brings news," the second Para said. "Para is twenty-four. The Syn are awake by thousands along the sky. Noc spoke to a Syn colony, but they will not help us; they all expect to be dead before the Eaters awake."

"Of course," said the first Para. "That always happens. And the Syn are plants; why should they help the Protos?"

"Ask Noc if he'll guide us to Shar," Lavon said impatiently.

The Noc gestured with its single short, thick tentacle. One of the Paras said, "That is what he is here for."

"Then let's go. We've waited long enough."

The mixed quartet soared away from the Bottom through the liquid darkness.

"No," Lavon snapped. "Not a second longer. The Syn are awake, and Notholca of the Eaters is due right after that. You know that as well as I do, Shar. Wake up!"

"Yes, yes," the old man said fretfully. He stretched and yawned. "You're always in such a hurry, Lavon. Where's Phil? He made his spore near mine." He pointed to a still-unbroken amber sphere sealed to a leaf of the water plant one tier below. "Better push him off; he'll be safer on the Bottom."

"He would never reach the Bottom," Para said. "The thermocline has formed."

Shar looked surprised. "It has? Is it as late as all that? Wait while I get my records together." He began to search along the leaf in the debris and the piled shards of his spore. Lavon looked impatiently about, found a splinter of stonewort, and threw it heavy end first at the bubble of Phil's cell just below. The spore shattered promptly, and the husky young man tumbled out, blue with shock as the cold water hit him.

"Wough!" he said. "Take it easy, Lavon." He looked up. "The old man's awake? Good. He insisted on staying up here for the winter, so of course I had to stay too."

"Aha," Shar said, and lifted a thick metal plate about the length of his forearm and half as wide. "Here is one of them. Now if only I haven't misplaced the other—"

Phil kicked away a mass of bacteria. "Here it is. Better give them both to a Para, so they won't burden you. Where do we go from here, Lavon? It's dangerous up this high. I'm just glad a Dicran hasn't already shown up."

"I here," something droned just above them.

Instantly, without looking up, Lavon flung himself out and down into the open water, turning his head to look back over his shoulder only when he was already diving as fast as he could go. Shar and Phil had evidently sprung at the same instant. On the next frond above where Shar had spent his winter was the armored, trumpet-shaped body of the rotifer Dicran, contracted to leap after them.

The two Protos came curving back out of nowhere. At the same moment, the bent, shortened body of Dicran flexed in its armor plate, straightened, came plunging toward them. There was a soft plop and Lavon found himself struggling in a fine net, as tangled and impassible as the matte of a lichen. A second such sound was followed by a muttered imprecation from

Phil. Lavon struck out fiercely, but he was barely able to wriggle in the web of wiry, transparent stuff.

"Be still," a voice which he recognized as Para's throbbed behind him. He managed to screw his head around, and then kicked himself mentally for not having realized at once what had happened. The Paras had exploded the trichocysts which lay like tiny cartridges beneath their pellicles; each one cast forth a liquid which solidified upon contact with the water in a long slender thread. It was their standard method of defense.

Farther down, Shar and Phil drifted with the second Para in the heart of a white haze, like creatures far gone in mold. Dicran swerved to avoid it, but she was evidently unable to give up; she twisted and darted around them, her corona buzzing harshly, her few scraps of the human language forgotten. Seen from this distance, the rotation of the corona was revealed as an illusion, created by the rhythm of pulsation of the individual cilia, but as far as Lavon was concerned the point was solely technical and the distance was far too short. Through the transparent armor Lavon could also see the great jaws of Dicran's mastax, grinding away mechanically at the fragments which poured into her unheeding mouth.

High above them all, Noc circled indecisively, illuminating the whole group with quick, nervous flashes of his blue light. He was a flagellate, and had no natural weapons against the rotifer; why he was hanging around drawing attention to himself Lavon could not imagine.

Then, suddenly, he saw the reason: a barrel-like creature about Noc's size, ringed with two rows of cilia, and bearing a ramlike prow. "Didin!" he shouted, unnecessarily. "This way!"

The Proto swung gracefully toward them and seemed to survey them, though it was hard to tell how he could see them without eyes. The Dicran saw him at the same time and began to back slowly away, her buzzing rising to a raw snarl. She regained the plant and crouched down.

For an instant Lavon thought she was going to give up, but experience should have told him that she lacked the sense. Suddenly the lithe, crouched body was in full spring again, this time straight at Didin. Lavon yelled an incoherent warning.

The Proto didn't need it. The slowly cruising barrel darted to one side and then forward, with astonishing speed. If he could sink that poisoned seizing-organ into a weak point in the rotifer's armor—

Noc mounted higher to keep out of the way of the two fighters, and in the resulting weakened light Lavon could not see what was happening, though the furious churning of the water and the buzzing of the Dicran continued.

After a while the sounds seemed to be retreating; Lavon crouched in the gloom inside the Para's net, listening intently. Finally there was silence.

"What's happened?" he whispered tensely.

"Didin does not say."

More eternities went by. Then the darkness began to wane as Noc dropped cautiously toward them.

"Noc, where did they go?"

Noc signaled with his tentacle and turned on his axis toward Para. "He says he lost sight of them. Wait—I hear Didin."

Lavon could hear nothing; what the Para heard was some one of the semitelepathic impulses which made up the Proto's own language.

"He says Dicran is dead."

"Good! Ask him to bring the body back here."

There was a short silence. "He says he will bring it. What good is a dead rotifer, Lavon?"

"You'll see," Lavon said. He watched anxiously until Didin glided backwards into the lighted area, his poisonous ram sunk deep into the flaccid body of the rotifer, which, after the delicately organized fashion of its kind, was already beginning to disintegrate.

"Let me out of this net, Para."

The Proto jerked sharply for a fraction of a turn on its long axis, snapping the threads off at the base; the movement had to be made with great precision, or its pellicle would tear as well. The tangled mass rose gently with the current and drifted off over the abyss.

Lavon swam forward and, seizing one buckled edge of Dicran's armor, tore away a huge strip of it. His hands plunged into the now almost shapeless body and came out again holding two dark spheroids: eggs.

"Destroy these, Didin," he ordered. The Proto obligingly slashed them open.

"Hereafter," Lavon said, "that's to be standard procedure with every Eater you kill."

"Not the males," one of the Para pointed out.

"Para, you have no sense of humor. All right, not the males—but nobody kills the males anyhow, they're harmless." He looked down grimly at the inert mass. "Remember—destroy the eggs. Killing the beasts isn't enough. We want to wipe out the whole race."

"We never forget," Para said emotionlessly.

## 2

The band of over two hundred humans, with Lavon and Shar and a Para at its head, fled swiftly through the warm, light waters of the upper level. Each man gripped a wood splinter, or a fragment of lime chipped from stonewort, as a club; and two hundred pairs of eyes darted watchfuly from side to side. Cruising over them was a squadron of twenty Didins, and the rotifers they encountered only glared at them from single red eye-spots, making no move to attack. Overhead, near the sky, the sunlight was filtered through a thick layer of living creatures, fighting and feeding and spawning, so that all the depths below were colored a rich green. Most of this heavily populated layer was made up of algae and diatoms, and there the Eaters fed unhindered. Sometimes a dying diatom dropped slowly past the army.

The spring was well advanced; the two hundred, Lavon thought, probably represented all of the humans who had survived the winter. At least no more could be found. The others—nobody would ever know how many—had awakened too late in the season, or had made their spores in exposed places, and the rotifers had snatched them up. Of the group, more than a third were women. That meant that in another forty days, if they were unmolested, they could double the size of their army.

If they were unmolested. Lavon grinned and pushed an agitated colony of Eudorina out of his way. The phrase reminded him of a speculation Shar had brought forth last year: If Para were left unmolested, the oldster had said, he could reproduce fast enough to fill this whole universe with a solid mass of Paras before the season was out. Nobody, of course, ever went unmolested in this world; nevertheless, Lavon meant to cut the odds for people considerably below anything that had heretofore been thought of as natural.

His hand flashed up, and down again. The darting squadrons plunged after him. The light on the sky faded rapidly, and after a while Lavon began to feel slightly chilly. He signaled again. Like dancers, the two hundred swung their bodies in midflight, plunging now feet first toward the Bottom. To strike the thermocline in this position would make their passage through it faster, getting them out of the upper level where every minute, despite the convoy of Protos, concentrated danger.

Lavon's feet struck a yielding surface, and with a splash he was over his head in icy water. He bobbed up again, feeling the icy division drawn across his shoulders. Other splashes began to sound all along the thermocline as the army struck it, although, since there was water above and below, Lavon could not see the actual impacts.

Now they would have to wait until their body temperatures fell. At this dividing line of the universe, the warm water ended and the temperature dropped rapidly, so that the water below was much denser and buoyed them up. The lower level of cold reached clear down to the Bottom—an area which the rotifers, who were not very clever, seldom managed to enter.

A moribund diatom drifted down beside Lavon, the greenish-yellow of its body fading to a sick orange, its beautifully marked, oblong, pillbox-like shell swarming with greedy bacteria. It came to rest on the thermocline, and the transparent caterpillar tread of jelly which ran around it moved feebly, trying vainly to get traction on the sliding water interface. Lavon reached out a webbed hand and brushed away a clot of vibrating rods which had nearly forced its way into the shell through a costal opening.

"Thank . . ." the diatom said, in an indistinct, whispering voice. And again, "Thank . . . Die . . ." The gurgling whisper faded. The caterpillar tread shifted again, then was motionless.

"It is right," a Para said. "Why do you bother with those creatures? They are stupid. Nothing can be done for them."

Lavon did not try to explain. He felt himself sinking slowly, and the water about his trunk and legs no longer seemed cold, only gratefully cool after the stifling heat of that he was breathing. In a moment the cool still depths had closed over his head. He hovered until he was reasonably sure that all the rest of his army was safely through, and the long ordeal of search for survivors in the upper level really ended. Then he twisted and streaked for the Bottom, Phil and Para beside him, Shar puffing along with the vanguard.

A stone loomed; Lavon surveyed it in the half light. Almost immediately he saw what he had hoped to see: the sand-built house of a caddis-worm, clinging to the mountainous slopes of the rock. He waved in his special cadre and pointed.

Cautiously the men spread out in a U around the stone, the mouth of the U facing the same way as the opening of the worm's masonry tube. A Noc came after them, drifting like a star shell above the peak; one of the Paras approached the door of the worm's house, buzzing defiantly. Under cover of this challenge the men at the back of the U settled on the rock and began to creep forward. The house was three times as tall as they were; the slimy black sand grains of which it was composed were as big as their heads.

There was a stir inside, and after a moment the ugly

head of the worm peered out, weaving uncertainly at the buzzing Para which had disturbed it. The Para drew back, and the worm, in a kind of blind hunger, followed it. A sudden lunge brought it nearly halfway out of its tube.

Lavon shouted. Instantly the worm was surrounded by a howling horde of two-legged demons, who beat and prodded it mercilessly with fists and clubs. Somehow it made a sound, a kind of bleat as unlikely as the birdlike whistle of a fish, and began to slide backwards into its home—but the rear guard had already broken in back there. It jerked forward again, lashing from side to side under the flogging.

There was only one way now for the great larva to go, and the demons around it kept it going that way. It fell toward the Bottom down the side of the rock, naked and ungainly, shaking its blind head and bleating.

Lavon sent five Didin after it. They could not kill it, for it was far too huge to die under their poison, but they could sting it hard enough to keep it traveling. Otherwise, it would be almost sure to return to the rock to start a new house.

Lavon settled on an abutment and surveyed his prize with satisfaction. It was more than big enough to hold his entire clan—a great tubular hall, easily defended once the breach in the rear wall was rebuilt, and well out of the usual haunts of the Eaters. The muck the caddis-worm had left behind would have to be cleaned up, guards posted, vents knocked out to keep the oxygen-poor water of the depths in motion inside. It was too bad that the amoebas could not be detailed to scavenge the place, but Lavon knew better than to issue such an order. The Fathers of the Protos could not be asked to do useful work; that had been made very clear.

He looked around at his army. They were standing around him in awed silence, looking at the spoils of their attack upon the largest creature in the world. He did not think they would ever again feel as timid toward the Eaters. He stood up quickly.

"What are you gaping at?" he shouted. "It's yours, all of it. Get to work!"

Old Shar sat comfortably upon a pebble which had been hollowed out and cushioned with spirogyra straw. Lavon stood nearby at the door, looking out at the maneuvers of his legions. They numbered more than three hundred now, thanks to the month of comparative quiet which they had enjoyed in the great hall, and they handled their numbers well in the aquatic drill which Lavon had invented for them. They swooped and turned above the rock, breaking and reassembling their formations, fighting a sham battle with invisible opponents whose shape they could remember only too well.

"Noc says there's all kinds of quarreling going on among the Eaters," Shar said. "They didn't believe we'd joined with the Protos at first, and then they didn't believe we'd all worked together to capture the hall. And the mass raid we had last week scared them. They'd never tried anything of the kind before, and they *knew* it wouldn't fail. Now they're fighting with each other over why it did. Cooperation is something new to this world, Lavon; it's making history."

"History?" Lavon said, following his drilling squadrons with a technical eye. "What's that?"

"These." The old man leaned over one arm of the pebble and touched the metal plates which were always with him. Lavon turned to follow the gesture, incuriously. He knew the plates well enough—the pure uncorroded shining, graven deeply on both sides with characters no one, not even Shar, could read. The Protos called the plates *Not-stuff*—neither wood nor flesh nor stone.

"What good is that? I can't read it. Neither can you."

"I've got a start, Lavon. I know the plates are written in our language. Look at the first word: *ha ii ss tuh oh or ee*—exactly the right number of characters for 'history.' That can't be a coincidence. And the next two words have to be 'of the.' And going on from there, using just the characters I already know—" Shar bent and traced in the sand with a stick a new train of characters: *i/terste/ /ar e/ / e/ ition.*

"What's that?"

"It's a start, Lavon. Just a start. Some day we'll have more."

Lavon shrugged. "Perhaps, when we're safer. We can't afford to worry about that kind of thing now. We've never had that kind of time, not since the First Awakening."

The old man frowned down at the characters in the sand. "The First Awakening. Why does everything seem to stop there? I can remember in the smallest detail nearly everything that happened to me since then. But what happened to our childhoods, Lavon? None of us who survived the First Awakening seems to have had one. Who were our parents? Why were we so ignorant of the world, and yet grown men and women, all of us?"

"And the answer is in the plates?"

"I hope so," Shar said. "I believe it is. But I don't know. The plates were beside me in the spore at the First Awakening. That's all I know about them, except that there's nothing else like them in the world. The rest is deduction, and I haven't gotten very far with it. Some day . . . some day."

"I hope so too," Lavon said soberly. "I don't mean to mock, Shar, or to be impatient. I've got questions, too; we all have. But we're going to have to put them off for a while. Suppose we never find the whole answer?"

"Then our children will."

"But there's the heart of the problem, Shar: We have to live to have children. And make the kind of a world in which they'll have time to study. Otherwise—"

Lavon broke off as a figure darted between the guards at the door of the hall and twisted to a halt.

"What news, Phil?"

"The same," Phil said, shrugging with his whole body. His feet touched the floor. "The Flosc's castles are going up all along the bar; they'll be finished with them soon, and then we won't dare to get near them. Do you still think you can drive them out?"

Lavon nodded.

"But why?"

"First, for effect. We've been on the defensive so far, even though we've made a good job of it. We'll have to follow that up with an attack of our own if we're going to keep the Eaters confused. Second, the castles Flosc builds are all tunnels and exits and entrances—much better than warm houses for us. I hate to think of what would have happened if the Eaters had thought of blockading us inside this hall. And we need an outpost in enemy country, Phil, where there are Eaters to kill."

"This is enemy country," Phil said. "Stephanost is a Bottom-dweller."

"But she's only a trapper, not a hunter. Any time we want to kill her, we can find her right where we left her last. It's the leapers like Dicran and Notholca, the swimmers like Rotar, the colony builders like Flosc that we have to wipe out first."

"Then we'd better start now, Lavon. Once the castles are finished—"

"Yes. Get your squads together, Phil. Shar, come on; we're leaving the hall."

"To raid the castles?"

"Of course."

Shar picked up his plates.

"You'd better leave those there; they'll be in your way in the fighting."

"No," Shar said determinedly. "I don't want them out of my sight. They go along."

## 3

Vague forebodings, all the more disturbing because he had felt nothing quite like them ever before, passed like clouds of fine silt through Lavon's mind as the army swept away from the hall on the Bottom and climbed toward the thermocline. As far as he could see, everything seemed to be going as he had planned it. As the army moved, its numbers were swelled by Protos who darted into its ranks from all sides. Discipline was good; and every man was armed with a long, seasoned splinter, and from each belt swung a stonewort-flake hand-axe, held by a thong run through a hole Shar had taught them all how to drill. There would probably be much death before the light of today faded, but death was common enough on any day, and this time it should heavily disfavor the Eaters.

But there was a chill upon the depths that Lavon did not like, and a suggestion of a current in the water which was unnatural below the thermocline. A great many days had been consumed in collecting the army, recruiting from stragglers, and in securing the hall. The intensive breeding which had followed, and the training of the newborn and the newly recruited, had taken still more time, all of it essential, but all irrevocable. If the chill and the current marked the beginning of the fall turnover . . .

If it did, nothing could be done about it. The turnover could no more be postponed than the coming of day or night. He signaled to the nearest Para.

The glistening torpedo veered toward him. Lavon pointed up.

"Here comes the thermocline, Para. Are we pointed right?"

"Yes, Lavon. That way is the place where the Bottom rises toward the sky. Flosc's castles are on the other side, where she will not see us."

"The sandbar that runs out from the north. Right. It's getting warmer. Here we go."

Lavon felt his flight suddenly quicken, as if he had been shot like a seed from some invisible thumb and forefinger. He looked over his shoulder to watch the passage of the rest through the temperature barrier, and what he saw thrilled him as sharply as any awakening. Up to now he had had no clear picture of the size of his forces, or the three-dimensional beauty of their dynamic, mobile organization. Even the Protos had fitted themselves into the squads; pattern after pattern of power came soaring after Lavon from the Bottom: first a single Noc bowling along like a beacon to guide all the rest, then an advance cone of Didin to watch for individual Eaters who might flee to give the alarm, and then the men, and the Protos, who made up the main force, in tight formations as beautiful as the elementary geometry from which Shar had helped derive them.

The sandbar loomed ahead, as vast as any mountain range. Lavon soared sharply upward, and the tumbled, raw-boned boulders of the sand grains swept by rapidly beneath him in a broad, stony flood. Far beyond the ridge, towering up to the sky through glowing green obscurity, were the befronded stems of the plant jungle which was their objective. It was too dim with distance to allow him to see the clinging castles of the Flosc yet, but he knew that the longest part of the march was over. He narrowed his eyes and cleft the sunlit waters with driving, rapid strokes of his webbed hands and feet. The invaders poured after him over the crest of the bar in an orderly torrent.

Lavon swung his arm in a circle. Silently, the following squadrons glided into a great paraboloid, its axis pointed at the jungle. The castles were visible now; until the formation of the army, they had been the only products of close cooperation that this world had ever seen. They were built of single brown tubes, narrow at the base, attached to each other in a random pattern in an ensemble as delicate as a branching coral. In the mouth of each tube was a rotifer, a Flosc, distinguished from other Eaters by the four-leaf-clover of its corona, and by the single, prehensile finger springing from the small of its back, with which it ceaselessly molded its brown spittle into hard pellets and cemented them carefully to the rim of its tube.

As usual, the castles chilled Lavon's muscles with doubt. They were perfect, and they had always been one of the major, stony flowers of summer, long before there had been any First Awakening, or any men. And there was surely something wrong with the water in the upper level; it was warm and sleepy. The heads of the Flosc hummed contentedly at the mouths of their tubes; everything was as it should be, as it had always been; the army was a fantasm, the attack a failure before it had begun—

Then they were spied.

The Flosc vanished instantly, contracting violently into their tubes. The placid humming of their continuous feeding upon everything that passed was snuffed out; spared motes drifted about the castle in the light.

Lavon found himself smiling. Not long ago, the Flosc would only have waited until the humans were close enough, and then would have sucked them down, without more than a few struggles here and there, a few pauses in the humming while the out-size morsels were enfolded and fed into the grinders. Now, instead, they hid; they were afraid.

"Go!" he shouted at the top of his voice. "Kill them! Kill them while they're down!"

The army behind him swept after him with a stunning composite shout.

Tactics vanished. A petaled corona unfolded in Lavon's face, and a buzzing whirlpool spun him toward its black heart. He slashed wildly with his edged wooden splinter.

The sharp edge sliced deeply into the ciliated lobes. The rotifer screamed like a siren and contracted into her tube, closing her wounded face. Grimly, Lavon followed.

It was pitch dark inside the castle, and the raging currents of pain which flowed past threw him from one pebbly wall to another. He gritted his teeth and probed with the splinter. It bit into a yielding surface at once, and another scream made his ears ring, mixed with mangled bits of words in Lavon's own language, senseless and horrible with agony. He slashed at them until they stopped, and continued to slash until he could control his terror.

As soon as he was able, he groped in the torn corpse for the eggs. The point found their life and pricked it. Trembling, he pulled himself back to the mouth of the tube, and without stopping to think pushed himself off at the first Eater to pass it.

The thing was a Dicran; she doubled viciously upon him at once. Even the Eaters had learned something about cooperation. And the Dicrans fought well in open water. They were the best possible reinforcements the Flosc could have called.

The Dicran's armor turned the point of Lavon's splinter easily. He jabbed frantically, hoping to hit a joint, but the agile creature gave him no time to aim. She charged him irresistibly, and her humming corona folded down around his head, pinned his forearms to his sides—

The Eater heaved convulsively and went limp. Lavon half slashed, half tore his way free. A Didin was drawing back, pulling out its seizing-organ. The body floated downward.

"Thanks," Lavon gasped. The Proto darted off without replying; it lacked sufficient cilia to imitate human speech. Possibly it lacked the desire as well; the Didins were not sociable.

A tearing whirlpool sprang into being again around him, and he flexed his sword arm. In the next five dreamlike minutes he developed a technique for dealing with the sessile, sucking Flosc. Instead of fighting the current and swinging the splinter back and forth against it, he gave in to the vortex, rode with it, and braced the splinter between his feet, point down. The results were even better than he had hoped. The point, driven by the full force of the Flosc's own trap, pierced the soft, worm-like body half through while it gaped for the human quarry. After each encounter, Lavon doggedly went through the messy ritual of destroying the eggs.

At last he emerged from a tube to find that the battle had drifted away from him. He paused on the edge to get his breath back, clinging to the rounded, translucent bricks and watching the fighting. It was difficult to make any military sense out of the melee, but as far as he could tell the rotifers were getting the worst of it. They did not know how to meet so carefully organized an attack, and they were not in any real sense intelligent.

The Didin were ranging from one side of the fray to the other, in two tight, vicious, efficient groups, englobing and destroying free-swimming rotifers in whole flocks at a time. Lavon saw no fewer than half a dozen Eaters trapped by teams of Paras, each pair dragging a struggling victim in a trichocyst net remorselessly toward the Bottom, where she would inevitably suffocate. He was astonished to see one of the few Nocs that had accompanied his army scourging a cringing Rotar with its virtually harmless tentacle; the Eater seemed too astonished to fight back, and Lavon for once knew just how she felt.

A figure swam slowly and tiredly up to him from below. It was old Shar, puffing hard. Lavon reached a hand down to him and hauled him onto the lip of the tube. The man's face wore a frightening expression, half shock, half pure grief.

"Gone, Lavon," he said. "Gone. Lost."

"What? What's gone? What's the matter?"

"The plate. You were right. I should have known." He sobbed convulsively.

"What plate? Calm down. What happened? Did you lose one of the history plates—or both of them?"

Slowly his tutor seemed to be recovering control of his breathing. "One of them," he said wretchedly. "I dropped it in the fight. I hid the other one in an empty Flosc tube. But I dropped the first one—the one I'd just begun to decipher. It went all the way down to the Bottom, and I couldn't get free to go after it—all I could do was watch it go, spinning down into the darkness. We could sift the mud forever and never find it."

He dropped his face into his hands. Perched on the edge of the brown tube in the green glow of the waters, he looked both pathetic and absurd. Lavon did not know what to say; even he realized that the loss was major and perhaps final, that the awesome blank in their memories prior to the First Awakening might now never be filled. How Shar felt about it he could comprehend only dimly.

Another human figure darted and twisted toward him. "Lavon!" Phil's voice cried. "It's working, it's working! The swimmers are running away, what's left of them. There are still some Flosc in the castles, hiding in the darkness. If we could only lure them out in the open—"

Jarred back to the present, Lavon's mind raced over the possibilities. The whole attack could still fail if the Flosc entrenched themselves successfully. After all, a big kill had not been the only object; they had started out to capture the castles.

"Shar—do these tubes connect with each other?"

"Yes," the old man said without interest. "It's a continuous system."

Lavon sprang out upon the open water. "Come on, Phil. We'll attack them from the rear." Turning, he plunged into the mouth of the tube, Phil on his heels.

It was very dark, and the water was fetid with the odor of the tube's late owner, but after a moment's groping Lavon found the opening which led into the next tube. It was easy to tell which way was out because of the pitch of the walls; everything the Flosc built had a conical bore, differing from the next tube only in size. Determinedly Lavon worked his way toward the main stem, going always down and in.

Once they passed beneath an opening beyond which the water was in furious motion, and out of which poured muffled sounds of shouting and a defiant buzz. Lavon stopped to probe through the hole with his splinter. The rotifer gave a shrill, startled shriek and jerked her wounded tail upward, involuntarily releasing her toe-hold upon the walls of the tube. Lavon moved on, grinning. The men above would do the rest.

Reaching the central stem at last, Lavon and Phil went methodically from one branch to another, spearing the surprised Eaters from behind or cutting them loose so that the men outside could get at them as they drifted upward, propelled by the drag of their own coronas. The trumpet shape of the tubes prevented the Eaters from turning to fight, and from following them through the castle to surprise them from behind; each Flosc had only the one room, which she never left.

The gutting of the castles took hardly fifteen minutes. The day was just beginning to end when Lavon emerged with Phil at the mouth of a turret to look down upon the first City of Man.

He lay in darkness, his forehead pressed against his knees, as motionless as a dead man. The water was stuffy, cold, the blackness complete. Around him were the walls of a tube of a Flosc's castle; above him a Para laid another sand grain upon a new domed roof. The rest of the army rested in other tubes, covered with other new stony caps, but there was no sound of movement or of voices. It was as quiet as a necropolis.

Lavon's thoughts were slow and bitter as drugged syrup. He had been right about the passage of the seasons. He had had barely enough time to bring all his people from the hall to the castles before the annual debacle of the fall overturn. Then the waters of the universe had revolved once, bringing the skies to the Bottom, and the Bottom to the skies, and then mixing both. The thermocline was destroyed until next year's spring overturn would reform it.

And inevitably, the abrupt change in temperature and oxygen concentration had started the spore-building glands again. The spherical amber shell was going up around Lavon now, and there was nothing he could do about it. It was an involuntary process, as dissociated from his control as the beating of his heart. Soon the light-generating oil which filled the spore would come pouring out, expelling and replacing the cold, foul water, and then sleep would come. . . .

And all this had happened just as they had made a real gain, had established themselves in enemy country, had come within reach of the chance to destroy the Eaters wholesale and forever. Now the eggs of the Eaters had been laid, and next year it would have to be done all over again. And there was the loss of the plate; he had hardly begun to reflect upon what that would mean for the future.

There was a soft *chunk* as the last sand grain fell into place on the roof. The sound did not quite bring the final wave of despair against which he had been fighting in advance. Instead, it seemed to carry with it a wave of obscure contentment, with which his consciousness began to sink more and more rapidly toward sleep. They were safe, after all. They could not be ousted from the castle. And there would be fewer Eaters next year, because of all the eggs that had been destroyed, and the layers of those eggs . . . There was one plate still left . . .

Quiet and cold; darkness and silence.

*In a forgotten corner of the galaxy, the watery world of Hydrot hurtles endlessly around the red star, Tau Ceti. For many months life has swarmed in its lakes and pools, but now the sun retreats from the zenith, and the snow falls, and the ice advances from the eternal ocean. Life sinks once more toward slumber, simulating death, and the battles and lusts and ambitions and defeats of a thousand million microscopic creatures retreat into the limbo where such things matter not at all.*

*No, such things matter not at all when winter reigns on Hydrot; but winter is an inconstant king.*

# 14 GREAT TALES OF ESP 30p

Cast your mind back.
Back to the early moments of remembrance.
Back to the pleasure, the pain,
the mystery and the uncertainty.

Stand naked before the Unknown.
Challenge its infinitude, wrestle in its servitude.
For it waits for your accomplishment.

*This is a book for those of you with the curiosity
and the courage to imagine experience
beyond the limits of the world you can see
and touch.*

**From Isaac Asimov, Robert A. Heinlein, Murray Leinster,
Frederic Brown, Zenna Henderson and others.**

Introduction by **John W. Campbell.**
Edited by **Idella Purnell Stone.**